GOD'S PLAN

FINDING YOURSELF *in* HIS GRAND DESIGN

HENRIETTA MEARS

From Gospel Light
Ventura, California, U.S.A.

Published by Regal
From Gospel Light
Ventura, California, U.S.A.
www.regalbooks.com
Printed in the U.S.A.

Library of Congress Cataloging-in-Publication Data
Mears, Henrietta C. (Henrietta Cornelia), 1890-1963.
God's plan : finding yourself in His grand design / Henrietta Mears. — [Rev. ed.].
p. cm.
Includes bibliographical references.
ISBN 978-0-8307-4562-3 (trade paper)
1. Providence and government of God—Miscellanea. 2. Providence and government of God—Devotional literature. 3. Bible—Criticism, interpretation, etc. I. Title.
BT96.3.M43 2008
231′.5—dc22
2008000005

Information on pages 7-10 adapted from Marcus Brotherton, *"Teacher"* (Ventura, CA: Regal, 2006), pp. 61-70, 91-99, and Earl Roe, *Dream Big: The Henrietta Mears Story* (Ventura, CA: Regal, 1990), pp. 132-142.

Quotation from Henrietta Mears on p. 10 from Ethel May Baldwin and David V. Benson, *Henrietta Mears and How She Did It!* (Ventura, CA: Regal, 1966), p. 288.

Quotation on pages 22-24 from Dr. E. Schuyler English, ed., *The Pilgrim Edition of the Holy Bible* (Oxford, U.K.: Oxford University Press, Inc., 1948). Used by permission.

1 2 3 4 5 6 7 8 9 10 / 15 14 13 12 11 10 09 08

Contents

Section Three: God's Plan Completed

FOREWORD

At the great testimonial dinner for Dr. Henrietta Mears held at the Hollywood Presbyterian Church in the spring of 1961, I was greatly impressed with the fact that almost invariably all who were gathered there addressed their beloved leader as "Teacher." And they so addressed her because this had been the pre-eminent characteristic of their relationship to Dr. Mears through the years, especially in her great college class that she so faithfully taught for a quarter of a century.

The honor of being known as "Teacher" to so many hundreds attending that dinner and to so many thousands more, many of them as missionaries living in countries around the globe, was not come by automatically. A true teacher has both a gift for teaching, as the New Testament acknowledges, and a determination to devote himself or herself to prolonged preparation for those teaching hours. I have heard, on good authority, that at the very beginning of her teaching ministry for the college class, Dr. Mears spent 20 hours a week in preparation for her 30-minute message on the Lord's Day!

Through the years, I enjoyed the great privilege of bringing messages to this class occasionally in the Sunday morning hour, more often in the Sunday evening meeting, and most frequently in their gatherings on Wednesday night. Often, for these evening meetings, I presented a series of messages on some particular subject, sometimes at Dr. Mears's own suggestion, such as a series on the book of Revelation. I must say, without reservation, that this was the most enthusiastic, most dynamic class of young people I have ever had the opportunity of teaching. They reminded me in so many ways of the Bible class I attended when a high school student at the Buena Memorial Presbyterian Church in Chicago, taught by the late Mr. Andrew Stevenson. The manner in which Dr. Mears would express her own appreciation for these messages made one take a silent vow that there was nothing she might ask one to do but that the task would be gladly undertaken.

There is no need here to describe her great work at Forest Home, or the tremendous influence of Gospel Light Publications, or her radiant leadership in conferences here and there. Where Dr. Mears was, there was enthusiasm, expectation and glorious cooperation. Everything she was vitally related to she dominated, but not as a dictator. You were not working *for* her, but working *with* her for the Lord. In my range of experience, Dr. Mears was the most inspiring woman leader in Christian causes that I have ever known. No one will ever take her place. We all miss her—no one more than I.

There is no need to say anything about the material in *God's Plan*. It will speak for itself. Material like this is more needed today than ever. May these pages of biblical interpretation and the conviction of the truthfulness of the Word of God on the part of those who use these studies prove the means of instructing many in the eternal realities of life in Christ. And may they confirm those who already have been taught, that together teacher and those taught may continue to build up the Body of Christ and help to make it possible for us all to give a reason for the hope that is within us.

Dr. Wilbur M. Smith (1894-1976)

Cofounder of Fuller Theological Seminary
Former professor of English Bible,
Trinity Evangelical Divinity School
Author of *Therefore Stand* and *Imminent Signs of the Times*

Introduction

In 1928, Henrietta Mears faced a difficult decision. A year before, she had taken a sabbatical leave from her teaching position at a high school in Minneapolis, Minnesota, to determine if she wanted to continue teaching or pursue another career. Remaining in the teaching field would require her to attend Columbia University to prepare for administration work. In the meantime, a pastor of a small church in Hollywood, California, had offered her a position as director of Christian education.

When doors began to open that pointed Henrietta in the direction of Hollywood, she sensed God's Plan for her life and accepted the position. She and her sister, Margaret, sold their home in Minnesota and headed out west. Slowly but steadily, she began to build a Sunday School program that would be as sound in administration as the finest school system in the country.

At the time, the typical method of conducting Sunday School classes was to simply corral the children into a single room and read them a story. Henrietta envisioned setting up a department for every age group with classes broken out by each child's specific age. Her ideas, though radical at the time, were effective—within two years, the Sunday School at the church grew from 450 to more than 4,000.

GOD'S
PLAN
DRAWN
GOD'S PLAN
OF THE AGES
Part 1
S 091 151

GOD'S
PLAN
REVEALED
GOD'S PLAN
OF THE AGES
Part 2
T 092 259

GOD'S
PLAN
COMPLETED
GOD'S PLAN
OF THE AGES
Part 3
S 093 154

GOD'S
PLAN
FOR MY
LIFE
S 094 150

From her work in the Minneapolis public school system, Henrietta had learned the importance of having quality curriculum. So she sent out requests to publishing houses and began to survey the Sunday School curricula that was available. Most of the materials were biblically sound, but the lessons were bland, with no pictures or activities for students to complete. Many were not geared toward any particular age. None that she found presented the material in a chronological manner.

When the supply of one curriculum for her students ran out and Henrietta received the new materials, she opened one lesson to read, "Paul survived his shipwreck because he had eaten carrots and was strong." She wrapped up the books and sent them back to the publisher. From this point on, she would write the lesson material for her Sunday School herself.

At first, Henrietta never had any intention of publishing and selling the materials. This changed one Sunday morning when Marion Falconer, a druggist from Anaheim, visited Hollywood First Presbyterian and demanded that Henrietta give him copies of the materials—or guarantee that they would be printed. Something in Mr. Falconer's plea struck a chord in Henrietta, and she promised that she would look into the matter.

Henrietta was eventually put in touch with Cary Griffin, a printer in nearby Glendale, California. Cary agreed to hold his bills for printing, except when he had to make a layout of cash, as for engravings. And so, Henrietta and Esther Ellinghusen, a gifted junior high teacher in the Los Angeles public school system whom Henrietta had recruited to write the lessons, began the process of writing and editing nine books for each quarter of the year.

In 1933, Gospel Light Press obtained its first copyright. One of the earliest curricula to be prepared by Henrietta was a series of teachings known as *God's Plan for the Ages*. "The purpose of the course," wrote Henrietta, "is to study God's plan of the ages as it is revealed in His Word. We want to give young people 'a reason for the faith that is in them.' Most people do not have a comprehensive grasp of the Scriptures. They do not realize that God has a plan in His dealings with His creatures."

The first quarter, "God's Plan Drawn," was released in 1934, followed by second and third installments, "God's Plan Revealed" and "God's Plan Completed," in 1935. Each quarter's materials included a student workbook (with illustrations, maps, puzzles and games) and an accompanying booklet for teachers (with various tips on how to structure the teaching time and lead a discussion of the topics presented). A fourth quarter, "The Challenges of the Christian Life," first issued separately in 1936, was incorporated into the course in 1940 and titled "God's Plan for My Life."

In 1958, the course was revised and updated to prepare students "who are confronted with new concepts in science, religion and philosophy . . . study and understand God's plan from creation through the consummation of all things, which He has made known through His Word." In 1971, the first three quarters from the teacher's portion of the course were adapted into a trade book and released as *God's Plan: Past, Present and Future,* with a new foreword by Dr. Wilbur Moorehead Smith, former professor of English Bible at Fuller Theological Seminary and Trinity Evangelical Divinity School.

The current edition of this work is based on the 1971 version but also incorporates information from the students' materials released by Gospel Light in 1958 and portions of "God's Plan for My Life." For ease in reading, the Bible version used in the book has been updated to *The New King James Version.* All attempts have been made to preserve Henrietta's unique style and terminology.

God's Plan is as relevant today as when it was first published more than 70 years ago. "My heart is thrilled when I see what the Word of God can do," Henrietta once said. "I have discovered that if the Bible is taught the way it should be that it will be like a powerful magnet drawing youth unto the Lord Jesus Christ. What a supremely superb Textbook we have!"

Section One:

God's Plan Drawn

1

God the Planner

For I am God, and there is no other; I am God, and there is none like Me, declaring the end from the beginning, and from ancient times things that are not yet done.

Isaiah 46:9-10

The trouble with so many people is that they begin at the wrong end of things. Let us begin at the beginning with God. God is the first and the last fact. No one can get either behind Him or beyond Him.

The Bible is the one great document that gives to us what men in ages past have learned about God. "Who made me" is the first and biggest question a little child asks as soon as he or she begins to think. The very first words in the Bible, "In the beginning, God" (Gen. 1:1), answer that question.

The key verse to what Genesis teaches is given in that first verse. It is a statement concerning eternity. Remember that eternity has no beginning and no end. For what lies back of man's experience, there are but three sources of information possible: (1) God's revelation in the Scriptures, (2) God's revelation in nature, and (3) God's revelation in Christ. Since God gave all of these sources, there can be no conflict among them.

The second must be interpreted by the other two; and the third can only be fully understood in the light of the first.

The Word of God is more interested in telling us *who* made the world than it is in telling *how* the world was made. It tells us the one thing we cannot find out ourselves: "In the beginning, God created." No other answer to this great question has ever been satisfactorily given.

God first came down to *create,* and then to *save.* Compare the work of God in creation and His work in redemption. He merely spoke and worlds were framed; but He had to suffer and die to save His creation. He made man by His breath; He saved man by His death.

Many scholars think that the Bible is inharmonious and full of errors. It is as though they took a record and bored a hole a little off center and put it on the machine to play. What disharmony results! The sound is indescribable. That is what many people do with the Bible. They take it from its inspired setting and have it revolve around their own speculations and ideas. But the Bible says, "In the beginning, God," not "In the beginning, man." The Bible is Christocentric—Christ-centered.

A watch was made that took 12 years to complete. It was the size of a quarter and a fourth of an inch thick. The metals were so amalgamated that they were unaffected by any change in the atmosphere. After 12 months, the watch had varied only 3 seconds. This was a wonderful piece of mechanism, but our God by the word of His mouth has set a great timepiece in the heavens, where billions of suns, moons and stars have revolved countless years without a second's variation!

The "Book of Beginnings" begins with God—creation begins with God. There is a tremendous sweep in these first few verses of Genesis, covering innumerable years. Everything points back to God, and yet how prone we are to forget Him! We do not count Him in the beginnings of all things, even in our little lives.

Our eyes are fixed on circumstances and things about us instead of on God. We say, "God? Of course, there is a God, but what about Him?" So many people live just within the little circle of their own experiences. It would do us all good if we would read Genesis 1:1 and stop after the word "God." Yes, in the very beginning of creation, in the beginning of the very first day, God was there. Is He in the beginning of every one of your days? What a difference it would make in your life if He were!

God's Timepiece Is Perfect

God's hand is in evidence in *all* His creation. A party had climbed to the top of the Matterhorn. They were admiring the grandeur and beauty all about them. One of the climbers had brought a microscope to study insect life. He looked through the microscope at the legs of a little fly. "See," he said, "the legs of the housefly in America are naked, but the legs of this little creature are covered with fur leggings. The same God who made this great mountain has attended to the comfort of the tiniest of His creatures, even supplying it with socks and mitts."

We cannot see God, but we can see evidences of Him in all His creation. Yes, it is true that "the heavens declare the glory of God; and the firmament shows His handiwork" (Ps. 19:1). Evolutionary process demands a first cause, a beginning. It cannot supply it. The evolutionist must tell us where the universe came from. No one can find anything in this universe that God has not first put there for man to find. God is the beginning of all. He is everywhere, but He can only be "seen" by our spiritual sight.

The Bible says "in the beginning, God." Evolutionists and philosophers admit naturally enough the eternity of elementary matter from which, they state, through a slow evolution everything has been produced—heaven, earth, man and even

God if He is necessary. Science deals only with phenomena or with the things that are perceived by the senses. That is, things we can see, feel, taste, smell or hear. Can God be seen by the human eye or by the most powerful microscope? Can He be caught in a test tube or weighed in the most delicate balance? "Can you search out the deep things of God" (Job 11:7)?

Science starts with some tremendous assumptions about the universe as to its laws and order, and these assumptions are made on pure faith. They never have been and never can be proved by scientific study. Yet the scientist never doubts them. He also keeps on using faith through much of his work. When an astronomer locates three points on the orbit of a planet, he constructs the whole orbit, looks for the planet at other points and confidently expects to find it there. With faith and imagination, he predicts and looks for the unseen. The astronomer by faith predicts an eclipse of the sun and tells the very day, the hour and the minute it will begin. This is only one of a thousand instances of facts that are predicated on faith.

Men cannot predict history or the future. They cannot foretell when a war will break out, because history is manmade. But astronomers, for instance, can predict just what will take place in nature, because the heavens are timed by God, and His timepiece is perfect.

A Vast Universe

The vastness of the universe that scientists keep discovering for us has immense space and speeds, masses and motions. The billions of suns and systems in the universe make man feel that he is only an infinitesimal speck on a tiny globe that is swimming around in the light of billions of suns. Can we think then, if there is a God, that He can have the least interest in such a tiny creature as man? No wonder the psalmist says, "What is man, that Thou art mindful of him?" (Ps. 8:4). The overpowering sense of the vastness of this universe makes us all feel the same way. But think of this: God has put into this infinitesimal man a mind that can study the vastness of His universe.

Astronomers used to tell us things that frightened us; now they see things that frighten them. We know that light travels at the rate of 186,000 miles per second. At this tremendous rate of speed, light takes about 1 $^{1}/_{4}$ seconds to reach the earth from the moon and about 8 minutes from the sun. From the nearest star, light travels 4 years on its journey to the earth. But to get here from the nearest spiral galaxy, light must travel 2 years. And from the farthest galaxy that can be photographed with the 200-inch telescope on Mt. Palomar, light travels for over one billion years before it reaches the earth.

Josephus, the great Jewish historian, said, "God adorned the heavens with the sun, moon and stars." How little did he realize that the Milky Way alone is composed of billions of stars and that it would take 100,000 years to go from one edge to the other traveling at the speed of light. Our earth and its solar system are only a speck in this vast ocean of stars. The Bible says in Genesis 1:31, "God saw everything that He had made, and indeed it was very good."

Real Science

The question is often asked, "Does science contradict the Bible?" True science and the Bible illuminate each other. Dr. Michael Pupin, a great physicist, once said, "If science does not assist me in a better understanding of the creation and a clearer personal relationship with Him; if science does not assist me in carrying out the Divine purpose, then I am a failure as a scientist."

If true believers knew science, and if scientists knew the Bible, there would be more Christian faith and more true philosophy. In the Bible there is no science that is manmade. The laws of God's Word spurn the ever-changing theories of men. Galileo numbered the stars in thousands. Did God ever make a mistake like that? Long before that, God had told Abraham to look up into the heavens. He promised Abraham a seed as innumerable as the stars (see Gen. 15:5). The early scientists thought the world was flat; that it rested on the back of a turtle. What does God's Word say? "He hangs the earth on nothing" (Job 26:7) and God "sits above the circle of the earth" (Isa. 40:22). Now that scientists have discovered that the stars are literally without number, their terminology fits in with the Scriptures. Had the account of creation been in accord with the science of Greece or Rome or the scholars of the Middle Ages, how utterly false it would have been!

We Can Know God

The design of the Bible is to reveal God's plan in the creation of the world and its redemption from sin by Jesus Christ. Let us begin where the Bible begins and trace the marvelous unfolding of His plan through the entire Word. As we see God's plan unfold, let us keep in mind that He is the divine architect. Let us see that God is great. The plan of the ages is a great and wonderful plan. It is comprehensive and complete. The God who made it is greater than His plan.

We look around us at the universe that the Lord has created. We see its beauty. We look through a telescope and we are made aware of the immensity of God's universe. We use a microscope and we are made aware of the detail and the intricacy of the universe. And our new awareness serves only to make us wonder how we fit into the whole marvelous work. But we have a place. And that place is made for us by the fact that God who made all things loves us and wants us to know Him.

We come to know Him through His creation. But it is so great that it awes us. We come to know Him through the Bible and we see that God is holy and we are sinful. Then we come to know Him through the Lord Jesus Christ and we learn that He loves us and wants us to be with Him for all eternity. He wants this so much that He has provided a way of salvation for us so that we will be fit to dwell with Him.

Yes, surely, we look at the universe and say, "Oh, Lord, how great You are." Then we look at the cross and say, "Wonder of wonders, He loves even me."

Daily Meditations

Sunday: "In the beginning, God"—Psalm 90:1-12

Monday: "Created"—Psalm 19:1-14

Tuesday: "The heaven and the earth"—Isaiah 40:12-22

Wednesday: The earth's foundation—Jeremiah 31:37; Hebrews 1:10-11

Thursday: The earth's measurements—Job 38:4-1

Friday: God knows us—Psalm 139:1-6

Saturday: God is great—Psalm 136:109

2

GOD THE ARCHITECT

You may know and believe Me, and understand that I am He. Before Me there was no God formed, nor shall there be after Me.
ISAIAH 43:10

"The fool has said in his heart, 'There is no God'" (Ps. 14:1). What? No God? A watch and no watchmaker? A building and no builder? A farm and no farmer? A school and no teacher? A creation and no creator? "He who sits in the heavens shall laugh" at such absurd atheism (Ps. 2:4). The sublime opening of the Bible announces the fact of God.

The Bible opens with the doctrine of God and, without discussing anything about Him, the first statement of Genesis makes Him the creator of the universe: "In the beginning, God created the heaven and the earth." The world is not self-creative or self-existent. There was a time when the world was not—a time when it was called into existence. This act required the creative power of an infinite God.

A famous astronomer produced a small model of the solar system, showing the earth, the moon and the planets moving abut the sun. One day, a famous atheist, who said he could not believe in God, saw the little model and asked the astronomer,

"Who made this beautiful model?"

"No one," was the astronomer's answer.

"No one?" echoed the atheist disgustedly. "Well, how did it get here then?"

"It just happened," the astronomer replied.

"Don't be so foolish," replied the atheist. "Such a perfect model could not just happen. Surely someone made it and put it here."

"I'm not half as foolish as you are," the astronomer coolly responded. "You can't believe this little model of the solar system just happened, but you profess to believe that the great universe, with the real sun, moon and stars, and the earth upon which we live, was not made by any hand and just happened in its place and is kept working without any guiding mind. Who is the fool?"

When we see anything, we naturally ask the cause of that thing. We see the world and ask how it came to be. Did it form itself, as evolutionists would have us believe? No more than nails, bricks or mortar can form into a house or building by themselves. There must be a builder. As the existence of a perfect model shows the existence of a designer, so this universe confirms the existence of God.

Human beings all over the world have a consciousness of God. Every person in Africa or the islands of the sea, every tribe, every known race of mankind has a belief in a supreme being. Medicine men from time immemorial have been the priests of religions that acknowledge a supernatural being. Such a universal result must have a cause. That cause is God Himself!

In the Beginning

As Paul walked down the streets of Athens, he saw men and women bowing down to statues. Among them he saw an altar with the inscription, "To the Unknown God." Paul told the people that the God they so ignorantly worshiped, unknown to them, was really the Lord of heaven and Earth. He told them that this God was the creator and showed them that God did not live in houses built by man. He told them that God did not need anything they could make with their hands, for He was the giver of life and breath, for "in Him we live and move and have our being" (Acts 17:28). Paul told the Athenians that they could not live unless God gave them their very breath. This God that they did not know was nearer to them than any idol of gold or silver. This "Unknown God" is the only God that can satisfy the poor human heart.

Someone once said, "A God capable of proof would be no God at all." We could no more prove the existence of God than prove that a thing is beautiful. It may be shown, but not proved. No one argument can be decisive, but there is great strength collectively to make us sure of His existence.

There is design in the universe. It is obvious that the existence of a watch not only proves a maker but also a designer. A watch is made for a purpose. So in this world, the design speaks of an intelligence that thought it out. How perfectly every blade of grass is formed and every snowflake is designed!

The greatest evidence of all is that of Scripture. It asserts, assumes and declares that the knowledge of God is universal. "The heavens declare the glory of God" (Ps. 19:1).

A man asked the chief of a desert tribe how he could believe in a God he had never seen. The chief answered, "This morning I walked outside of my tent and saw the tracks of a camel in the sand. I looked around. I couldn't see a camel, but I knew one had been there. Just so, I see the handiwork of God everywhere in this universe and I know that He exists."

In Genesis 1:26 we read, "Let Us make man in Our image, according to Our likeness." Note the fact that the plural form of the name of God is used with the singular objects, the words "image" and "likeness." The plural form of the name conveys the idea of the Trinity, and the singular object that of unity. This is God speaking of Himself as a trinity. He says "us" and "our."

Although we know that God exists in three persons–*God the Father*, the architect of the universe (see Acts 15:18); *God the Son*, the builder (see John 1:1-13; Eph. 3:9; Heb. 1:20); and *God the Holy Spirit*, the beautifier and giver of life (see Job 26:13; 33:4)–the Bible tells us that "the LORD one" (Deut. 6:4). The word "one" in this Scripture is used in a collective sense, much as "crowd," "flock" and "group" are all understood to mean more than one. The idea of "one" in this verse means the same thing–one God existing in three persons. The Hebrew word *echad*, meaning "one," is the word that is used to describe the oneness of God.

The Old Testament in particular emphasizes the unity of God (see Deut. 6:4; Isa. 44:6; Exod. 20:3). That God is one and that there is none other is the forceful testimony of more than 50 passages in Scripture. A great truth in the Old Testament is the prominence given to the doctrine of the unity of God. By unity, we mean that the divine nature is undivided and there is but one infinite and perfect God. There are three persons in the Godhead, but one God. We believe in one God–not three.

The New Testament emphasizes the Trinity. This is evident from the following verses: the baptism of Jesus (see Matt. 3:16-17); the baptism formula (see Matt. 28:19); the apostolic benediction (see 2 Cor. 13:14); and the fact that Christ Himself teaches it (see John 14:16). As a passage from *The Pilgrim Edition of the Holy Bible* states:

> A type of the Trinity is the sun. Let us see how it pictures for us God the Father, God the Son, and God the Holy Spirit.
>
> The great ball called the sun, [more than] ninety million miles away, no one has ever seen–not even

astronomers. All we see is the light from it; for it is only the light and the chemical power of the sun that come to earth.

Just so, no man has seen God the Father at any time. But as astronomers have learned a great deal about the sun by studying the sunlight, so we can learn a great deal about God the Father by getting to know God the Son, Jesus Christ, who came to earth. Like the sunshine, He is called "the brightness [outshining] of [God's] glory" (Hebrews 1:3).

And just as the sunlight *is* the sun, so Jesus Christ *is* God. For example: On a cloudy day the sun suddenly shines out. All the children cry with joy, "There is the sun!" They do not mean that the great ball in the sky has come into their classroom. That would be absurd. It is the sunlight that they see. But the sunlight and the sun are one, and we call them both, "the sun." So God the Father, and God the Son are one. We call both "God," for both are God.

But there is a third element in the sun—its chemical power. On bright spring days the children's wraps come off, and they rush out to visit the garden plots where weeks before, they planted seeds. They find the tiny green shoots peeping up. What made them grow? "The sun," they say. But they really mean the chemical power in the sunshine. What do children need to make them grow in a normal way? "The sun," we say. Yet again, we mean the chemical power in the sunshine. That power is distinct from the sun and from the sunlight, yet it is one with them. And we speak of it, too, as "the sun," for it *is* the sun.

The Holy Spirit is like that. He is a distinct Person, yet He is one with God the Father and God the Son. He is God the Holy Spirit. He quietly works in hearts, unseen, and unknown except by the wonders that He does in giving life, and the life of God, to those who, will receive it.

God was not alone in making this world, nor was He alone in His plan to save the world. "For God so loved the world that He gave His only begotten Son" (John 3:16), and then the Holy Spirit was sent to bear witness of that great truth and to make us new creatures in Christ Jesus.

The Attributes of God

The Scriptures tell us that there are certain qualities that belong to God alone. They are what He is and always has been.

God Is Spirit

"God is Spirit, and those who worship Him must worship in spirit and truth" (John 4:24). We learn to know God not only from His works but also from His words. Every one of us can recognize the voices of speakers whom we have never seen. We are acquainted with their personalities through their voices. And so we can know God without seeing Him. We know Him through His Word, and we can say, "whom having not seen, [we] love" (1 Pet. 1:8).

Some people think that when we say God is spirit, we do not believe that God is a person. When we say that someone has a fine personality, we do not mean he is fine looking. That has nothing to do with features or body. It is the man himself, the spirit of the man who dwells within that body. So although God is spirit, He is a person.

God Is Infinite

"Great is the Lord, and greatly to be praised; and His greatness is unsearchable" (Ps. 145:3). It is difficult for man's mind to comprehend the infiniteness of God. The psalmist says His greatness is unsearchable. He is without limits of any kind—without end, boundless, immeasurable. He truly is worthy of our praise!

God Is Unchangeable

"Jesus Christ is the same yesterday, today, and forever" (Heb. 13:8). It is wonderful to know that in this world where everything is changing constantly, God remains the same.

The sun is not fickle or partial because it melts wax but hardens clay. The change is not in the sun, but in the object it shines upon. When a man bicycling against the wind turns about and goes with the wind instead of against it, the wind seems to change. But it is really the man's direction that has changed.

Scripture often says that God repents of what He has done, but let us look at it. God's unchanging holiness requires Him to treat the wicked differently from the righteous. When the righteous become wicked, His treatment of them must change.

Divine repentance is therefore the same principle acting differently in altered circumstances. God ever hates the sin and ever loves the sinner. God's character never changes, but His dealing with people change as they change from ungodliness to godliness and from disobedience to obedience.

God Is Love

"He who does not love does not know God, for God is love" (1 John 4:8). Christianity is the only religion that sets forth God as love. The gods of other religions are often depicted as being angry, hateful beings that are in constant need of appeasing. If you went to India to the great temple of the goddess Kali, you would see a horrible creature with wild eyes. Her red tongue, thirsty for blood, hangs to her waist and there is a necklace of skulls about her shoulders. She waits to be appeased by the blood of animals. This is a picture of how some people of other religions think of their gods. But our God's love is greater than we can ever comprehend. God desires the salvation of all men.

God Is Holy and Eternal

"You shall therefore consecrate yourselves, and you shall be holy; for I am holy" (Lev. 11:44). No one but God can truthfully say, "I am holy." He is perfect; His holiness is unchanging. Because He is holy and worthy of praise, He wants us to sanctify ourselves and be holy. God is also timeless–of infinite duration and without beginning or ending. He is "from everlasting to everlasting" (Ps. 90:2)

God Is Omnipresent

"Where can I go from Your Spirit? Or where can I flee from Your presence? If I ascend into heaven, You are there; If I make my bed in hell, behold, You are there. If I take the wings of the morning, And dwell in the uttermost parts of the sea, Even there Your hand shall lead me, And Your right hand shall hold me" (Ps. 139:7-10).

God is everywhere present. We are told that He is in heaven, His dwelling place (see Matt. 6:9); that Christ is at His right hand (see Eph. 1:20); and that God's throne is in heaven (see Ps. 11:4). Just as the soul is present in every part of the body, so God is present in every part of the world. A speaker stands on the platform. His bodily presence is there, but his personality is felt as far as his voice can be heard. God says His throne is in heaven, but His personality and power are felt throughout His entire creation.

God the Father is especially manifested in heaven. Jesus taught us to pray, "Our Father in heaven" (Luke 11:2). God the Son became flesh and dwelt among us. "For in Him dwells all the fullness of the Godhead bodily" (Col. 2:9). The body of every believer is the temple of the Holy Spirit. He is closer to us than our breathing and nearer to us than our hands or feet.

God Is Omniscient

"Great is our Lord, and mighty in power; His understanding is infinite" (Ps. 147:5). God knows the end of everything from the beginning. We are like a person standing by a river in a low place who can see only that part that is passing him. But the man who is high up in a mountain lookout may see the whole course of the river, how it rises and how it runs. Thus it is with God. From His place in the heavens, He can see just how every event is going to turn out. God knows all things. Remember, you cannot hide anything from God.

God Is Omnipotent

"With men this is impossible, but with God all things are possible" (Matt. 19:36). God can bring to pass everything that He wills. He *is* able to do all things. The God to whom we pray is able to do for us exceedingly abundantly above all that we can ask or think (see Eph. 3:20).

We can never fully understand the greatness of God, but at least we know that God is greater than the universe He created. Yet His very greatness includes His ability and desire to care for the smallest of His creatures. Not a sparrow falls without His knowledge. Even the very hairs of our heads are all numbered. His greatest undertaking is seen in His provision for the salvation of His creation.

What is God like? We want to know. The question has been asked through the ages. Many answers have been given. Some of them are false. All of them were incomplete until the Lord Jesus Christ came and explained, "He who has seen Me has seen the Father" (John 14:9).

God Is Worthy of Our Worship

We cannot talk about our God this much without realizing that He is worthy of our worship. But how do we worship God? What does worship mean?

The Bible tells us that we should fear the Lord. This is found in many places of the Bible. Ecclesiastes 12:13 says, "Let us hear the conclusion of the whole matter: Fear God and keep His commandments, for this is man's all." To "fear the Lord" means to recognize His holiness and to realize how great He is and how unworthy we are to have His love.

Sometimes we forget that God is holy and we treat Him as we would treat one of our earthly friends. God is our friend, that is true, but He is also our God and we should respect and honor Him. He says, "Be still, and know that I am God" (Ps. 46:10). The problem with most of us is that we are seldom still long enough to learn anything.

The worship of the true and living God is the highest expression of which man is capable. We worship Him by waiting upon Him in silence as we realize who He is and what He does. We can worship Him in prayer. Christians can worship Him by singing His praise and hearing about Him. We can worship Him wherever we are. Remember to do as Jesus Christ commanded: *Worship Him in spirit and in truth* (John 4:24).

Daily Meditations

Sunday: God is one God—Deuteronomy 6:4; Isaiah 44:6-8; 1 Corinthians 8:4-6; 1 Timothy 2:5

Monday: God is a triune God—Matthew 3:16-17; 28:19; 1 Corinthians 12:3-6

Tuesday: God knows all—Psalm 139:1-6; Isaiah 48:5-8

Wednesday: God has all power—Psalms 107:25-29; 139:14-19

Thursday: God is everywhere—Psalm 139:7-12;
Jeremiah 23:23-24; Acts 17:24-28

Friday: God is love—1 John 4:8-16

Saturday: God alone should be worshiped—Isaiah 6:1-8

3

God Reveals His Plan

For prophecy never came by the will of man, but holy men of God spoke as they were moved by the Holy Spirit.
2 Peter 1:21

Have you ever thought what you would know about God and His plan for the ages and for you if you had no Bible? Think about it for a moment. You could not say that you know about Christ or the Holy Spirit, or the love of God, or heaven, or salvation, or so many other things. If we are to know many of the things that God wants us to know, He had to provide a way to tell us. That way is the revelation of His plan in the book we call the Bible.

When we think of God, we must remember that He is "the Beginning and the End . . . who is and who was and who is to come" (Rev. 1:8). Our minds are too limited to understand fully all of the great truths of God's plan, but we are assured that they are true because God tells us so in the Bible. God's plans extend throughout all eternity, but His plans also include our lives for today and tomorrow.

Can we believe what the Bible says? We probably have an immediate reaction to that question. We say, "Of course!"

Yet have we ever stopped long enough to realize how amazing it is that we can believe it? In the first place, the last book of the Bible was completed about A.D. 95 or 96, more than 1,900 years ago. The 66 books of the Bible were written over a period of 1,400 years and by 40 different writers. These men, in most cases, had never met each other. They came from different backgrounds and cultures. Some of them spoke different languages. There is no human explanation as to why the Bible is a unit and how all of it has the same message. The Holy Spirit is the only answer.

The Bible Is True

The Bible is an old book, but its teachings are up to date. In fact, its teachings are so timely that many of them have never been understood. For example, the Bible says in 2 Peter 3:10-11, "But the day of the Lord will come as a thief in the night; in which the heavens shall pass away with a great noise, and the elements shall melt with fervent heat; both the earth and the works that are in it will be burned up. Therefore, since all these things will be dissolved, what manner of persons ought you to be in conduct and godliness?" Until our modern era, no one had experienced anything like what Peter described. Then an atomic explosion was seen for the first time. Now we know that these words can very literally come true.

Could Peter have known about nuclear explosions through his own intelligence? Of course not. But God knew all about atomic energy long before man ever thought about it. As late as the year 1926, a dictionary gave the definition of an atom in these words: "Particle of matter so small as to admit of no division." In the first century A.D., the Holy Spirit had Peter describe something that man could not understand in the twentieth century.

Does this mean that the Bible is a science textbook? No. The purpose of the Bible is to reveal the love and holiness of God for sinful people in order that they can be saved through our Lord Jesus Christ and dwell forever with God. The central theme of the Bible is not humans or even knowledge; the central theme is Christ. He is on every page of the Bible. He said, "In the volume of the book it is written of Me" (Heb. 10:7). The Bible was not written as a textbook of science or history, but no true science or history disagrees with it. When the Bible mentions a fact of science or an event of history, that which it says is true.

If the Bible agreed with the science of former years, it would not be the Word of God. How ridiculous are the statements in the ancient writings concerning science! Even the Koran, which was written centuries after Christ, tells us that the earth is anchored to mountains with cables.

History tells us that the Roman Catholic Church deposed Vergilius for believing that the earth was a globe and that Galileo was compelled to recant for believing that the earth moves. The Chaldeans believed that the earth was a living creature, and the Egyptians taught that the sun was a great crystal reflecting the light of the earth. How wonderful it is to know that the Word of God is absolutely free from all of these unscientific statements and these ridiculous hypotheses.

Man could never have written the first chapter of Genesis, because the scientific truth of it was not discovered until centuries later and it gives us a record of things that never were seen by man. Men have tried to discover some errors in it, but they cannot.

The Bible Reveals God's Plan

The glory and majesty of God are certainly seen in creation. Paul says in Romans 1:20, "For since the creation of the world His invisible attributes are clearly seen, being understood by the things that are made, even His eternal power and Godhead." We can look around us and see that God is orderly and that He does all things well.

But when we say that God so loved the world that He gave His only begotten Son, we know this only because God's Word tells us so. Nothing in creation tells us how to become a Christian. Looking at the beautiful mountains will not make us realize that we are sinners and need a Savior. Tracking the stars through a telescope will not tell us that the God who created all things has a plan for us. Watching cells divide under a microscope will never help us find God's will for our lives. All of these truths we know only from God's Word.

When we seek to discover what we can about God's great plan, we discover that the source of all we find out will be—the Bible. It will be our authority and the final answer to all of our questions.

Why do we believe that the Bible is such a good source book? One reason we have already discussed: the Bible is true. It claims to be the Word of God and the Holy Spirit bears us witness that this is true. Another reason is that we believe that the Bible is inspired. Second Peter 1:21 puts it like this: "Holy men of God spoke as they were moved by the Holy Spirit." What does this mean?

Second Timothy 3:16 states, "All Scripture is given by inspiration of God." "Inspiration" means that God directed the writers so that they wrote what He wanted them to write. This does not mean they were secretaries who transcribed the dictation of someone else. God used their natural talents, their abilities and their interests, but at the same time He guided what they wrote so that the final message was free from errors. God gave us an inspired book because He wanted us to have His Word on which we can depend and know His plan of the ages.

How do we know that the Bible is inspired? In the first place, it claims inspiration. Over and over again these words appear: "Thus says the LORD," and "the word of the LORD came to me," and similar phrases. It has been estimated that this kind of phrasing appears 3,800 times in the Old Testament. In the first five books of the Bible, written by Moses, the words, "The LORD spoke unto Moses," appear 95 times.

Second, the Bible's trustworthiness testifies to its inspiration. The events that it prophesies come to pass. The history that it relates is true; the scientific data is accurate. The Bible has in it hundreds of fulfilled prophecies. Here are a few concerning the Lord Jesus:

- He was to be born of the tribe of Judah (see Gen. 49:10; Luke 3:33) of the house of David (see Isa. 9:7; Matt. 1:1).
- He was to be born in Bethlehem (see Mic. 5:2; Matt. 2:1) and come out of Egypt (see Hos. 11:1; Matt. 2:14-15).
- He was to cry out, "My God, My God, why have You forsaken Me?" (see Ps. 22:1; Matt. 27:46).
- He was to die for sinners (see Isa. 53:12; Rom. 5:8) and be raised from the dead (see Ps. 16:10; Luke 24:36-48).

And on and on to a total of 90 prophecies concerning Christ's life and death.

Finally, Christian experience helps us to know that the Bible is from God. Let me explain this with an illustration.

Suppose that you are eating some ice cream when a friend happens to come by.

"What are you eating?" he asks.

"Ice cream," you reply.

"I do not believe you," he says.

"Try it for yourself," you answer. When he tries it, he knows that you are right.

Someone may ask you, "How do you know that the Bible is true?"

You answer, "I have tried it and I find that the Lord speaks to me from it." There is no answer to such an argument.

What Should We Do About the Bible?

We have seen that the Bible is the only source for finding God's plan and that it is a reliable source of information. We have seen that the Bible is the inspired Word of God. Now the question is, "What should we do about it?" Really, there seems to be only one obvious answer: We should read and study it. Do you do that? Do you spend time every day reading of God's Word to see what it can teach you each day?

One thing you must remember: Begin with prayer. First, ask the Lord to send His Holy Spirit to help you to understand what you read. When you finish reading, thank the Lord for helping you. If you don't entirely understand something, read it over and over. Then write down your question and ask someone else to help you. Don't say, "I can't understand the Bible." The Holy Spirit will help you to understand it if you will let Him. The Lord promised, "The Helper, the Holy Spirit, whom the Father will send in My name, He will teach you all things" (John 14:26).

What a privilege we have to study the inspired Word of God. Just think! We have in our possession the words of the great God who created and cares for all things. But sometimes we treat His words with less concern than we do the comic strips. Isn't it a disgrace how little interest we show in finding out what God has said? Remember, the Bible reveals God's plans. Let us read it to discover those plans.

Daily Meditations

Sunday: God is a great planner—Psalm 95:1-5

Monday: God plans for people—Joshua 1:7-9

Tuesday: God plans for Christian living—Colossians 3:14-17

Wednesday: God reveals His plans by the Spirit—1 Corinthians 2:9-15

Thursday: God reveals Himself in Christ—John 1:1-4,14

Friday: God's Word is inspired—John 7:14-14; 2 Timothy 3:16

Saturday: God's law is perfect—Psalm 19:7-11

4

God's Angels: Messengers and Servants

Praise Him, all His angels . . . let them praise the name of the Lord, for He commanded, and they were created.

Psalm 148:2,5

There is an old hymn that says, "I want to be an angel and with the angels stand."

Do you want to be an angel when you die? If you do, I am afraid you are never going to make it. God has something much better for you than being an angel. God's children will reign with Him; angels serve Him.

Statements like the words of the hymn quoted above have given a very wrong idea of just what angels are. People have an idea that those who have died have been given a pair of wings and a harp and now are angels. This is a common mistake; it is not what the Scriptures teach. It is true that all Christians who die trusting in the Lord Jesus Christ as Savior are in His presence in heaven, but they are not angels. The Bible teaches that angels are a distinct class of beings who have never been human beings. They are ministering spirits (see Heb. 1:14).

Our Lord said that human beings after they die and rise from the dead "are like angels of God in heaven" (Matt. 22:30) in the matter of marriage and giving in marriage. This shows that human beings in heaven are *like* angels in this respect, but they are not angels. Know this: Christians will no more become angels when they die than they will become birds or fish. Believers in Christ are called saints; they are never called angels in the Bible.

When Were Angels Created?

Many people wonder why the Bible does not tell when angels were created, but many great Bible teachers believe that they were included in the general creation spoken of in the first verse of Genesis: "In the beginning God created the heaven and the earth."

There is another opinion based on Genesis 2:1, which says, "Thus the heavens and the earth, and all the host of them, were finished." The Hebrew word for "host" is *sabba* and is used especially of military ranks. This heavenly host that God created are angels. We are led to believe that angels are intellectual creatures, that they have great minds and live in a supernatural world, and that they are obedient servants and faithful messengers of the Lord God.

When God created the heavens and the earth, He created a great number of spiritual beings. In Gethsemane, after Jesus had been arrested and Peter had cut off the high priest's ear, the Lord told this impulsive disciple to put up his sword: "Do you think that I cannot now pray to My Father, and He will provide Me with more than twelve legions of angels?" (Matt. 26:53).

The apostle John on Patmos said that in the vision given to him, "I heard the voice of many angels around the throne, the living creatures, and the elders; and the number of them was ten thousand times ten thousand, and thousands of thousands" (Rev. 5:11). This last clause means myriads and myriads. Their number is well nigh infinite, and they are almost unlimited in their power (see 2 Kings 19:35; Acts 5:19; 12:7,23).

Although the angels are spirits and do not have flesh and blood (see Ps. 104:4; Heb. 1:14), they often assume a visible form and appear to people. Many times we read that angels talked with people (see Gen. 19:1; Judg. 2:1; 6:11-22; 13:3,6; John 20:12-13; Luke 1:26; Acts 7:30; 12:7-8).

What Are Angels?

Angels are a distinct order of creation. The word "angel," which literally means "messenger," is used in Scripture with reference to three distinct kinds of beings. First, it is used with reference to God Himself. We find Him called "the angel of the Lord." The word "angel" is also used in reference to men messengers, and finally to a host of spiritual creatures whom we generally think of as angels.

The Angel of the Lord

How marvelous to think that over and over again in human history God has come down to be a "messenger," or herald, in His dealings with people!

It was God Himself, as "the Angel of the Lord" (Gen. 22:11), who called to Abraham out of heaven and told him not to take the life of Isaac. In the same chapter, we read that the Angel of the Lord called to Abraham out of heaven the second time and said, "By Myself I have sworn . . . because you have done this thing, and have not withheld your son, your only son, in blessing I will bless you, and in multiplying I will multiply your descendants as the stars of the heaven and as the sand which is on the seashore" (Gen. 22:16-17).

The expression "the Angel of the LORD" in a great number of Bible passages plainly refers to God—that is His title. The angel of the Lord appeared to Hagar in the wilderness (see Gen. 16:10). It is a most interesting study to look up all the passages that refer to "the angel of the Lord" (see Gen. 16:1-13; 21:17-19; 22:11-16; 31:11-13; Exod. 3:2-4; Judg. 2:1; 6:12-16; 13:3-22).

Messengers

We find the Bible full of instances in which the Lord used angels to minister to His children and serve Him. Sometimes the Greek word for "angel" is used in Scripture for men. Messengers can be men or angels (see Luke 7:24; Jas. 2:25; Rev. 1.20; 2:1,8,12,18; 3:1,7,14).

A Great Host of Spiritual Creatures

The third group of beings for whom the Scriptures use the word "angel" are not spoken of as human beings but are a great host of specially created spiritual beings. They were created with perfect freedom of will, and so angels, like human beings, can sin. They, too, can depart from the laws of God, for every bit of God's creation exists under the dominion of law. Thus, this last class of angels is divided into two groups: (1) those who serve God, and (2) the fallen angels who followed Satan in his revolt against God (see 2 Pet. 2:4; Jude 6; 1 Cor. 6:3). The Bible states distinctly that some angels sinned. They broke the laws placed on them by God, were driven from their high estate in heaven, and were changed into evil angels.

The angels who serve God are exceedingly numerous (see Matt. 28:53; Heb. 12:22; Rev. 5:11). Their place is around the throne of God (see Rev. 7:11). Their special work is to minister to those who shall be heirs of salvation (see Heb. 1:13-14). We find wonderful examples of their ministry in 1 Kings 19:5-8, Psalm 34:7, Daniel 6:22, Matthew 2:13 and Acts 5:19.

Servants of the Lord

Angels are always ready to do the bidding of God. One service that the angels render is to bear God's messages. It was an angel who confided God's plan to Gideon for him to be the deliverer of Israel from the Midianites (see Judg. 6:11-22). It was an angel who revealed to Daniel the messages recorded in the book that bears his name (see Dan. 10). An angel told Zacharias of the coming birth of John the Baptist (see Luke 1:5-14). An angel announced both to Mary and to Joseph that Mary should be the mother of the world's Redeemer (see Matt. 1:20-21; Luke 1:26-38). An angel directed the praying Cornelius to send for Peter who would show him the way of salvation (see Acts 10:1-6). And it was an angel who brought the message of God to Philip. He directed Philip to leave his work in the great city of Samaria and go to the desert to talk to one man (see Acts 8:26-29).

Ranks of Angels

There are gradations in the ranks of these spiritual beings. They are called angels, cherubim and seraphim. They all may have individual names, but only Michael and Gabriel are mentioned in the Bible.

Michael, whose name means "who is like unto God," was the great archangel of heaven. The archangel defends the holiness of God and fights against Satan (see Dan. 10:21; Jude 9; Rev. 12:7). Gabriel, whose name means "the mighty one," was entrusted with many wonderful heavenly messages. He was God's special messenger who announced Jesus' birth to Mary (see Luke 1:26-38) and John's birth to Zacharias (see Luke 1:5-25).

What about the group of angels called "cherubim"? What is their task? This group seems to be concerned with carrying out God's judgment. We read of them in connection with the expulsion of Adam and Eve from the Garden of Eden (see Gen.

3:24). Another group of angels, called "seraphim," seem to be concerned with the worship of God (see Isa. 6:2-7).

Angels have also another task to perform. The Bible says, "Are they not all ministering spirits sent forth to minister for those who will inherit salvation?" (Heb. 1:14). Just think! God says in His Word that His angels are to watch over us, for we are heirs of salvation.

When God created the angels, He put them in a special heavenly sphere above the sphere of men. It is said that man is made "lower than the angels" (Heb. 2:7). When Christ came down to earth, He took a place "lower than the angels" (Ps. 8:5; Heb. 2:7,9) so that He might lift the believer into His own sphere above the angels (see Heb. 2:9-10). Angels were created to be the servants of the most high God, but we were created to be His companions (see Matt. 26:53; John 15:l5).

Angel Ministry

The Holy Spirit's work with the children of God is spiritual, while the angels seem to be limited to physical service. Angels laid hold of Lot and led that lingering man out of the doomed city of Sodom (see Gen. 19:15-16). When Elijah was tired and weak from hunger, it was an angel who told him to sleep. When he awoke, an angel fed Elijah on food that this heavenly messenger had prepared (see 1 Kings 19:5-7). It was an angel that delivered Peter out of prison on the very night before his execution (see Acts 5:19-20). (See also Exodus 23:20 and read the beautiful verse in Psalm 34:7.)

Angels Execute Judgment

Not only do the angels keep a watch over the children of God, but they also execute the judgment of God. Angels stood guard at the entrance to the Garden of Eden with a flaming sword (see Gen. 3:24). When David sinned and God punished the people, He made use of a pestilence by the hand of an angel to slay thousands of the Israelites (see 2 Sam. 24:16). The story of the great army of Sennacherib is another illustration of the work of angels to execute judgment (see 2 Kings 19:35). And at the end of the age, we are told that "the Son of Man will send out His angels, and they will gather out of His kingdom all things that offend, and those who practice lawlessness, and will cast them into the furnace of fire" (Matt. 13:41-42).

Angels Ministered to Christ

Much is told in Scripture of the ministry of angels to the Lord Jesus Christ when He was here on this earth. After He had defeated the devil at the time of His temptation, "the devil left Him, and behold, angels came and ministered to Him" (Matt. 4:11). When the Lord was in the garden of Gethsemane, sweating as it were great drops of blood, "an angel appeared to Him from heaven, strengthening Him" (Luke 22:43). Angels ministered to the bodily needs of the Lord when He was here on this earth suffering the limitations of human flesh.

When Christ returns to this earth in power and great glory, the angels will accompany Him (see Matt. 25:31; 2 Thess. 1:7). How inconceivably glorious will be that day when innumerable beings like the shining ones described in Revelation 10:1 and Matthew 28:3 shall come together with Christ, who outshines them all. They shall suddenly appear, coming in the clouds of heaven to this earth! This is not speculation but a literal fact that will take place one day.

Angels Minister to Believers

Throughout the Bible, we frequently read of the work that angels do for those who are obedient to the Lord. For example, in Jacob's vision at Bethel, the angels were seen assuring Jacob of

God's love and care (see Gen. 28). Revelation 8:3-4 says that angels have a part in the presentation of prayers to God. Let us not confuse this with the work of the Lord Jesus Christ as our mediator. We can come to God the Father only through Christ (see John 14:6). Certainly, this means in prayer as well as our coming to know God through Christ. We are not to pray to angels or to worship them. We pray only to God; we worship only God. But in some way, angels have a part.

The Angels Rejoice

Of the 39 books in the Old Testament, 16 expressly refer to angels and several other books refer to them without specifically using the word "angel." Angels are mentioned by name in 17 of the 27 books of the New Testament. In total, angels are mentioned 108 times in the Old Testament and 165 times in the New Testament.

As we read of the work of the angels, one characteristic comes to our attention repeatedly: The angels obeyed the commands of God. Psalm 103:20 says, "Bless the Lord, you His angels, who excel in strength, who do His word, heeding the voice of His word." How much more we should be obedient to the commands of God! The angels are His servants, but we are His children.

The angels rejoice over one person who comes to Christ for forgiveness of sin (see Luke 15:10). We, too, should rejoice when someone comes to Christ, for we know the joys of having our sins forgiven. We understand how truly wonderful it is to pass from death into eternal life through faith in the Lord Jesus Christ.

The Lord has a great angelic host who praise Him, serve Him, obey Him and rejoice with Him. Let us join with them in praise to our God. Let us serve the Lord with gladness and obey

His commandments. Let us rejoice with Him over the salvation of those who come to Him.

Daily Meditations

Sunday: Angels worship God—Nehemiah 9:6;
Philippians 2:11; Hebrews 1:1-16
Monday: Angels are ministering spirits—Acts 12:7-11;
27:23-24; Hebrews 1:7-14
Tuesday: Angels tell the will of God—Daniel 8:15-17; 9:20-23; 12:1-7
Wednesday: Angels execute the will of God—Numbers 22:21-35;
Matthew 13:39-42
Thursday: Angels ministered to Christ—Matthew 4:11; Luke 22:39-45
Friday: Angels are subject to Christ—Ephesians 1:20,22;
Colossians 1:15-17; 2:10
Saturday: Angels attend Christ at His second coming—
Matthew 16:27; 25:31; Mark 3:38; 2 Thessalonians 1:7

5

SATAN, THE PROUD ANGEL

But even if our gospel is veiled, it is veiled to those who are perishing, whose minds the god of this age has blinded, who do not believe, lest the light of the gospel of the glory of Christ, who is the image of God, should shine on them.

2 CORINTHIANS 4:3-4

People like to joke about the devil. No one enjoys this more than the devil himself. He doesn't want people to believe that he really exists, for if they deny his existence, he can do his worst. Some people do not think that it makes any difference whether they believe in a personal devil or not. Let us see what God's Word says concerning Satan and then draw our conclusions from that. Satan does not want the light of Scripture thrown on him, for God's Word is true.

Satan is a created being. He was placed in the "garden of God," on "the holy mountain of God" (Ezek. 28:13,14). Who is this one who was clothed in the beauty of heaven and who lived upon the holy mountain of God? He was the anointed cherub, the wisest and fairest of all God's creatures, who rebelled against God and drew down after him a great host of heaven.

The Prince of the World

The one that we now call Satan was once the most beautiful angel of heaven, named Lucifer, but his beauty and brightness were more than he could bear. Lucifer was given a throne; therefore, he must have had a kingdom with lesser angels to serve him (see Isa. 14:12-13). Since his fall, he has been called the "ruler of the demons" (Matt. 9:34), "ruler of this world" (John 12:31; 14:30; 16:11), "god of this age" (2 Cor. 4:4), and "prince of the power of the air" (Eph. 2:2). He has innumerable servants to do his bidding (see Matt. 7:22-23; Luke 11:14-19; 2 Cor. 11:14-15).

What was Satan's sin? Paul tells us the cause of Lucifer's fall. It was the sin of pride (see 1 Tim. 3:6). In his pride, Satan imagined that he might be like God (see Isa. 14:12-14). How was his pride punished? God ruined Lucifer's dream of power, and he was cast from heaven.

Our Lord said, "I saw Satan fall like lightning from heaven" (Luke 10:18). When lightning falls or strikes, it brings ruin; and when Lucifer fell, one-third of the angels of heaven fell with him (see Rev. 12:4-9). What a terrible sin Lucifer's pride was, and what a terrible result it had!

The greatest sin today is the sin of self-will. This sin is always instigated by Satan. How different is the mind of Christ (see Phil. 2:5-8). Jesus said, "Behold, I have come to do Your will, O God" (Heb. 10:9). Satan's plan has always been to work against God's will. Christ came to destroy the work of the devil, the author of evil (see Gen. 3:1-6,14,24).

Satan set up his will against God's will, and he lifted up his heart because of his beauty and brightness. In Isaiah 14:13-14, notice that five times Lucifer says "I will": "*I will* ascend into heaven, *I will* exalt my throne above the stars of God; *I will* also sit on the mount of the congregation on the farthest sides of the north; *I will* ascend above the heights of the clouds, *I will* be like the Most High" (emphasis added). Here is Lucifer's sin: His will, not God's will, was his desire.

Sin is selfish. Think about it for a minute and see if that is not true. When people lie, they do it because the truth would belittle them or hurt them. When people steal, it is because they want what belongs to another. When people gossip, it is to make someone else appear in a bad light and them to appear in a good light. Sin is always selfish. In the center of the word "sin" is "I."

Fallen Angels

A great part of the angels led by Satan were changed from angels of light to angels of darkness, and the others to demons. All their wonderful gifts were turned into hatred, envy and jealousy toward God, who had driven them out of heaven. How foolish it is for anyone or any creature to rebel against God! These angels could not succeed against God, even if perhaps they were numbered by hundreds of millions. So, they vented their wrath upon the earth.

The Bible teaches that no man can break God's laws without punishment. God's laws break men. If any scientist breaks the laws that govern the dividing of an atom, he or she may be killed. If a person falls out of a second story window, the law of gravity pulls that individual to the ground and he or she is hurt. God's laws are fixed. We cannot change them.

The angels that fell seem to be in two groups. One group is even now reserved in chains awaiting God's judgment. Second Peter 2:4 states, "God did not spare the angels who sinned, but cast them down to hell and delivered them into chains of darkness, to be reserved for judgment." Jude 6 states, "And the angels who did not keep their proper domain, but left their own habitation, He has reserved in everlasting chains under darkness for the judgment of the great day." This group of angels must have done something so displeasing to God that He took away their freedom. Neither of these verses describes just what that sin was, but it was terrible enough to make God take such drastic action.

Then there is another group of fallen angels that are called "demons." Demons are the wicked angels who are at liberty in this world and who spend their time tormenting us and tempting us to sin against God (see Eph. 6:12). There are many demons. These are the messengers of the devil, and they go about doing their master's bidding (see Mark 5:13-16).

Satan's Work Today

Gradually, the picture of why there is evil in the world is becoming clearer. Satan is the author of sin. It is his work and the work of his demons that bring such horrible things to pass from day to day. One look at a daily newspaper will convince anyone that the devil is at work.

We know that Satan began as one of the angels and about the sin he committed against God. Now let us see what he is like today.

The Bible has many words to describe him. In 1 Peter 5:8, he is described as "a roaring lion, seeking whom he may devour." A lion is not an animal to play with. It is dangerous to try to pet one or to attempt to feed one by hand. Do you and I realize that it is just as dangerous to "fool" with the devil? Some people talk about him lightly as if he were a naughty child. People try to brush him off and ignore him. However, a lion that is running loose cannot be ignored. We better not ignore the devil.

Satan is a powerful enemy. He is clever and he knows all the tricks. To ignore him gives him an opportunity to get us to fall for his tricks. In Jude 9, Michael the archangel contended with him, but Michael knew better than to try to fight him alone. This verse says that Michael said to the devil, "The Lord rebuke you!" The best way to face a lion is with a weapon that you know is strong enough to destroy him. The Lord Jesus Christ and the Word of God are the only weapons the devil fears. We cannot defeat him in our own strength, but the Lord Jesus can.

In 2 Corinthians 11:14, the devil is called an "angel of light." Satan is a very real being and not the imaginary creature we see pictured as a red demon with a long tail, horns and a pitchfork. The devil likes us to think of him like that. He likes it because that is *not* what he is like. It is similar to a thief sending the police to look for a black convertible when he is making his getaway in a green sedan. The thief can slip by and the police will never know it. That is just what the devil does. He appears as something good so that we will not recognize sin. He is really like a wolf in sheep's clothing. He looks like an angel, but he tempts us to sin, like the devil he is.

Remember that the devil is intelligent. Even his temptations are clever. He would not think of tempting you to murder someone; that is against your nature. But he might tempt you to lie about someone, as this is something you may possibly do. Satan will not suggest that you sin by doing something that is completely beyond the realm of possibility. He will tempt you to sin by doing the thing that you want to do but which is opposed to God's will.

The devil often comes to us as an angel of light and suggests that we compromise just a little with what we know is right. He suggests that we are too tired to get up and read our Bible in the morning. He hints that we are too sleepy to pray before we go to bed. He tells us not to bow our head in the restaurant to ask the Lord's blessing on our food. "After all," the devil says, "you may be laughed at. The others won't understand. God knows that you are thankful; ask the blessing with your eyes open so no one will know." The devil tells us not to be so sold out to Christ as to live for Him at work, at school and around home. He says people will think that we are fanatics. "Don't talk about the Lord," he suggests. "Don't give to the Lord's work." And so on and on the temptations go. Satan suggests compromise instead of an out-and-out stand for the Lord Jesus.

There is still another way in which he appears as an angel of light. He has people talk about religion, even quote from the Bible, and yet they deny the Lord Jesus Christ. They call Him just a good man or a great teacher, but they do not believe He is the Son of God, the second person in the Trinity. Beware of anyone who denies the deity of Christ. Guard against the tricks that the devil uses. Ask the Lord to keep you alert to recognize them. "Put on the whole armor of God, that you may be able to stand against the wiles of the devil" is the command of God that Paul gives us in Ephesians 6:11.

Resisting the Devil

What is the armor of God? The rest of the passage in Ephesians 6:10-17 will tell us. We are to have a belt of truth—that means no place for deceit in our lives. We are to put on the breastplate of righteousness—we often think of righteousness as something that we cannot have, but the truth is that as Christians we have the righteousness of Christ. We are to put on the shoes of the preparation of the gospel of peace—that means that we are always ready to tell the way of salvation wherever we are. We are to take the shield of faith—after all, it is only by trusting in Christ for strength that we can keep from the devil's power. We are to wear the helmet of salvation—we must know for sure that we are Christians. We must know it because God tells us so in His Word, and His Spirit bears witness with us that we are His children (see Rom. 8:16).

This is our defensive armor. Our only offensive weapon is the Sword of the Spirit, which is the Word of God. Christ resisted Satan by quoting words from the Scriptures (see Luke 4:4). The psalmist said, "Your word I have hidden in my heart, that I might not sin against You" (Ps. 119:11). With this equipment, we are ready to face the temptations of the devil. Just notice one thing: There is no protection for our backs. We do not retreat in the Christian life; we march always as an offensive army.

One more name for the devil is found in Revelation 12:10: "the accuser of the brethren." He is at work in this role today. This is a law term; it means he is the prosecuting attorney against us. In 1 John 2:1 there is another law term, but this time it applies to Christ. He is called our "advocate," or the defense attorney. This is a picture of a courtroom. God is the judge. Into the court comes the devil. "One of your children has sinned," he says to God. "Your own Word says that 'the soul who sins shall die' (Ezek. 18:4). What are you going to do about it?"

God is a holy judge. His law must stand; sin must be punished. If we have sinned, we deserve death. But before God can pass judgment upon us, the Lord Jesus steps forward. "Just a minute," He says. "I died for that one. He is one of My children. I have forgiven that sin."

The Judge looks at the accuser, and then turns to the Advocate. "Not guilty!" He says. And the devil is defeated again.

The Doom of Satan

Not only is the devil defeated in the court of heaven when he tries to accuse us, but his defeat will be complete some day. When the Lord Jesus comes back and judgment is passed upon those who refused the offer of salvation, the devil will also be judged. He and his angels will stand trial.

This time, the Judge will pass sentence. "And the devil, who deceived them, was cast into the lake of fire and brimstone . . . and they will be tormented day and night forever and ever" (Rev. 20:10).

Ever since Satan tempted Adam and Eve in the Garden of Eden, he has been under a special curse. You see, the serpent was cursed "more than every beast of the field" (Gen. 3:14). The curse said that the serpent was to eat dust. Isaiah 65:25 says that much of the animal world is to be changed, but not the serpent. Read the verse: "The wolf and the lamb shall feed together, the lion shall eat straw like the ox, and dust shall be the serpent's food." The lake of fire into which the devil and his angels are to be thrown was prepared especially for them (see Matt. 25:41).

The works of the devil are to be destroyed. In fact, that is the purpose for which Christ came: "For this purpose the Son of God was manifested, that He might destroy the works of the devil" (1 John 3:8).

The defeat of Satan is sure, for the Bible tells us so. Our victory is secure in Christ. The Bible tells us that God will make us victorious in Christ. "Thanks be to God, who gives us the victory through our Lord Jesus Christ" (1 Cor. 15:57).

Daily Meditations

Sunday: Satan, the anointed cherub—Ezekiel 28:13-19

Monday: Satan's fall—Isaiah 14:12-20

Tuesday: Wicked angels are punished—Jude 5-10

Wednesday: The disguises of Satan—2 Corinthians 2:11; 11:13-14; James 4:7

Thursday: The condition of mankind—John 8:44; 1 John 3:8-10

Friday: The armor of God—Ephesians 6:10-17

Saturday: The doom of Satan—Revelation 20:1-10

6

God's Creation of the Universe

In the beginning God created the heavens and the earth.
GENESIS 1:1

How do you think we would get along if we tried to live on the theory of not believing anything that we did not understand? Most people do not understand all about electricity, but the whole world believes in it and uses it. We do not understand what it is that makes one seed grow and another seed die, but we believe in life in the growing seed, even though we cannot understand it.

Many people in this world say they do not believe in God or the Bible because they cannot understand it all. Do you really think that is sensible? The wisest and ablest people in the world are those who are ready to listen to what God tells them, to use what He has given them and to believe in Him and His love.

How can we know that God created the universe even though we weren't there when He created it and we cannot understand all about it? If we will look closely, we will find the name of the One who was both architect and builder of this universe. Where do we first see it? In the first verse of the Bible. Nature itself gives evidence of God as a great architect everywhere—in the rocks, in the flowers, in the birds and in the stars. Nobody but God could have made a world like this.

An automobile has the name of its manufacturer on it. Pens, washers, and almost everything else bears the trademark of its maker. Just so, the skies are filled with stars that only God could have made.

Did Chance Bring About this Universe?

"The heavens declare the glory of God . . . the firmament shows His handiwork" (Ps. 19:1). We cannot understand how God made this universe, but it isn't reasonable to think that mere forces made such an intricate, beautiful, carefully planned world without a great mind to direct those forces. According to Genesis 1:3, God just spoke and it was done. God used the forces of the universe that He created to bring about marvelous results.

Although we solve problems in mathematics with just 10 digits, we do not try to put a lot of numbers into a hat and shake them around to solve the problems. We know that it takes the 10 numbers plus our *minds* to work out the correct answer. If a poet wants to write a beautiful poem, he does not put a lot of letters of the alphabet into a hat and shake out a poem. All the letters are used to tell us his thoughts, but he arranges those letters with his *mind* to make the beautiful things we call poetry.

We see the boulders that physical geographers say the great glaciers made, coal that was formed out of buried trees and ferns, and coral that has built up islands. When we study geology, we learn about many of the forces that God used in the building of this universe. Some try to tell us that this marvelous universe was brought into being by chance. Do you think that this would be sufficient cause? Then God is the sufficient answer.

In a plant where telephones are manufactured and assembled, people and machines work on an assembly line to put together the many parts of a telephone. You could shake these parts together in a tub for the next 17 million years, but you would never have a telephone. So we know that it would be impossible for the more than 90 elements of which this universe is made to bring themselves together by mere chance to form this wonderful world in which we live.

It took the mind of God, plus the elements, to create this universe. A mechanic may have all the parts of an automobile lying at his feet, but it will take his mastermind to make an automobile out of them. The steam engine and the airplane and the skyscraper are the products of *mind,* not chance. This universe is infinitely greater and more complex than the greatest manufactured product that the most intelligent human being could think of creating.

Is Evolution the Answer?

Some people who try to explain the fact of creation without God have worked out a theory called "evolution." The dictionary defines "theory" as a proposed explanation whose status is still conjecture. The theory of evolution tries to explain *how* creation happened without God. This theory maintains that life started with the first bit of matter and from it all other life came. Life then evolved or progressed so that man came from lower forms of life. The Bible does not teach this.

One real problem of biological evolution is this: From what source did the first bit of matter come? When the evolutionist has gone back as far as he can, he still must find the source of the first matter. The Christian's answer is that *in the beginning God created the heavens and the earth.* There was no matter until God made it by the power of His word.

Some theistic evolutionists (evolutionists who believe in God) believe that God did create the first bit of matter, but since then a process of evolution has been in effect. This raises the question, Where is the relationship between the lowest forms of animal life and the highest forms of plant life? Where is the "missing link" between plants and animals?

Plants were created on the third day; animals on the fifth day. "Then God said, 'Let the earth bring forth grass, the herb that yields seed, and the fruit tree that yields fruit according to its kind . . .' so the evening and the morning were the third day. So God created great sea creatures and every living thing that moves, with which the waters abounded, according to their kind, and every winged bird according to its kind . . . so the evening and the morning were the fifth day" (Gen. 1:11,13,21,23).

God's law is each kind "according to its kind." Apple trees always bring forth apples, never lemons. There are various types of apples, but they are always apples. Luther Burbank, an American botanist, horticulturist and pioneer in agricultural science, made a better potato in 1872, but it was still a potato. He crossed peaches and plums to make nectarines, but botanically they were the same kind of fruit. He could never have crossed peaches and pears, because they are in different species. People may change and improve a species, but they cannot change one species to another. Dr. Etheridge, a curator of the British Museum, once said, "In all this great museum there is not one particle of evidence of transmutation of species."

Do you know that climbing beans always grow up a pole from left to right? If people reverse them, they will die. It is not necessary to plant a seed right side up. God made each seed so that it always grows upward. Striped watermelons always have an even number of stripes. Citrus fruits always have an even number of sections. An ear of corn always has an even number of rows.

Would these rules be true if plants, animals and humans came about by accident? No indeed, they were no accident. God is the only creator. He made all things Himself; He made this great unchanging law that each kind reproduce *according to its kind*.

Biological evolutionists say that there is a missing link between man and lower forms of life. If this link could be found, they believe that they could explain the evolution of man. However, this link will always be missing, because it does not exist. Edward Conklin, a professor of biology at Princeton University, said this about creation: "The probability of life originating from accident is comparable to the probability of the Unabridged Dictionary resulting from an explosion in a printing factory."

The perfection and orderly arrangement of every part of creation shows that the Creator was infinitely wise and great. Our earth with all its plant, animal and human life did not just happen to come into existence. It was all planned by God and created according to that plan. "God saw everything that He had made, and indeed it was very good" (Gen. 1:31).

Creation of the Heavens and the Earth

Of course, there was a time when there were no heavens and no earth. There was a time when there was only God. When the heavens and earth were formed, God formed them. They did not happen into being; God made them. Everything that exists by creation, God made. In Colossians 1:16 we read these words: "For by Him all things were created that are in heaven and that are in earth, visible and invisible, whether thrones or dominions or principalities or powers." All things were created through Him and for Him. The earth was created in six "days," or periods of time.

The First Day

In Genesis 1:3-5, we find that by the word of God the darkness was dispelled by the light. God separated light from darkness, for light and darkness cannot mix.

Name all the different kinds of light you know–sunlight, electric, candle, fire, match, lightning bug, glowworm. All trace back to the sunshine and to God. What is light, anyway? Strike a match. Now blow it out. Where did the light go when it went out? You say, "I don't know." Some people do not believe what they do not understand. Then, what is light?

Notice that there is no mention of any means used by God except His word. There is only the simple statement of the fact . . . and it was so.

The Second Day

In Genesis 1:6-8, we find that God "divided the waters." The firmament was made by the separation of the salt waters beneath and the fresh waters above. Here is another mystery that is hard to understand. Great clouds floating overhead carry tons of water. What keeps them there? Why don't they drop? God just spoke, and there the water hangs "divided" until He is ready to have it come down and bless the earth. God established the natural law that makes all this possible.

In Job 37:16, we find this question: "Do you know the balance of clouds, those wondrous works of Him who is perfect in knowledge?" Just think what wonderful balancing this must be. Thousands of tons of water hang suspended in the sky. Certainly, only God can do anything as wonderful as balancing clouds.

Job 14:18-19 teaches us the work of erosion and gives us a good definition of exactly what takes place in a landslide. Job 26:7 tells us clearly that the earth is suspended, that God "hangs the earth on nothing." Job 28:25 teaches us an interesting fact concerning the wind having a weight and the balance of water upon the earth and in the sky. This idea of evaporation is also found in Ecclesiastes 1:7. Isaiah 40:22 teaches us that the earth is a sphere.

How wonderful it is to realize the wonders of this world God made and the greatness of the Book that reveals the truths to us.

The Third Day

In Genesis 1:9-13, we find that the land appeared as it emerged from beneath the water. The dry land made plant life possible, "the fruit tree that yields fruit according to its kind" (v. 11). This is the law of growth that God established and has been so ever since. We do not look for apples on a pear tree. We do not plant carrots and expect potatoes. God said, "according to its kind."

Each thing that God created was to reproduce after its own kind. Instead of increasing in number, species have decreased; nature shows a downward tendency. Retrogression of species certainly is well established. God made so many types of plants that even at this time there are about 250,000 species. God made desert plants, called "belly plants," so small that only the trained eye ever sees them. And yet these plants bloom with a beauty that is amazing. There is a Desert Calico flower that has petals of white, pink and purple, yet the entire blossom is less than two-tenths of an inch across. The Rock Gila has such tiny flowers that the insects cannot get inside of them. Only God could make such delicate blossoms.

By comparison, God made the massive redwoods of northern California. These are the largest trees in the world. One of them, the General Sherman, is nearly 280 feet tall. It takes about 20 people with outstretched arms to reach around the trunk. When the Lord Jesus was here on Earth, this tree was about 2,000 years old. Surely only God could make such a tree.

The Fourth Day

In Genesis 1:14-19, we read that the two great lights for the earth were set "for signs and seasons, and for days and years." God created the sun, moon and stars by just the words, "Let there be lights in the firmament" (v. 14).

The sun is nearly 93 million miles away from the earth. The temperature on its surface is about 12,000° F. If the sun were closer, life on the earth would be impossible. If it were farther away, the earth would be too cold for life to exist. God put the sun in just the right place.

The sun is about 865,000 miles in diameter—not a very large body as stars go. In fact, the star Betelgeuse in the constellation of Orion is more than one million times as big as the sun. The sun appears so bright because it is so close to the earth. If it were as far away as the stars in the Big Dipper are, we could not see it without a telescope.

Does God Care About Us?

Everywhere about us is evidence of God's creation, an orderly creation that God brought into being. Of course, when we look at the vastness of the universe, it is easy for us to sometimes wonder, *Does the Creator of all things know or care about me?* We feel like David when he said, "When I consider Your heavens, the work of Your fingers, the moon and the stars, which You have ordained, what is man that You are mindful of him, and the son of man that You visit him?" (Ps. 8:3-4). Yet we know that David knew that God did care for him (see Ps. 23).

The great Bible story of beginnings is the story of God preparing a place for humankind. Just think of this: God made humans to have dominion over all of His creation. "You have made him to have dominion over the works of Your hands; You have put all things under his feet" (Ps. 8:6).

God does care for us. He does want to lead and guide us. He wants our love and fellowship. In truth, the question is not with God; the question is with us. Do we want God to lead us? Will we follow when He tells us what He wants us to do?

Daily Meditations

Sunday: God created the heavens and the earth—Genesis 1:1-8

Monday: Dry land and heavenly bodies—Genesis 1:9-19

Tuesday: Christ created all things—John 1:1-14

Wednesday: The universe reveals God's power—Psalm 104:1-9

Thursday: God has a plan for all nature—Psalm 104:1-9

Friday: God's wisdom—Psalm 104:19-24

Saturday: Worship the Lord—Psalm 104:25-35

7

God's Creation of Living Things

So God created man in His own image; in the image of God He created him; male and female created He them.
Genesis 1:27

"When I consider Your heavens, the work of Your fingers, the moon and the stars, which You have ordained, what is man that You are mindful of him, and the son of man that You visit him?" These were the observations of David in Psalm 8:3-4. The greatness of the universe certainly makes us realize that our God is a great God. The creator is always greater than His creation. By the word of His power, all the things that we see around us were made.

The Word of God tells us not only what God created but also that God's creation was an orderly one. Before humans, God created animals. Before animals, God created plant life. Before plant life, God made minerals. Humans were the last in order of creation. There was method, profession and intelligence in creation. God prepared the earth before He made humans and put them there.

All the world about us was made by God. Everywhere and in everything we see His handiwork. We see it in the greatness of creation; we see it in the size and scope of creation; we see it in the order and design as well as in the continuation of natural laws that He has set up.

What makes for this order and certainty in the universe?

The law of chance cannot produce such order as we find in the creation of the universe. In creation, we see evidence of a mind capable of planning and thinking. This mind must belong to someone who has the knowledge and power to create and who is able to control all that He created. Blind force, chance, evolution—none of these can do the job. The only answer is that God created the universe and all the things in it. This is just what the Bible teaches.

Creation of Living Things

The Bible teaches that God created everything in six days, and on the seventh day He rested. During the first four days, or periods of time, God created the universe and plant life. God continued His work of creation for two more days to fulfill His purpose for the universe, and especially for the world.

The Fifth Day

Genesis 1:20-23 tells of the creation of animal life in the water and in the air. Again, God says that each is to bring forth "according to its kind."

God created fish that range in size from a tiny minnow to a great whale. The whale is the largest living thing that man has ever seen, perhaps larger even than the prehistoric monsters. The main artery of the whale is a pipe large enough to hold easily a full-grown man.

God made birds to fly in the heavens. Lightness and buoyancy, of course, were important. The great creator knew this, so He made the bones of the birds so that they may be filled with air as a sponge is filled with water. In fact, the whole body is inflated like a balloon.

Even the feathers that cover the bird are marvelous examples of ingenuity. Each feather is a series of amazing locks—as many as one million on a large feather. These locks hold the feather together. If the feather is torn, the bird "preens" it back together again. Take a feather and pull it apart in one place. Then carefully, with just a slight amount of pressure, run the tear between your thumb and finger. Repeat two or three times and the locks will spring again into place and the torn area will be mended.

The Sixth Day

In Genesis 1:24-27, we see that there were a great many things that God made on this sixth day of creation. The Bible says that all the creeping things were made. Do you know that for each of the stars you can see on a clear night, God has created 100 different species of insects?

On the sixth day, animals and man were also created. The climax of all creation is man. God did not create him until He had prepared a place for him. We may think that we are not very important when we look at the vastness of this universe, yet man, we are told, was made in God's image. He can think God's thoughts after Him. He can do God's will. He can respond to God's love.

Did you ever wonder why we are made as we are? God made our bodies for the kind of life we live on this earth. Scientists declare that it would be practically impossible to improve the biological construction of the human body. For example, if our bodies were much larger, our hands and fingers would be too large and clumsy for fine work, such as watchmaking or sewing. Two eyes are better than one for judging distance and shape. No wonder the psalmist said, "I will praise You, for I am fearfully and wonderfully made" (Ps. 139:14).

The purpose of creation was the preparation of a home for man. The world was made for man to enjoy. His needs from the animal and vegetable world had been provided before he was created. How wonderful that the light, the heat, the moisture and earth, essential for plant and animal life, came first. This reveals that God is infinite in wisdom and power and is infinite in His love to us. What we do owe Him! What can we do without Him?

The Bible describes the creation of man like this: "So God created man in His own image; in the image of God He created him" (Gen. 1:27). And again, "The LORD God formed man of the dust of the ground, and breathed into his nostrils the breath of life; and man became a living being" (Gen. 2:7). The rest of the creation God made by the word of His power, but man was made in a special way: He breathed life into him.

At the beginning, God gave man a position that he could never attain by himself. When God created man, He gave him dominion. Make a mental list of the things over which man was to rule. How does man rule the earth? It yields to him all its precious treasures at his bidding; it helps his grain and fruit to grow. How does he rule over animals? They become obedient to his commands. They do what he wants them to do. They serve as food. How does man rule over the seas, including rivers and lakes? They carry his ships. They turn his water wheels to make electricity. They give him water to drink. How about the sun? It warms him and lights him on his way. It puts life into his corn and wheat as they grow. "Created in the image of God" is a thought that should be remembered. In mind and spirit and in dominion over nature, man is the glory and crown of creation.

Human ingenuity has invented the telephone, the X-ray machine, bridges and tunnels and has even harnessed the power of lightning. With every great business enterprise, somewhere a person with a handful of brains a little bigger than two fists controls it all, his or her shoulders back and head up! All other creatures grovel with their heads down. Only man lifts his face upward to God.

There are two accounts of man's making. The first in Genesis 1 merely makes the statement that man was made. The second in Genesis 2 goes back over the story and adds certain particulars. It tells how he was made; where his home was to be (a garden), what his work was (cultivating the soil), what his relation to God should be (that of simple obedience). It tells of the bringing to him of his life companion and helpmate, who was taken out from close to his own heart.

In all of God's creation, there was no other creature like Adam. The Lord God brought the animals to Adam to be named. Genesis 2:20 says, "So Adam gave names to all cattle, and the birds of the air, and to every beast of the field. But for Adam there was not found a helper comparable to him."

The Lord said that it was not good for man to be alone (see Gen. 2:18), so God provided a helpmate for him. God made Eve for Adam. The Lord took a rib from Adam and from it "made into a woman, and He brought her to the man" (v. 22). It was God who made marriage and the home. Marriage is blessed of God and should be treated as a sacred bond.

The Seventh Day

"Then God saw every thing that He had made, and indeed it was very good" (Gen. 1:31). On the seventh day, God ended the work He had done and rested (see Gen. 2:2). God rested because His work in creating the heavens and the earth was completed, not because He was tired.

The Power of Choice

Although Adam and Eve were created without sin, God gave them the power to choose between right and wrong. They did not have to choose right, but they did not have to choose to do wrong, either. They had a free will. They could do as they chose.

God placed them in a perfect place, the Garden of Eden, and told them to keep it for Him. They had the freedom and use of the whole Garden, with one exception. God said, "Of every tree of the garden you may freely eat; but of the tree of the knowledge of good and evil you shall not eat, for in the day that you eat of it you shall surely die" (Gen. 2:16-17).

God wanted Adam and Eve to obey Him, but He gave them the right to choose to obey. He did not make them obey. The Lord God gives us the same power of choice. We do not choose whether to eat of the fruit of a certain tree, but we are faced with the fact that God does not make us obey Him. He asks us to do so, and then leaves the choice up to us.

We are faced with other choices as well. One of life's great choices is the work we do. Another great choice is the person whom we will marry. But the greatest choice concerns the Lord Jesus Christ. Will we decide to be for Christ or against Him? The consequences of this choice are very plain: If we decide against Christ, we will be barred from heaven forever (see Matt. 10:32-33), but if we decide for Him, we will become God's children and will have heaven for our eternal home (see John 3:36).

Many years ago, Patrick Henry made a great choice. He said, "Give me liberty or give me death." He preferred death to slavery. He made his choice. Some years ago, Adolph Hitler was warned not to attack Poland. He made his choice, attacked, and World War II began. Soon after, Japan chose to attack the United States, and the United States entered the war. In each case, a different choice could possibly have been made.

If you are a Christian, you have already made the greatest choice—Jesus Christ is your Savior. But every day you are faced with more choices. Make your choice only when you are sure that what you decide will please our Lord and Savior. Seek His will in prayer and in the study of the Bible. Consult with Christian leaders, talk it over with your pastor, and get their advice. Then, when you know the right choice, do it.

Daily Meditations

Sunday: God creates life—Genesis 1:20-31

Monday: The Garden of Eden—Genesis 2:1-17

Tuesday: The creation of Eve—Genesis 2:18-25

Wednesday: Man's dominion—Psalm 8:1-9

Thursday: Man should praise God—Psalm 139:14-18,23

Friday: Man's position in Christ—Ephesians 1:15-23

Saturday: Man's future paradise—Revelation 22:1-5

8

Sin Mars God's Plan

Through one man sin entered the world, and death through sin, and thus death spread to all men, because all sinned.
Romans 5:12

A young man was trying to get another to go into a bar and have a drink with him. "We may as well have a good time," said the first. "We must see life as it is."

"No," answered the other. "To know life is to know it at its best. You had better come with me to church and learn something about life as it ought to be."

Which one was right? Why?

We can be sure of one thing—God wants life to be what it ought to be. If anyone tries to show us that real life is something other than the life the Lord has told us He wants us to live, we should be on our guard.

Where Sin Begins

God created Adam and Eve to have fellowship with Him. In the cool of the day, God talked with them in the Garden of Eden. Many people have been interested as to where this garden was located. The majority of scholars have placed it in the valley of the Tigris and Euphrates Rivers.

You could never find a more ideal home for man. It is still a beautiful spot. The tall date palms grow and provide the inhabitants who live in their shade with almost every necessity of life. Pelicans and storks abound along the banks of the Euphrates and Tigris, and fish can be found in great numbers in the rivers and marshes of the region.

In man's hand was placed the power of dominion over all things that God had created. Even the beasts of the field were obedient to the will of our first parents. That dominion lasted until sin entered the world. As we mentioned in the last chapter, Adam and Eve were created perfect, with sinless natures, but they *could* sin because God had given them the power of choice. It was possible for them to sin, just as it was possible for them not to sin. God wanted humans to choose to obey Him rather than choose not to obey Him.

The first temptation to do wrong came through a serpent. All through the Bible "serpent" is the word used for Satan. The serpent was the most subtle, or wisest, of the animal creation (see 2 Cor. 11:3; Rev. 12:9,14-15; 20:2).

The serpent was the most beautiful creature, and the devil wanted to hide himself behind something good. He wanted to use the best thing that he could find. He almost always hides behind something good. Someone has said that "good" is the worst enemy of the "best." What does this mean? It means that often we are fooled into accepting the thing that is not too bad instead of doing God's will that is best.

The devil is the master deceiver (see 2 Cor. 11:13-14; Eph. 6:11-12; 2 Thess. 2:9). He blinds the eyes of those that believe not (see 2 Cor. 4:4). The first temptation of Eve began with questioning what God had told her to do. What did the serpent say that Eve could eat if she wanted to? "He said to the woman,

'Has God indeed said, "You shall not eat of every tree of the garden"? . . . You will not surely die. For God knows that in the day you eat of it your eyes will be opened, and you will be like God, knowing good and evil'" (Gen. 3:1,4-5).

This is how sin comes into the human heart. The devil takes delight in misinterpreting God. He tries to make us think that God is holding back on us. He tells us to pay no attention to God but just do what we think is right. The serpent put in Eve's heart the wicked, terrible thought that some other plan than God's was the best. Does Satan ever do that now? How? Has he ever done it to you?

The devil always promises to give us that which he never does. He says, "Take this way for fun, success and real joy." Instead, like Adam and Eve, we get death. Satan makes sin appear to be what it is not. It seems to be beautiful at first, but later it holds us in its clutches. Many people say, "I thought I was having a good time, but see where it brought me."

There is a constant warfare between good and evil—between God's plan for us and Satan's designs upon us. There is no end to the fight on Earth. However, God has promised that wherever there is a temptation, there is also a way out. In 1 Corinthians 10:13, Paul writes, "No temptation has overtaken you except such as is common to man; but God is faithful, who will not allow you to be tempted beyond what you are able, but with the temptation will also make the way of escape, that you may be able to bear it."

Talented people need to be especially on guard against the wrong use of their talent. Why does the possession of a talent almost always open the way to temptation? Because everybody has a strong point that, if it is not guarded, becomes a gateway to temptation.

The temptation often comes to question God's goodness. Don't ever question God's love. You can always be sure that God does what is best for you. You may not always understand, but you can always be sure that God's care is so great that He can keep you from falling. Never doubt God's love.

Yielding to Temptation

God said that if Adam and Eve ate of the tree of the knowledge of good and evil, it would only bring sorrow. Satan asked Eve the question, "Has God indeed said?" (Gen. 3:1), and Eve answered Satan. She didn't need to answer him; he wasn't after information. He was just trying to raise a doubt in her mind. The tempter was only trying to make Eve question God's goodness and to shake Eve's simple faith in God's love.

First a question and then a lie—that is the way the devil works. The tempter began with a mean, insinuating question about God's love and then a flat contradiction of what God had said. Eve doubted God. Her eyes looked; she saw. That was the beginning of it all. Then she argued with herself and reached out her hand.

Notice that one step led to another. Each step got progressively worse. First there was a lingering look; second, a yearning desire; third, a yielding to action. This sin began with the eye, then the mouth, then the mind, and then finished with the hand as Eve plucked the fruit. We need to watch our eyes. The eye opens the door to most of the sin that is done. Eve's eye opened the door to her appetite.

In 1 John 2:16, we read, "For all that is in the world—the lust of the flesh, the lust of the eyes, and the pride of life—is not of the Father but is of the world." These three categories are the very ones that the devil used to tempt Eve. She sinned with her eyes, for in Genesis 3:6 we read that the fruit "was pleasant to the eyes." She sinned with her mouth, or the lust of the flesh, for she saw that the tree "was good for food." She sinned with her hand, for she took the fruit. She thought that it would make her wise. This was the pride of life.

Does sin generally affect others besides the one doing the sinning? It is all too true that when we sin, someone we love will suffer. Eve's hand did two things: It took the fruit and then gave it to her husband. Sin is so selfish! No one ever sins alone. If we take hold of a sooty, black stick and then take hold of someone else's hand, that person's hand will be blackened also. So will everything that we touch. We'd better stop before we do the thing that is wrong.

Adam blamed Eve, and Eve blamed the serpent. Why do we blame others for our wrongdoing? It's so easy for us to give an excuse for what we do instead of confessing that the act is sin and asking God to forgive us. We must learn not to blame others for what we do and just face the truth. God knows all about it, anyway. We can't fool Him!

What is the penalty for sin? "For the wages of sin is death, but the gift of God is eternal life in Christ Jesus our Lord." God said in Genesis 2:17 that if Adam and Eve ate of the fruit of the tree, they would surely die. Did they? Consider this: Our life is from God. Whatever separates us from Him cuts us off from life. If we cut off a branch of a tree, the branch is dead. It has been separated from its source of life. It may not look dead immediately, but just wait a few days. Adam and Eve died because they would now be separated from God.

When Adam and Eve questioned and disbelieved God's word, they lost fellowship with Him and were driven from their beautiful home. What a train of misery followed upon their unbelief! Six terrible results came upon the whole world when they chose to sin:

1. The ground was cursed (see Gen. 3:17-19).
2. There would be suffering in childbirth (see Gen. 3:16).

3. Humans would now have to toil in order to live (see Gen. 3:19).
4. There would be physical and spiritual death (see Gen. 3:3,19; Rom. 5:12).
5. There would be fear of God instead of fellowship with Him (see Gen. 3:8-11).
6. Humankind was expelled from the Garden (see Gen. 3:22-24).

How sad it is that Adam and Eve chose to break God's law. But then, don't you and I also break God's law? Or, to be more correct, you and I are broken by God's law. God did not make puppets of men. He gave each one of us a free will.

Sin Must Be Punished

The temptation to sin came to Adam and Eve from an outside source, but the sin itself was an act of their own determination. The first sin was very much like every sin that has been committed. It was a positive disbelief in the word of the living God, a belief in Satan rather than a belief in God.

It is helpful to note that the same kinds of temptation that came to Adam and Eve came to Christ in the wilderness (see Matt. 4:1-11), and these same kinds of temptations have come to men ever since (see 1 John 2:15-17). The devil came to Christ with the temptation that He should turn the stones into bread. Certainly, this was an attempt to make Christ sin by yielding to the lust of the flesh.

Next, the devil told the Lord Jesus to cast Himself down from the pinnacle of the Temple. Here was a temptation to yield to the sin of the pride of life. Finally, the devil showed the Lord all the kingdoms of this world and said to Him, "All these things I will give You if You will fall down and worship me"

(Matt. 4:9). What an example of a sin to yield to the lust of the eyes. The devil makes great offers. He even dared make them to Christ!

The whole world was affected by Adam and Eve's sin and their fall (see Rom. 8:19-22). All people since the Fall, without respect to position or class, have been sinners before God. "There is none righteous, no, not one" (Rom. 3:10). "Therefore, just as through one man sin entered the world, and death through sin, and thus death spread to all men, because all sinned" (Rom. 5:12).

The entire nature of humankind has been brought under the condemnation and curse of sin. Our understanding is darkened (see Eph. 4:18). Our hearts are deceitful (see Jer. 17:9). Our minds and consciences are defiled (see Titus 1:15). Our flesh is defiled (see Gal. 5:17). Our will is enfeebled (see Rom. 7:18). And we are destitute of any qualities that meet the requirements of God's holiness (see Rom. 7:18).

A Promised Redeemer

When Adam and Eve realized that they were naked, they tried to make their own covering. What did they use? "Then the eyes of both of them were opened, and they knew that they were naked; and they sewed fig leaves together and made themselves coverings" (Gen. 3:7). They tried to hide from God by their own works, but that could not count with God.

But in Genesis 3:21, we find that God gave them a covering of skin. This new clothing that God gave to Adam to replace the covering he made himself shows that the shedding of blood is necessary for suitable covering for sin, not only for Adam and Eve, but for the whole human race. "According to the law almost all things are purified with blood, and without shedding of blood there is no remission" (Heb. 9:22).

In the same chapter that records this story of sin is the promise of victory over it. God is never late. Genesis 3:15 says, "I will put enmity between you and the woman, and between your seed and her Seed; He shall bruise your head, and you shall bruise His heel." Here is the first promise in Scripture—a promise of a Savior. Notice carefully a great truth of Scripture is mentioned in this first promise: the Redeemer of the race is to be the seed of the woman.

The covering of skins that God provided to Adam and Eve to cover themselves pointed forward to Christ's death on Calvary. An animal had to die. Remember, "the wages of sin is death" (Rom. 6:23). Sin had to be punished. Christ took the punishment for it in His death. All the sacrifices of animals before His death were pictures of what He would do. The cross of Calvary stands so related to all the ages that the sacrifice of Jesus Christ once and for all fulfilled the promise of a Redeemer and provided salvation to all who believe since the very Fall of man. Christ was "the Lamb slain from the foundation of the world" (Rev. 13:8).

Sin in Our Lives

What is sin? How can we know when we are sinning? Why is sin so terrible? What does it do to us? The Bible has many answers to these questions. We are told that sin is the transgression of the law (see 1 John 3:4) and that all unrighteousness is sin (see 1 John 5:17). The omission of that which we know to be good is sin (see Jas. 4:17). Whatever is not of faith is sin (see Rom. 14:23).

It is the Holy Spirit who convicts us of sin (see John 16:8-9). It is the Word of God that tells us what we must do to keep from sin. Sin is terrible because God hates it (see Isa. 13:11). It separates us from Him (see Isa. 59:1-2) and keeps us from heaven (see Rev. 21:27). It brings forth death (see Rom. 6:23; Jas. 1:15).

From the story of the first temptation told in Genesis 3:1-6, we can answer the question, What is sin? Do you think Adam and Eve knew that they had sinned? What verse in the third chapter of Genesis says that they did? They disobeyed God by not believing His word. Unbelief is the worst sin.

When we do sin, what are we to do? "If we confess our sins, He is faithful and just to forgive us our sins and to cleanse us from all unrighteousness" (1 John 1:9). Isn't that a wonderful promise that the Lord has given to us? He will forgive us if we come to Him.

So never allow sin to remain unconfessed. Tell God immediately what you have done and ask His forgiveness.

Daily Meditations

Sunday: The temptation of Eve—Genesis 3:1-7

Monday: Sin must be punished—Genesis 3:8-19

Tuesday: The results of sin—Genesis 3:20-24

Wednesday: All are guilty of sin—Romans 5:12-19

Thursday: All have sinned—Romans 3:10-23

Friday: Christ died for our sin—Romans 5:1-11

Saturday: Christ forgives our sin—1 John 1:1-10

9

The Results of Sin

For the wages of sin is death, but the gift of God is eternal life in Christ Jesus our Lord.
Romans 6:23

If we could legislate and get a perfect environment for people, give them plenty of food and plenty to wear, would people be good? Certainly the Garden of Eden had a perfect environment, but did it produce perfect people? We need a new nature for a new home.

Let's go over the effects of Adam and Eve's sin upon the world. What was man's sin? What great promise of the Savior was given?

When Adam and Eve ate of the tree of the knowledge of good and evil, their eyes were opened and they knew that they were naked in God's sight; that is, that they were sinners (see Gen. 3:7). Now that humans had knowledge of good from evil, they must do good and refrain from evil. Knowledge always brings responsibility.

Is it true that the knowledge of good makes us do good? How many times we know exactly what is right! Our conscience speaks to us, but we deliberately do wrong. Even the smallest child knows that it is wrong to steal cookies or to spend the pennies out of his bank. But does that keep him or her from doing it? No, the child just waits until his mother steps out of the room. Everyone has a conscience that tells him or her what way is right, but humans have continually failed to obey its dictates. For more than 1,600 years God observed the condition of humankind. He tested people in every possible way, but as we read in Genesis 6:12, "All flesh had corrupted their way on the earth."

A Self-Centered Race

How different the whole world had become as a result of the Fall. The animals had become ferocious, and humans were fearful of them. Thorns and thistles had grown. Humans had become great upon the earth, but what did God say about them? "Then the LORD saw that the wickedness of man was great in the earth, and that every intent of the thoughts of his heart was only evil continually" (Gen. 6:5).

From the very beginning of the civilization that Adam and Eve tried to set up, sin was working. Humankind's perverse selfishness produced its deadly fruit. All sin has its roots in and grows up out of unbelief. Humans were now *self-centered* instead of *God-centered.* Self is the heart of all sin, whether in Satan or in man. God is the center of true life and should be its beginning and end.

Remember the record with the hole in it a little off center? What a terrible noise it made. Instead of beautiful music, there was nothing but discord. Now, if the record is put back on the machine exactly on center, the discord is turned into lovely music. The record has not been changed at all. All the difference is in the center. God wants our lives to be a beautiful symphony of music. Everything He creates and plans is beautiful. He plans our lives with Himself as the center. If we have self as the center, we find that our days are full of confusion and unhappiness.

Adam and Eve's first children after being driven out of the Garden were Cain and Abel. No doubt their father and mother taught them about God and told them about the covering of skins that had been given to them by God. This covering required the shedding of the blood of animals as a proper covering for their sin and shame.

As Cain and Abel grew to be young men, they brought their own offerings to the Lord. Cain's was a bloodless sacrifice of the best fruit of his own labor. Abel brought a lamb for a sacrifice. Here are two distinct and opposite types of offerings: the one offers nothing but the shed blood, and the other offers the best of his works. Which one brought the better offering, Cain or Abel? "By faith Abel offered to God a more excellent sacrifice than Cain, through which he obtained witness that he was righteous, God testifying of his gifts; and through it he being dead still speaks" (Heb. 11:4).

No doubt God had clearly taught people how to approach Him. It is seen in the fact that Abel offered unto God a more excellent sacrifice than Cain. Abel offered the sacrifice of blood as God had commanded. Cain represents all those who believe that they can come to God and please Him with an offering of a good life and "doing the best they can." How many there are today who think they can come to God and please Him this way! Abel represents those who know that only through faith in the shed blood of Jesus Christ, the Lamb of God, can they really please their heavenly Father.

God could not accept Cain's sacrifice. "He did not respect Cain and His offering. And Cain was very angry, and his countenance fell. So the LORD said to Cain, 'Why are you angry? And why has your countenance fallen? If you do well, will you not be accepted? And if you do not do well, sin lies at the door.

And its desire is for you, but you should rule over it'" (Gen. 4:5-7).

We can learn a great deal here about sin. When God is not pleased, it is clear evidence that sin is lurking around somewhere. God hates sin and will always fight it. When God is not pleased, we want to find out what is wrong. Sin always wants to be the master and have its own way. Sin has such an ugly spirit. If it cannot rule, it will do its best to ruin.

Cain saw that his brother's offering was accepted, but his was not. His jealous disposition did not let him seek in himself the cause of the failure, but made him look to his brother. He showed his spirit in his countenance. Those who nurse jealousy only cultivate awful misery. How unhappy the jealous person is! Look at the work of jealousy in the home, in school and in business.

The first death in the world was a murder that grew out of anger. The victim was an innocent and good man, and the murderer was his brother. Oh, the blackness of sin! A little talk out in the field, a flaring up of anger, a blow, and then *murder!*

How are we going to avoid Cain's fate? He is not the last man that was ruined by a bad disposition. The Bible says that hating is the same as murder (see Matt. 5:21-22). How quickly God's questions follow sin. "Where are you, Adam?" "Where is Abel your brother?" Lies were the answers to both the questions. One sin always calls for another. Our hope is found in 2 Corinthians 5:17: "if anyone is in Christ, he is a new creation; old things have passed away; behold, all things have become new."

Results of Humankind's Civilization

As time went on, Adam's children, grandchildren and great-grandchildren grew to be men and women. People built up a civilization of their own, which came to naught (see Gen. 4:16-24). After Cain killed his brother, Abel, he fled to Nod, where he built the city of Enoch. Cain's wicked generation ended with Lamech, another murderer. These wicked, worldly sons were cattle owners (see Gen. 4:20), musicians (v. 21) and workers of art in brass (v. 22). Humans lived upon the earth, and their wickedness was very great. Genesis 4–5 shows the development and results of sin in family life, and Genesis 6–8 shows the results in the experiences of the race.

In this age of new responsibilities, humankind went downward through its lusts. How evil they were! Compare Cain's line and Seth's line (see Gen. 4:1-24 and 4:25–5:32). The fifth from Cain was a murderer, so the line of Cain begins with murder and ends with murder (see Genesis 4:8,23). Seth's line, however, ends with one who walked with God. What a difference! God gave Seth to Adam and Eve to take Abel's place, and his was a godly line.

It was through the line of Seth that the Messiah promised in Genesis 3:15 was to come. The greatest teaching of all Genesis 3 is in this fifteenth verse. This is the first Messianic promise. The Redeemer of the race was to be "the seed" of the woman. The entire Bible is occupied with the development and fulfillment of this promise of a coming Savior. Christ was to be born of a virgin, and He would come to put an end to the works of the devil though His death and resurrection.

The fifth from Seth was a man named Enoch. The Bible says the he "walked with God" (Gen. 5:22). He was the one who was taken to heaven without dying, for "God took him" (v. 24). His son was Methuselah, the oldest man who ever lived. His son was Lamech, whose son was Noah.

God's Provision in Judgment and in Forgiveness

Noah's grandfather, Methuselah, was 243 years old when Adam died. Noah's father, Lamech, was 56 years old when Adam died.

What wonderful stories Noah's father and grandfather must have told Noah about the first man and woman and the beginning of life on this earth! Lamech died five years before the Flood and Methuselah died the year of the Flood.

Noah lived on the earth for 600 years during the same time Methuselah lived, and Methuselah lived on the earth with Adam for more than 250 years. Thus, Methuselah, Noah's grandfather, must have also told Noah many stories and given him much information about the beginning of life on this earth. Noah had all this information during the Flood. Noah lived 350 years after the Flood and passed all of this information along to his children and grandchildren.

During the time that Noah lived on the earth, the Bible says that man's sin was very great (see Gen. 6:5,11-12). Yet it is good to see that even in the midst of such sin and wickedness, there was one man who walked with God. God could say to Noah, "Make yourself an ark of gopherwood . . . and cover it inside and outside with pitch" (v. 14). In the Garden, a *covering* for the sin of Adam and Eve was provided, and now Noah was furnished a place of *protection,* an ark.

We must begin where the Bible begins if we want to trace the marvelous unfolding of God's plan of redemption through Christ, the central fact of the Bible. Remember, the Bible was not written to give us the history of the race. There is very little history of the age before the Flood. Of all the children of our first parents, it only mentions three names: Cain, Abel and Seth. *The Bible is only for one purpose—the unfolding of the plan of salvation.*

The fact of man's disobedience is clearly set forth. The fact of sin in the world is indisputable. It is wonderful that God's provision for forgiveness is also indisputable.

Turn to Romans 5:12-14. Here is set forth in plain language the condition of the world without God. Here is the picture of the family of Adam. Here is our picture, for we also are the family of Adam. Now read Romans 5:15-21. Here is God's provision for forgiveness. In the death of Christ, those who are sinful can be made righteous.

Do you realize that God has also provided for us to come to Him whenever we have done something that has displeased Him? Do you remember when you were little and you did something that your mother had told you not to do? For a little while, it was not pleasant to be around her, because the fellowship between you and your mother had been broken. Then, when you finally decided that this was not so good, you went to your mother and told her you were sorry. She forgave you, and at once you felt better.

It is the same way with the Lord. When we sin, we are not comfortable with God; we do not want to study His Word. We find it is hard to pray. But the Lord has said, "If we confess our sins, He is faithful and just to forgive us our sins and to cleanse us from all unrighteousness" (1 John 1:9). There is no other way. Christ is the only one who can and will forgive us and cleanse us from our sin.

Daily Meditations

Sunday: Man's sin—Genesis 6:1-7

Monday: God's grace—Genesis 6:8–7:1; Romans 5:20

Tuesday: This is a warning—Luke 17:22-37

Wednesday: The blood sacrifice is necessary—Hebrews 9:16-22,25-28

Thursday: Christ's Blood offered—Hebrews 9:11-15; 1 Peter 1:18-19

Friday: Man's unrighteousness—Romans 3:9-20

Saturday: God's righteousness—Romans 4:3-7; 5:15-21

10

God's Judgment in the Flood

The Lord *said, "My Spirit shall not strive with man forever, for he is indeed flesh."*
Genesis 6:3

We plant a garden that we hope will be beautiful. As soon as the seeds begin to grow, we must watch for weeds. If we are careless, the weeds will spread until the whole garden is filled with them and they choke out all the good plants that are growing there. If we want a good garden, we must constantly pull out the weeds.

Sin is like a weed that spreads throughout the garden. It will choke out all the good in our lives if we allow it to grow. When Adam and Eve sinned through disobedience and brought sorrow and suffering to the world, this seed of sin began to grow and spread, until we find Cain sinning even worse than his father or mother. Sin started with one person, but it was not long until all had sinned and fallen short of the glory of God (see Rom. 3:23).

At first, only two people broke God's commandments. Then many more were sinning, and there soon was great wickedness upon the face of the earth. There was a lack of concern among the people for God's commandments. They continued in their way of life with no thought of God. Their only goal was pleasure. Eventually, humankind fell so far below God's standard that He was grieved and sorry that He had ever created them (see Gen. 6:6).

God's masterpiece of creation had been marred by sin. Being a holy God, He could not allow this sin to go unpunished.

One Righteous Man in the Crowd

As God looked down upon all these wicked people, He found one righteous man in the crowd named Noah and honored him for his goodness. It is a great thing to have God pick a person out of the crowd to do His work. Can you think of any men or women you know who were evidently selected from the crowd to lead people to safety and success?

Perhaps God will some day pick you out of the crowd for His work. You say, "No chance." But He may, just the same. Read what He says in John 15:16: "You did not choose Me, but I chose you." Think of Noah. He had great faith, for he built for the rain while the sun was shining. He had great courage, for he kept building even though he was laughed at and treated with contempt. If God has work for you to do, He will want you to have faith and courage.

Punishment always follows sin. When Adam and Eve first sinned against God, what punishment followed? "So He drove out the man; and He placed cherubim at the east of the garden of Eden, and a flaming sword which turned every way, to guard the way to the tree of life" (Gen. 3:24). When their son Cain committed an even greater sin, how did God punish him? "And [God] said . . . now you are cursed from the earth, which has opened its mouth to receive your brother's blood from your hand. When you till the ground, it shall no longer yield its strength to you. A fugitive and a vagabond you shall be on the earth" (Gen. 4:10-12). When sin increased on the earth, how did God punish the sin of the race? "So the Lord said, 'I will destroy man whom I have created from the face of the earth, both man and beast, creeping thing and birds of the air' " (Gen. 6:7).

Think about it like this: Once, there was a rose bush that grew in a beautiful garden. Its blossoms were glorious, but one day the gardener saw that a blight had attacked his favorite bush and death was slowly but surely creeping down several large branches toward the root. The gardener knew what had to be done. Bending over the bush, the gardener cut away those blighted branches. Was he unkind? What was his purpose? The gardener was saving the good portion of the bush. In a similar way, the Lord was saving the righteous family of Noah by the Flood. Because sin, disease and contagion had earned for the people the wages of death, the Great Gardener in justice had to cut off the blighted branches before they affected Noah's family. Was it done in anger or revenge? It was Jehovah's righteousness and care for His obedient children.

The only way that God could show His justice was by destroying those who had hopelessly corrupted His creation. The Flood was God's righteous act toward humankind—toward that generation and all generations.

Warning of Judgment

In Genesis 6:14-16, we see that God planned to save Noah and his family in order to make a new beginning. He told him to build a strong boat, or "ark," the lower part of which was to be similar to a great river barge. The upper part was to have a roof like a house.

Notice the directions for building the ark and the warning Noah proclaimed during the construction. Picture in your mind

Noah's friends questioning and ridiculing him. One of them might have come up to Noah and said, "Hey, what is that you're building?"

"An ark."

"What's an ark?"

"It's some sort of boat."

"You don't need a boat around here; we're miles and miles from any water."

Noah might have answered, "There will be plenty of water one of these days. God is going to send a flood."

"We've never had a flood, whatever that is," the man would reply.

I am sure that Noah would warn that man and everyone who came near him to repent of his sin and to ask God's forgiveness. But the people just laughed and walked away. It is no wonder that God took such drastic means to cleanse the earth.

In the midst of wickedness so vile as to be unbearable to God, Noah remembered God and remained faithful. *First Noah remembered God, and then God remembered Noah.* Although he had been surrounded by such corruption for years, Noah had "found grace in the eyes of the LORD" (Gen. 6:8). God took Noah into His confidence and told him what he must do to prepare for the future.

There is a great lesson here. Noah was told to do something that seemed unreasonable. He was told to do something that cost his time, his money and his reputation. Nothing could seem more foolish than to build that great ship on dry land for a flood that seemed improbable.

Yet in the hour of crisis, Noah was prepared. How many times Jesus warned us to watch and pray lest temptation find us a ready victim when it comes. This is wonderfully illustrated in the great crisis in Noah's life. He passed through it safely because he was ready for it when it came.

It is not enough to believe that God is good. We must believe that it is good to do what God says even if we cannot see the outcome. So Noah did everything just as God had commanded. The ark was completed. Then Noah, his family and the animals entered, and God shut the door of the ark. He shut Noah in to keep him and his family safe, and He shut out the water. Remember, this God who sent the Flood is the same God who sent His Son to save sinners. He has not changed between that day and the day of crucifixion and our day. This is the kind of God He is. This is what He thinks of sin, and this is why He cares for those who trust Him.

The Size of the Ark

The ark was a flat-bottomed, rectangular construction, "The length . . . three hundred cubits, its width fifty cubits, and its height thirty cubits" (Gen. 6:15). We cannot know the exact size of the ark, because the size of the "cubit" (the ancient unit of measure) varied from 18 to 22 1/2 inches. However, figuring on the smaller measurement of 18 inches for the cubit, we know that the ark was at least 450 feet long, 75 feet wide and 45 feet high, with a possible displacement of 43,000 tons. That means that it was larger than many ships today. (Note that the Chaldean cubit was 22 1/2 inches, so if this was used, the ark was even larger.)

The ark had three stories, with each floor divided into many rooms. The ark was covered inside and out with pitch to make it waterproof. It may have taken Noah as long as 120 years to build it (see Gen. 6:3).

Notice that the number of animals was two of each *kind* (not variety), and seven pairs of each clean kind. If half the space of the ark had been filled with food and the required number of every true species now inhabiting the world were stored in the other half, 175 cubic feet of space would be given for each individual. (A 200-pound man requires only 15 cubic feet.) To be sure, there were one million kinds of living things on the earth. Many of the living creatures lived in the water, and about five-eights of the remainder were insects.

When all were safely inside the ark, the Flood came. This was no ordinary rainstorm. The Bible says that the windows of heaven were opened, the waters above the firmament poured down upon the earth, and the seas overflowed the land from below (see Gen. 7:11). For 40 days and nights, the waters fell. This was one cause of the Flood—it rained—and there was also a geological cause—the fountains of the deep were broken up.

It is wonderful to realize that all during the Flood, each little bird in the ark was just as safe as the big elephant. It was not the elephant's size and strength that made him safe; it was the ark that kept each animal from harm. In like manner, it is not our personal importance or even our good works that will save us from punishment from sin. The Lord Jesus Christ is the only one who can do that.

God's Agreement with Humans

The waters covered the land for many months, but finally they began to subside. The dry land appeared again, and the ark settled on the mountains of Ararat (see Gen. 8:4).

There is a wonderful climax in this lesson: God made an agreement with man. Think of the wonder of it! He explained to man what He intended. He even set up a reminder for Himself in the heavens (see Gen. 9:12-13).

When did God make this covenant with Noah? It was after Noah had reached the land, built an altar and sacrificed an offering upon it in thanksgiving to God for deliverance and to ask for protection in the future. What answer did God make to Noah's prayer? He promised never to destroy the earth again by water. What was the sign that God gave of this covenant that

He made with Noah? The rainbow. This rainbow was a sign of God's covenant with Noah.

Of what should this rainbow remind us every time we see it? The rainbow is another of many visible signs that illustrate spiritual truths, such as the Passover lamb, the Bronze Serpent, Gideon's fleece, and so forth. Remember, God always keeps His covenants with man. God always does what He says.

God's Word is the one sure thing we have in this world. God says, "I will remember My covenant" (Gen. 9:15). That is God's strong point. In fact, there is only one thing that God will not remember (see Jer. 31:34). God did not forget Noah for a second. He was planning the judgment of the sinners and the salvation of His child, Noah, at the same time. God never forgets those who put their trust in Him.

When the ground had become dry, God bade Noah and his family to go out. Noah's first act was not an act of rejoicing only but also one of thanksgiving to God for the salvation of himself and his family. He erected an altar and made a sacrifice of thanksgiving that was pleasing to God.

This was a great covenant that God made with Noah, but not nearly so great as the one that He made with us. Remember, at the time the Lord Jesus instituted the Lord's Supper, He said, "For this is My blood of the new covenant, which is shed for many for the remission of sins" (Matt. 26:28). How much greater is this token of a covenant than is the rainbow. God promised Noah that He would not destroy the world with a flood, but He promised to us eternal life. "And this is eternal life, that they may know You, the only true God, and Jesus Christ whom You have sent" (John 17:3).

Noah was able to partake of the covenant of the rainbow because He obeyed God. We are partakers of the new covenant by being obedient to the command of God in the accepting of Jesus Christ as our Lord and Savior.

A New Test

God gave into humans' hands the control of every living thing on Earth and in the seas. The responsibility was to govern the earth righteously for God, but humans failed, and so God ended their rule. The world was full of anarchy and rebellion. This brought on the judgment of Babel, confusion of tongues and dispersion. This terrible judgment came because of humankind's daring and rebellious attempt to become independent of God.

Under the Noahic Covenant, humankind is subjected to a new test. Under this test, humans are to be governed by other humans; for the first time, human government is to be established (see Gen. 9:6). Humans now become responsible to govern the world for God. That responsibility rested upon the whole race. We have become accustomed to the thought that the Jewish race alone was in possession of all the ordinances of God, but there were neither Jews nor gentiles at this time. These are basic, fundamental laws of God upon which human government rests.

Daily Meditations

Sunday: Sin—1 John 3:1-10
Monday: Christ's warning—Luke 17:22-37
Tuesday: The ark of safety—Genesis 7:1–8:19
Wednesday: Noah's altar—Genesis 8:20-22
Thursday: God's covenant—Genesis 9:9-17
Friday: A new covenant—Hebrews 8:6-13
Saturday: Future judgment by fire—2 Peter 3:3-13

11

When Man Ruled Himself

Everyone proud in heart is an abomination to the Lord*; though they join forces, none will go unpunished.*
Proverbs 16:5

Noah's family stepped out of the ark and into a world judged of sin and wickedness. They could expect God's blessing as long as they obeyed Him. What a responsibility they had! What would they do? God told Noah's family exactly what they had to do. They had to (1) replenish the earth with people, (2) take dominion over all the animals, (3) use animals for their food, (4) take green herbs (plants) for their food, and (5) obey God's law of a life for a life.

Noah was the connecting link between the antediluvian and postdiluvian world (before and after the Flood). The sons of Noah were the fathers of the various nations and races (see Gen. 10:32). Generally speaking, Ham and his sons took possession of Africa, Arabia and Palestine; Shem and his five sons settled in Persia, northwest of Mesopotamia to Asia Minor; and Japheth and his family settled in areas north (Europe) and west (Asia).

Humans Govern Themselves

After Noah's long confinement in the ark, his first act was to glorify God by erecting an altar and sacrificing burnt offerings upon it. It was then that God entered into an appropriate covenant with him, telling Noah that He would never again destroy the earth with a flood. God said in Genesis 8:21, however, that man's heart would continue to be evil from his youth. How sadly true this is!

Noah became a husbandman and planted a vineyard in Mesopotamia. Sometime later, he drank too much of the wine and was overcome. How sad that the man who had erected an altar in thanksgiving to God should be found drunk and naked! His sons discovered him in a shameful condition. Ham laughed at his father's shame, but Shem and Japheth took a garment and, without even looking at their unconscious father, covered him. God put a blessing upon Shem and Japheth for honoring their father (see Gen. 9:26-27) but cursed Ham's sons for ridiculing and making known their father's shame (see Gen. 9:25).

After the Flood, the families of the earth traveled together in groups as they journeyed from one place to another and sought the best pasture for their flocks. In their travels, they at last arrived in a fertile land known as the Plain of Shinar. It is not surprising to read in Genesis 11:2 that "they dwelt there." Soon, they thought up a plan of making bricks out of the soil of the plain, for there were no stones in the region.

So, they had "brick for stone, and they had asphalt for mortar" (Gen. 11:3). Because they were so successful in making bricks, they said to themselves, "Come, let us build ourselves a city, and a tower whose top is in the heavens; let us make a name for ourselves, lest we be scattered abroad over the face of the whole earth" (Gen. 11:4). God had told man to "fill the earth" (see Gen 9:1), which meant to repopulate it. He wanted people to disperse themselves. Instead, they migrated in a compact group and tried to become very powerful.

The Messianic Line

Shem had been selected as the new head of the Messianic line (see Gen. 9:26-27). It is possibly this distinction of Shem in being divinely selected in the line of the Messiah that gave rise to jealousy on the part of the sons of Ham and Japheth. It is also possible that this is the reason they said, "Let *us* make us a name," for the word "Shem" signifies "name." It was the races of Ham and Japheth, no doubt, that engaged in the Tower of Babel enterprise.

Nimrod, son of Cush, grandson of Ham, was a great warrior and builder. He was the first king to rule this earth. Nimrod taught men that instead of worshiping God, they should depend upon themselves for happiness and success. In order to strengthen this belief, he began to build a huge tower, which is called the Tower of Babel. This was entirely contrary to the will of God.

God saw that people were becoming more and more wicked in idolatry and that unless He intervened in some way, humans would never scatter over the earth and cultivate it as He had planned. So He razed Nimrod's kingdom to the ground, confused the people's tongues and scattered them with different languages over the face of the earth. This broke up their social intercourse and ended in the dispersion at Babel.

This left the Shemites (or Semites) in the East, and their separation from the others is peculiarly significant. How long these races dwelt together we have no way of knowing, but it was no doubt a long time. This belongs to what is known as the "prehistoric" age.

Language Development

How foolish it is to try to explain the history of languages without referring first to the record in Genesis 11:5-9! This passage teaches us that language is not the offspring of gibberish and jargon. Neither is diversity of tongues accidental variation or blind evolution!

Variety of tongues is not ideal–it is "babel"–and is doomed to be destroyed. Diversity of language is confusion; a judgment upon human defiance of God's law that people should scatter and repopulate the earth that He had made for their enjoyment. God tempered His judgment with mercy. He did not disrupt families. As we mentioned at the beginning of this chapter, the seed of Ham found their home in Africa, Arabia and Palestine, where they dwell to this very day. Shem settled in Persia and from Mesopotamia to Asia. Japheth inherited Europe and Asia.

Babylon and Egypt were founded by Ham (see Gen. 10:6-20). Assyria was founded by Shem (see Gen. 10:11-12,21-31). The European nations were founded by Japheth (see Gen. 10:2-5). (See also the diagram at the end of this chapter.)

The Cause of It All

Look back over the story as it is told in Genesis 11 again. What brought about this judgment of God? What exactly had the people done?

First, as we have already seen, they were disobedient. Remember, the Lord had told Noah that he and his sons were to replenish the earth. Not just a part of the earth, but *all* of it. The sons of Noah were to be the fathers of nations (see Gen. 10:32). Instead, as they journeyed from the east, they found a plain in the land of Shinar and dwelt there. This is the same kind of sin that Adam and Eve committed. The people after the Flood were disobedient to the commands of God. When you think about it carefully, you will see that many sins begin with disobedience to God.

Second, these people were proud. They were more interested in assuring fame for themselves than they were in obeying the Lord. In Genesis 11:4, we read that they wanted to make a name for themselves. These people felt the necessity of being famous. They wanted others to be aware that they were around.

Is not this often a cause for our sinning? Public opinion and public acclaim are strong influences upon most of us. We don't want to go against the crowd. We want people to like us and think well of us, so we do things that we know are not the very best. This need for approval is often the underlying cause for much of what we do.

Third, these people wanted to get to God in their own way. In the same verse in Genesis that we just read, the people said that they wanted to build a tower that would reach to heaven. Some Bible students believe that these people were worshipers of the heavens and that around the top of this tower were to be placed the signs of the zodiac. Whether this is true is hard to say, but we do know that the people wanted to make their own way to worship God.

God is only pleased with those who worship Him in Spirit and in truth. Jesus said, "I am the way, the truth, and the life. No one comes to the Father except through Me" (John 14:6). If we love the Lord because He has saved us, we know that nothing we can do with the works of our hands will gain access to heaven. We know that we must come to God in His way.

- SHEM—Peoples in Persia and areas NW from Mesopotamia to Asia Minor
  - Elam—Persians in S. Persia (Iran)
  - Asshur—Assyrians in Assyria (Iraq)
  - Arphaxad—Hebrews in Chaldea (Iraq)—Abraham
    - Ishmael
    - Isaac
      - Esau—Edomites
      - Jacob—Hebrews
  - Lud—Lydians in Central Asia Minor (Turkey)
  - Aram—Aramaic-speaking people in Syria and Mesopotamia (Iraq)

- HAM—Peoples in Africa, Arabia and Palestine
  - Cush—from lower Mesopotamia (Iraq), through SW Arabia, to Ethiopia
    - Nimrod, his son, was the first king on earth, founder of the kingdom of Babylon (Genesis 10:8-9).
  - Mizraim—Egyptians in Egypt
  - Phut—Libyans and Mauritanians in NE Africa
  - Canaan—Canaanites, Phoenicians and other people of early Palestine: Jebusites, Amorites, Girgashites and Hivites in Palestine and Syria
    - These are the people whom God commanded the Israelites to destroy completely because of their idolatry (Deuteronomy 9:1-5).

- JAPHETH—Peoples in areas north and west—Europe and Asia
  - Gomer—N. Asia Minor (Russia)
    - Cimmerians and Armenians
  - Magog—general term for both the land and people of the north
    - Scythians, Caucasians (Tartars and Russians)
  - Madai Media (Iran)
    - Medes and some Persian tribes
  - Javan—eastern Greece and western Asia Minor (Turkey)
    - Possibly also Spain (Tarshish)
      - Greeks, Etruscans, Romans, Cyprians, Macedonians, Rhodians
  - Tubal—Asia Minor (Turkey) and around the Black Sea
    - Tibareni and Tartars
  - Meshech—Cappodocia and E. Phrygia (Turkey)
    - Moschi and Muscovites
  - Tiras—NE Asia Minor (Turkey)
    - Thracians

Daily Meditations

Sunday: A new government—Genesis 9:1-6

Monday: Man's failure—Genesis 11:1-9

Tuesday: The slavery of sin—Romans 6:14-23

Wednesday: Some do not know God—Romans 1:18-23

Thursday: Rulers should honor God—Ezra 7:25-28

Friday: Pray for those in authority—1 Timothy 2:1-4

Saturday: Evil rulers will be punished—Psalm 2:1-12

12

God Chooses a People

I will make you a great nation; I will bless you and make your name great; and you shall be a blessing.
Genesis 12:2

Every four years in the United States, there is a day set aside when the American people choose a leader for the next four years. The greatest honor that can be conferred upon any person in the United States is to be chosen by his or her fellow citizens to this high office. Many boys and girls who are born in this land dream of the prospect of one day being president of this country.

This is indeed a great honor, but how immeasurably greater it was for God to choose one person out of all the people of the world to be the founder of His people. This man was to be known through all the ages as "the friend of God."

No man is more widely known than he, and none is more greatly revered. Jewish, Muslim and Christian people alike all point to him as the father of their faith. From him came the Hebrew people, through this people came the Christ, and through Christ all the earth has been blessed, with increased blessing yet to come.

God Calls Abram

Out of the dispersed descendants of the builders of Babel, God called one man, Abram, with whom He would enter into covenant (see Gen. 12:1-3). In other words, God and Abram formed a partnership. God commanded, and Abram was to carry out His directions. It was a partnership of marvelous fellowship that would pay great dividends.

At the Tower of Babel the people had failed, but God's eternal purpose was not going to fail. God had created man for fellowship with Himself. He has never lost sight of that original plan, and He will never be satisfied until it is fully realized and His people are again with Him in His paradise. Remember, God created humans in innocence and fellowship with Him and put them in paradise. Some day, humankind will find themselves again in paradise, in perfect fellowship with their Creator.

Abram lived in the land of Ur of the Chaldees. For hundreds of years, people read the biblical story of Abram and that he came from Ur, but no one knew where Ur was located. Therefore, some people believed that there was no such place. However, in 1922 archaeologists discovered the city of Ur. Their excavations revealed that this place not only existed but also that it was a great city with extensive water and sewer systems, paved streets, and other luxuries. Clay tablets were found that led scholars to believe that there was a system of education in place. Some tablets contained multiplication tables; others problems in division, work in square and cube root and even reading lessons.

Due to these discoveries, we now know that Ur was a city on the western side of the lower Euphrates and that it was the seat of culture and magnificent worship. But the worship was idolatry. The chief deity was the moon god. Abram was probably a member of a heathen family there (see Josh. 24:2). The Lord called this man out from his home to go into the Land of Promise. Humans had so displeased God that He had determined to select a people for Himself. This time, however, instead of destroying the people, God chose to pick out one man and separate him for Himself.

Somebody has said, "When the Lord found one man in all the world who was ready to do just exactly as He directed, He was ready to begin history anew, and take a fresh start with that man in blessing a whole race." Wherever there is a young person today with Abram's spirit, God wants that individual and will use him or her.

A Great Turning Point

So Abram left Ur. He didn't know exactly where he was going, and he didn't know what the next step was to be. Genesis 11 and 12 mark the turning point in God's dealings with humankind. Up to this time, history had dealt with the whole Adamic race; there was neither Jew nor Gentile, but all one in the first man, Adam. But now, humanity was a vast riverway from which God took a small stream, the Hebrew nation. It was through this stream that He wanted to bless the world.

The emphatic word is "blessed." Abram was to be blessed of God. He, in turn, was to be a blessing to others. Blessing would go out to others in proportion as they blessed Abraham. However, if Abram were to be a blessing, he first had to be obedient to the call of God. This was not an easy thing to do. It meant breaking social ties, overcoming prejudices, being misunderstood and enduring criticism. As we mentioned, Abram's people were idolaters, and he would have been regarded as peculiar, maybe even fanatical. He was standing for the true God and for pure worship, and, like Noah in his day, he had to stand practically alone. He had to obey God in doing a thing that seemed ridiculous to the people around him.

Abram was obedient simply because God asked him to be. God needed him, so he went. This characteristic of obedience is found in the lives of Moses, of Joshua, of Elijah, of Gideon, of John the Baptist, of Dr. Livingstone, of Martin Luther and of the missionaries who have gone out—and, yes, of the Son of God Himself!

It isn't always easy to be obedient. But Abram "went out, not knowing where he was going" (Heb. 11:8). No doubt Abram had lived all his life in the city of Ur. He had doubtless been born there (see Gen. 11:27-28.) Now the Lord was telling him that he should leave his home.

There seemed only one wise way to travel, and that was north along the river Euphrates. The little group consisting of Abram, his wife, Sarai, his father, Terah, and his nephew, Lot, traveled along the river for 430 miles until they came to the city of Haran. Abram disobeyed the Lord to the extent that he brought his family with him. God had said to leave his family and kindred behind (see Gen. 12:1). It was wrong for him to stop at Haran. It is also wrong to stop when God says to keep going.

We do not know how long Abram stayed at Haran, but finally his father, Terah, died and God called Abram again. He was to move on to a place that God would show him. Think of what it must have meant for Abram to start out with his wife and nephew and servants and move away from the river out into the desert. The next step was Shechem, which was more than 300 miles away. Surely, the only thing that kept Abram going was God's promise that He would show him a new land.

The call of Abraham was the beginning of a new development in the Messianic line. The line had run through individuals from Seth to Shem, covering a period of many centuries. Now it was to take on a national form, and Abram was selected as the head of that nation, the Hebrews.

The chosen nation was born in faith and sustained by faith—the faith of its great head, Abram. Hold firmly in mind that from Genesis 12 to Matthew 12:45, the Scriptures have Israel in view.

Heirs of Promise

God made a great covenant in Genesis 15:18 with Abram and his descendants. They were to become distinctly "heirs of promise." The covenant was one of grace, and not because they deserved it (see Gen. 12:1-3). The descendants of Abram had but to abide in the Land of Promise, Palestine, to inherit every blessing. This was the condition for blessing that God set down.

At last, Abram arrived in the land he had been promised. Where was this land that God gave to his heirs? Roughly, it extended from Dan to Beersheeba and from the river Jordan to the Mediterranean Sea. In this land, Abram and his children lived for many years and became great and powerful.

Abram is one of the great men of the Bible. He was not great because he never disobeyed or because he never made a mistake, for he did both of these things. No, he was great in the sight of God because he believed God. "He did not waver at the promise of God through unbelief, but was strengthened in faith, giving glory to God, and being fully convinced that what He had promised He was also able to perform. And therefore 'it was accounted to him for righteousness'" (Rom. 4:20-22).

The covenant that God established with Abram was to be a lasting covenant with only one condition: the people would abide in the land that God would give them. God told Abram to remain in the Promised Land for blessing, but when famine came, off he went into Egypt (see Gen. 12:10). Egypt is a type of the world. Many Christians try to substitute the things of this world for lost spiritual power. In doing so, they get out of the place of blessing.

Sometimes God *permits* us to do things that He does not *direct* us to do. There is a great difference between the directive and the permissive will of God. Our heavenly Father will often permit us to do the things that He would never direct us to do, because we are so determined to have our way.

Abram was 75 years old when God promised that He would make of him a great nation. When he was 99 years old, God changed his name from Abram to Abraham, which means "father of many nations"(see Gen. 17:5). When he was 100 years old, Abraham's son, Isaac, was born and the promise began to be fulfilled.

Isaac had two sons, Esau and Jacob. Remember the story of Jacob and his 12 sons, resulting in the removal of the children of Israel out of the Land of Promise into Egypt? In Egypt they lost their blessing, but not their covenant. God renewed His covenant with Isaac and Jacob (see Gen. 26:1-5; 28:13-17). These three are called the patriarchs of the covenant. You know how often you read of the "God of Abraham, Isaac and Jacob." No other names are included.

God performed that which He had promised. The land was given to the seed of Abraham. He was the father of a great nation. And in the coming of the Messiah from Abraham's race, all the nations are blessed.

Joseph, the son of Jacob, is often called by some Bible teachers the "Messianic patriarch," so perfect is he in his typology of Christ. Not a fault of his is on record. He is the connecting link between God's dealing with a particular family and God's blessing a nation.

Have Faith to Believe

God directed Abraham in many of the paths that he took. The Lord brought him all the way from Ur to the Promised Land.

The Lord gave him a son and promised Abraham that his name would be great.

The times that Abraham went his own way were always times of trouble and judgment. But after each one of Abraham's excursions outside of God's directive will, he came back to the Lord and asked for forgiveness. Let us not think for a minute that God commended Abraham for disobedience. But the Lord did commend Abraham for his faith and trust that He would do that which He had promised.

Remember that Abraham had to wait 25 years from the time that God first promised to make him a great nation until his son, Isaac, was born and the promise began to be fulfilled. It is no wonder that this man is commended for his faith in the Lord's word. You and I become impatient when we must wait one day for something that we want; just imagine waiting 25 years!

It couldn't have been easy for Abraham to wait for God to give him a son. Waiting is never easy. Patience of any kind is a hard virtue to attain. When we want something, we want it now. We don't like to wait. But the Bible says in James 1:3-4, "Knowing that the testing of your faith produces patience. But let patience have its perfect work, that you may be perfect and complete, lacking nothing."

If we ask the Lord for something and we do not receive it immediately, we feel that the Lord has said no to our request. Yet this may not always be the case. The Lord often answers our prayers, "wait awhile." In His own good time, He gives us those things that He has promised and those things that are needful for our lives. Abraham's faith in God's word earned him God's praise.

Remember, the Lord is pleased by faith. Rest then in His will, knowing that He never makes mistakes.

Daily Meditations

Sunday: God chooses a man—Genesis 12:1-9

Monday: God's covenant with Abraham—Genesis 15:18; 17:1-8

Tuesday: The place of blessing—Genesis 13:14-18; 26:1-3

Wednesday: Abraham's faith rewarded—Romans 4:1-8,13-22

Thursday: God gives responsibility—Hebrews 11:23-29

Friday: God's blessings depend on obedience—Leviticus 26:3-13

Saturday: Blessing in hard places—Genesis 39:1-23

13

God Gives the Law

Therefore by the deeds of the law no flesh will be justified in His sight, for by the law is the knowledge of sin.
Romans 3:20

Everything that God makes is perfect. If you examine the tiniest creature or one of millions of snowflakes under a microscope, you will find absolute perfection and order. So it is with the Law of God. As David said, "The law of the Lord is perfect" (Ps. 19:7).

The Israelites had promised to obey *all* that God told them to do. They had not done even the very simple things that God required before the Lord had told Isaac that he was to remain in the Promised Land if he were to be blessed. Abraham took at least two trips into Egypt, and then his grandson Jacob went down there to live. Jacob transported the whole family, 70 of them, into Egypt. Within a comparatively short time, the Israelites were in bondage. Only the intervention of God through Moses brought about their deliverance (see Exod. 3–13).

Through lack of faith to remain in the Land of Promise, this Abrahamic family went down into Egypt and brought upon themselves the long judgment of bitter bondage. From the day when God first told Abraham what He wanted to do for him and what He wanted to do for the whole world through his descendants, down to the day when Moses was summoned up into the sacred mount, God had been seeking, establishing and reestablishing special covenants with that chosen family that was now a great multitude.

God had bound Himself by a blood covenant to this people. They had accepted the covenant. Now, He could not go any further in bestowing His blessings until the people clearly understood what they had to do to make these blessings possible. They could receive continued blessing only as they lived true to all that the covenant of love stood for.

From Egypt to Mt. Sinai

Seventy Israelites went to Egypt (see Gen. 46:26-27), but 400 years later, Moses led out 600,000 men (see Exod. 12:37). With their families, there must have been a multitude of about 2.5 million people.

Traveling along the coast is the shortest route to make the trip from Egypt to Canaan, but God did not send His people this way because the coastal section was inhabited by the Philistines (see Exod. 13:17-18). The Israelites had been slaves for so long that they did not know how to fight hostile people. So the Lord sent the people across the Red Sea and down the Sinai Peninsula to Mt. Sinai, and then up the other side. The Lord does not always lead us the shortest way, but He always leads us the way that is best for us.

At last, the people came to the mountain of God, Mt. Sinai. Of all the Israelites, Moses was probably the only one who had ever been there before. In fact, it was there that Moses first encountered the Lord in the burning bush (see Exod. 3:1–4:19).

Now, the Lord told Moses that He would appear on Mt. Sinai. To prepare for His appearance, the people were to purify themselves and put on clean clothes. God warned them, "Take heed to yourselves that you do not go up to the mountain or touch its base. Whoever touches the mountain shall surely be put to death" (Exod. 19:12).

At last, the day came when the Law would be given (see Exod. 19:16-20). Just imagine how the people must have felt. Think of all of those people coming from their tents and standing at the foot of Mt. Sinai.

Two and one-half million people are a lot of people. Some of the states in this country do not have that many people within their borders. The camp probably covered the equivalent of at least 48 city blocks. Gathered together at the foot of the mountain, there would probably have been almost one square mile of people.

The tension probably reached a tremendous pitch even before the mountain began to smoke. Then followed the thunders and lightning, an earthquake, and the command of Moses that the trumpets begin to sound throughout the camp. Louder and louder the sound grew until the whole earth seemed to resound. What must it have been like? How must those Israelites have felt? How must Moses have felt when God called him to come up the mountain and meet the Lord God?

This was the setting for the giving of the Law. God was about to tell the people what He required of those who wanted to please Him.

God First

Law is wonderful. We would not want to live in any country where there was no law, where law was not enforced, or where lawbreakers were not punished. On the other hand, law is terrible, for there must always be punishment for breaking the law.

God's purpose in giving His people the Law at Mt. Sinai was to give them knowledge of their sin. The laws given by God are basic to all moral teaching, even in our present age.

The Ten Commandments are divided into two groups. The first four concern our relationship to God, while the last six give rules to govern our relationship with our fellow man. The Lord Jesus Christ summed the Ten Commandments up in the two great commandments. The first dealt with our relationship with God: "You shall love the LORD your God with all your heart, with all your soul, and with all your mind" (Matt. 22:37). The second dealt with our relationship with people: "You shall love your neighbor as yourself" (v. 38). The Ten Commandments have never been changed. The only difference is that now we have the power of the indwelling Christ to help us to keep them.

The first command that God gave was a requirement of absolute and complete allegiance to Himself (see Exod. 20:3). What would you think of a soldier who tried to serve in two different armies at the same time? If we try to divide our allegiance, we cannot serve God, nor can He help us in the way that He wants to.

If a man wants to enlist in the army of the United States, he must sign his name to a solemn agreement. If a man wanted to enlist in the army of the Lord, he, too, must enter into an agreement. Moses was trying to lead an army of the Lord through a campaign in the wilderness. It was necessary to enter into an agreement with the Lord if they were to serve Him.

Paul says the Law "was added because of transgressions" (Gal. 3:19). When God gave the Law, it did not take away the covenant of promise. It was *added* because of the transgressions. How long was it intended to last? Paul answers, "till the Seed should come to whom the promise was made" (Gal. 3:19).

What purpose does the Law serve? Law shows what is right and wrong and helps people to do what is right. Through the

Law is the knowledge of sin. "But the Scripture has confined all under sin, that the promise by faith in Jesus Christ might be given to those who believe" (Gal. 3:22). Remember, Paul says in Romans 3:23 that "all have sinned and fall short of the glory of God" and that the whole world is guilty before God. But this is the gracious purpose of God "that the promise by faith in Jesus Christ might be given to those who believe" (Gal. 3:22). Paul adds, "Therefore the law was our tutor to bring us to Christ" (v. 24).

Law Breakers

The people heard the words of the Lord and answered, "All the words which the LORD has said we will do" (Exod. 24:3). Unfortunately, the history of Israel in the wilderness is one long record of violation of the Law. The discipline of the nation by law ended in the judgment of the nation by captivity. The 10 tribes of Israel were taken captive by Assyria (see 2 Kings 17:5-23), and Judah was later taken captive by Babylon (see 2 Kings 25:1-11).

Israel failed to appreciate the grace of God in delivering them from Egypt. God had gone down, seen their trouble and come to deliver them (see Exod. 3). The people could do nothing. They were slaves in bitter bondage, but God carried them out as on eagles' wings (see Exod. 19:4). This is real grace! They did nothing themselves to gain their freedom.

For more than 1,000 years, Israel was under the rigor of the Law. Yet Law cannot save a person—it can only show him or her that he or she is a sinner. We look in the mirror and discover that our face is dirty and that our hair is disheveled, but the mirror neither dirties our face nor musses our hair, and it cannot cleanse our face and comb our hair. It has only one power: *to reveal our condition.*

Now, the Law does not make a person a sinner, nor does it have the power to cleanse a person from sin. It does one thing: It shows that person how unable he or she is to live up to the standard that God expects of His children. There was one who could keep the Law at every point, and He was our Lord and Savior Jesus Christ. He paid humankind's penalty for disobeying God's law and gave His life upon the cross.

If we want to please God, the only possible way to do it is to let Christ live in us. As the apostle Paul said, "For to me, to live is Christ, and to die is gain" (Phil. 1:21). Only Christ can live a Christian life through us. We just have to allow Him to move in and take possession of our lives.

Your life is your own. No one else can live your life. It is your own private property and it belongs to no one else. Therefore, only Christ can live a Christian life. A Christian life is Christ's life. It is His life. The wonderful thing is that He wants to live His life in you. "God willed to make known what are the riches of the glory of this mystery . . . which is Christ in you, the hope of glory" (Col. 1:27).

Law and Grace

God's perfect Law is such a hard and irrevocable standard that you and I can never attain its fulfillment. We may try to keep the Law, but it is impossible. Even if we manage somehow to keep ourselves from doing certain acts that it forbids, Christ says that evil thoughts are sin (see Matt. 5:21-22). So, even if we can control some of our actions, we cannot control our thoughts. If our thoughts are sinful, we are sinners. The Bible says in Proverbs 23:7, "For as he thinks in his heart, so is he."

People sometimes say, "I have never committed a very big sin, so I don't think God will condemn me." Again, the Bible has the answer: "For whoever shall keep the whole law, and yet stumble in one point, he is guilty of all" (Jas. 2:10). In God's sight, there are no big sinners and no little sinners. All the world is guilty before His requirements of holiness.

At the Bureau of Standards in Washington, D.C., there is a yardstick. It is kept in a place where temperature cannot affect it. This is the standard for all yardsticks. It is exactly three feet long. If any yardstick does not match this exactly, it is not a true yard. God's Law is a yardstick. Against it go your life and mine; if we do not match it exactly, we cannot satisfy God's requirements.

Oftentimes, we hear it said that someone has broken a law. Really this is not exactly true; rather, the law has broken that person. If a person falls out of a third-story window, he or she does not break the law of gravity; the law of gravity breaks him or her. The law is demanding; if we do not fulfill it, it breaks us.

This is a terrible condition in which to find ourselves. God's Law demands perfection, but we are not perfect. God's Law demands absolute obedience, but we are disobedient. We are in a hopeless condition. But God did not leave us there. "For what the law could not do in that it was weak through the flesh, God did by sending His own Son in the likeness of sinful flesh, on account of sin: He condemned sin in the flesh, that the righteous requirement of the law might be fulfilled in us" (Rom. 8:3-4).

In ourselves, we are sinners under condemnation of death. In Christ, we are the children of God and possessors of eternal life. Think again of the fear that must have been upon the Israelites when they awaited the giving of the Law. What a privilege is ours to come to Christ without fear, knowing that He will not reject us. He said, "The one who comes to Me I will by no means cast out" (John 6:37). How thankful we should be to God for the gift of eternal life. Have you thanked Him recently for all that He has done for you? Why not do it now?

Daily Meditations

Sunday: A life of bondage—Exodus 1:5-14

Monday: Deliverance from bondage—Exodus 14:13-28

Tuesday: The people choose the Law—Exodus 19:3-8

Wednesday: The Law—Exodus 20:1-26

Thursday: The purpose of the Law—Galatians 3:19-24

Friday: Christ kept the Law—Romans 10:4-10

Saturday: Peace with God—Romans 5:1-11

Section Two:

God's Plan Revealed

14

God's Dealings with the Jewish Nation of Old

Therefore know that the LORD *your God, He is God, the faithful God who keeps covenant and mercy for a thousand generations.*
DEUTERONOMY 7:9

Does God ever get discouraged? He surely had reason to be in His dealings with His chosen people. The history of Israel begins with the glorious supernatural entry of Israel into the Promised Land but ends with the pitiable downfall of Israel and Judah as the people are led out into captivity by pagan and godless nations.

Other nations come and go, but Israel lives on. The Jews are the "generation that will not pass away." God says of Israel, "Though I make a full end of all nations where I have scattered you, yet I will not make a full end of you" (Jer. 30:11). The Jews, scattered everywhere and dwelling in our own midst, are but one more proof that both the Old Testament and the New Testament are true.

The history of Israel is a testimony to the Bible's historic truth. In His present customs, in His very separateness, we see the impress of events that teaches us God's hand rests on the life of His people.

One of the most startling facts in connection with the Jewish race is their attitude toward Christianity. We know that the gospel was preached first to the Jew ("the Jew first" is a common expression in Scripture—see Romans 1:16). We also know that all the apostles, without exception, were Jews and that many of the first preachers were Jews. Yet the nation as a whole rejected Christ (see John 1:11). This people had been trained to know God's mind and had been prepared for the coming of Christ. How can we explain this rejection?

The Condition of the Jewish Nation

Read carefully the words of Isaiah 53:1-3. The Jews thought that the crucifixion of Jesus of Nazareth disproved all the claims that He was the Christ. Yet seven centuries before His blood was shed, it was declared that they would behold this event. The text of Isaiah 53:4-6 told them of it all.

Do you realize that the rejection of the Messiah by Israel is one of the outstanding features in the prophetic Scriptures concerning the Lord? If the Jews had accepted Jesus, He would not be the Messiah of the Old Testament. The Jews' scorn of this Nazarene is their unconscious testimony He is the Messiah.

The dispersion of the Jewish race was universal and has long been one of the common facts of history. "The LORD will scatter you among all peoples, from one end of the earth to the other, and there you shall serve other gods, which neither you nor your fathers have known—wood and stone" (Deut. 28:64).

Today, the Jewish people are found in every land from north to south, from east to west. *There is no other nation under the stars to whom these words could fit.* We have British Jews, German Jews, Italian Jews—there is not a nation of which the Jew is not a part.

There are Jewish communities in India and the Far East. There are Algerian Jews and groups in Australia and New Zealand.

Their preservation has been incredible. Although wanderers over the face of the earth and deprived of their own homeland, yet they have been kept a distinct and separate race (see Lev. 26:44). They have been massacred by the millions, yet they have endured.

Rome treated them cruelly. Josephus says that during the Jewish War, 1,356,460 were slain and 101,700 were carried away captive, besides the many lost due to famine and massacre. During the First Crusade in 1096, Jewish communities along the Rhine and Danube rivers in Europe suffered horribly. In World War II, 6 million Jews were killed under the Nazi regime in the Holocaust. Yet when undergoing the heaviest persecution, the Jewish race has always increased greatly in number.

They are a separate people, although this has not always been their desire (see Ezek. 20:32). But it has been God's desire. Though scattered among the nations, yet they "dwell alone" (Deut. 28:64; Num. 23:9).

There is a fact about Israel's history that puzzles many—namely, the exalted position given her in the Word of God and the humble place she has occupied among the nations of the world. The Bible sets the chosen people before all other people—the leader of all leaders, the prince among nations. Secular history, on the other hand, has given them no recognition whatever. Until World War I, they played no significant part in the affairs of nations and claimed no interest except among Bible students. Since that time, the state of Israel has been founded. The greatness of Israel was foretold in promise long before there was any possibility of its fulfillment.

God has always had great plans for His chosen people. It was through this people that Christ was to come in the flesh. The Old Testament is filled with promises that God made to them, including the promise God made to Abraham that He would give him a land and make his name great. Everyone should know this promise and its statements (see Gen. 12:1-3; 13:14-15). The promise was repeated to Isaac, and again to Jacob, making three famous covenants (see Gen. 26:3-4; 28:13-15). Centuries passed, and it appeared that God had forgotten His promises to Abraham, Isaac and Jacob and had abandoned His chosen people. But our God never forgets.

God has kept Israel alive in the world from Abraham's day to ours that in a glorious time yet to come He may summon her into her promised position in Christ Jesus her Messiah. Israel's physical captivity in Assyria and Judah's in Babylon were only types of the spiritual bondage of sin in which they both were living. They were already captives.

The Promised Land

How do we know that this land of Palestine was given to the Jewish people? In Genesis 17:7-8, God said to Abraham, "I will establish My covenant between Me and you and your descendants after you in their generations, for an everlasting covenant. Also I give to you and your descendants after you the land in which you are a stranger, all the land of Canaan, as an everlasting possession; and I will be their God."

God not only made this covenant with Abraham but also with his descendants after him. These are the title deeds to the Promised Land, recorded not in any registrar's office in a courthouse but in hundreds of millions of Bibles now extant in more than 2,400 languages and dialects of the earth, God's own Holy Word. And His Word can never fail (see 1 Kings 8:56).

God gave His chosen people many promises of blessing if they would be obedient to His Word, but He also gave them many warnings of the results that would follow if they sinned and were disobedient. Deuteronomy 28:1-14 gives a great list of the blessings that would attend the Israelites as the result of their obedience. Many of these were definitely fulfilled in their national life, up to the time when they reached the zenith of their history during the reign of Solomon.

However, if they were disobedient, God told them, "I also will walk contrary to you in fury; and I, even I, will chastise you seven times for your sins . . . I will lay your cities waste and bring your sanctuaries to desolation, and I will not smell the fragrance of your sweet aromas. I will bring the land to desolation, and your enemies who dwell in it shall be astonished at it. I will scatter you among the nations and draw out a sword after you; your land shall be desolate and your cities waste" (Lev. 26:27,31-33). The scattering of the Jewish people has been one of the commonplace facts of history.

The Kingdom

Under the leadership of Moses and Joshua, the people of Israel remained true to the Lord. Of course, there were times when they were drawn away by their own desires, but the Israelites generally followed the Lord under the leadership of these two great men of God.

After the death of Joshua, the Israelites forgot God. We read this description of their actions in Judges 2:12: "And they forsook the LORD God of their fathers, who had brought them out of the land of Egypt; and they followed other gods." Over and over again, the people acted the same way (see Judg. 2:14-19).

To lead the people in righteousness, God sent men and women called "judges" to them. While a particular judge lived, the people followed the Lord, but when the judge died, the people returned to their own ways and no longer followed the Lord. The last verse of the book of Judges describes accurately the ways of the Israelites: "Everyone did what was right in his own eyes" (Judg. 21:25).

The Lord eventually stopped revealing His will to the people. Finally, we read of the state of the people in these words: "The word of the LORD was rare in those days; there was no widespread revelation." Then Samuel was born in answer to the prayer of his mother, Hannah. To him, God once more revealed His will. We read, "Then the LORD appeared again in Shiloh. For the LORD revealed Himself to Samuel in Shiloh by the word of the LORD" (1 Sam. 3:21).

Samuel served the Lord as a judge over Israel for all the days of his life. When he grew old, he appointed his sons as his successors, but "his sons did not walk in his ways" (1 Sam. 8:3). So the Israelites came to Samuel, now an old man, and asked for a king. Samuel was hurt that the people did not want him, but the Lord spoke to Samuel and said, "Heed the voice of the people in all that they say to you; for they have not rejected you, but they have rejected Me, that I should not reign over them" (1 Sam. 8:7).

The first king of Israel was Saul of the tribe of Benjamin, but he did not do right in the sight of the Lord, and so God ended his reign. After Saul came the greatest of Israel's kings, the shepherd David. To this young man, the Lord God added another of His great promises: The kingdom of David was to be "forever." The covenant the Lord God made with David is summed up in the words of 2 Samuel 7:16: "Your house and your kingdom shall be established forever before you. Your throne shall be established forever."

Thus it was that the royal line of David was begun. Throughout all the years of the kingdom of Judah, the descendants of David ruled in Jerusalem. Further, God promised David, "My mercy shall not depart from him [David's son], as I took it from Saul, whom I removed before you" (2 Sam. 7:15).

The son of David, Solomon, was the last king to rule over all the tribes of Israel. Solomon's kingdom was great and rich. His reign was a time of peace and prosperity.

The Divided Kingdom

Upon the death of Solomon, the kingdom was divided. Ten tribes made Jeroboam, a servant of Solomon, their king and formed the kingdom of Israel, with Samaria as its capital. The kingdom extended from Bethel in the south to Dan in the north. In size, the kingdom was comparable to the state of New Hampshire. The two tribes of Benjamin and Judah recognized Solomon's son, Rehoboam, as their king. Jerusalem remained the capital of that kingdom, now known as Judah. This kingdom was smaller in area, being about the size of Connecticut.

In the years that followed, the descendants of David continued upon the throne of the southern kingdom, but the northern kingdom had many ruling houses. None of them followed the Lord God completely. Only the house of David remained true. Its history, too, had some blots of sin upon it, but there were a few rulers in Judah who worshiped the Lord God.

During this time, God raised up prophets–such as Jonah, Amos, Hosea, Obadiah and Joel to the 10 tribes of Israel, and Isaiah, Micah, Nahum, Habakkuk, Zephaniah and Jeremiah to the tribe of Judah–to foretell to the people the captivity of the nation if they refused to return to their God (see 2 Kings 17:13-14). The prophets also told them of the Messiah who would come in suffering and in glory (see Isa. 53).

The Captivity

Finally, after the Jews had rejected the prophets' message, the Assyrian army under Sennacherib captured the city of Samaria,

THE ORDER OF THE PROPHETS IN RELATION TO THE EXILE OF ISRAEL

This is the order of the prophets of old
As they came to God's people His plans they foretold.
While some before exile gave message of warning
And told of a nation in bondage and mourning.
Ezekiel and Daniel in exile's dark way
Kept Israel from wandering from God's Word away.
And when they returned to their homeland once more
God raised up three prophets their land to restore.

I. PROPHETS BEFORE THE EXILE

(1) To Nineveh
- Jonah, 782-753 B.C.

(2) To the ten tribes, Israel
- Amos, 786-746 B.C.
- Hosea, 748-690 B.C.
- Obadiah, 870-850 B.C.
- Joel, 835-796 B.C.

(3) To Judah (and Benjamin)
- Isaiah, 783-705 B.C.
- Micah, 738-690 B.C.
- Nehum, 661-612 B.C.
- Habakkuk, 625-597 B.C.
- Zephaniah, 640-608 B.C.
- Jeremiah, 626-587 B.C.

II. PHROPHETS DURING THE EXILE

Ezekiel, 592-571 B.C.
Daniel, 604-536 B.C.

III. PROPHETS AFTER THE EXILE

Haggai, 520 B.C.
Zechariah, 520-480 B.C.
Malachi, 455 B.C.

the capital of Israel, in 722 B.C. and deported its people. The city of Samaria had been under siege for three years (see 2 Kings 17:5). The list of sins of which Israel was guilty is a long one. The Lord condemned the people for doing such sins as walking in the statutes of heathen nations, doing secretly those things that were not right, setting up images, serving idols and other gods, and so forth (see 2 Kings 17:7-12).

Those who were deported from the northern kingdom never came back. There was no national spirit and no one to lead the effort in rebuilding the walls of Samaria. The captives were scattered. A few of the lower classes had been left behind, and the king of Assyria sent people of other conquered nations to Palestine. These people did not worship the Lord, "Therefore the LORD sent lions among them, which killed some of them" (2 Kings 17:25).

A few of the people from the northern kingdom returned to intermarry with the tribes that had made the land their home. These people intermarried and so began the nation of Samaritans. Remember that this is the group of people the Jews so despised because they were part Jew and part Gentile. At last, the king sent a priest of Israel that he might teach the people of the Lord God. The Bible describes the people in these words: "They feared the LORD, yet served their own gods—according to the rituals of the nations from among whom they were carried away" (2 Kings 17:33).

About 150 years after the northern kingdom had been taken captive, Judah, the southern kingdom, was taken away because of her foolish kings and brought down before the vengeance of Babylon. Jerusalem, the capital of Judah, was completely destroyed by King Nebuchadnezzar in 586 B.C. Nebuchadnezzar carried most of the population away to Babylon, but unlike Sargon in his dealings with Israel, Nebuchadnezzar allowed the children of Judah to preserve their unity in their land of exile.

God said that Judah's captivity should be 70 years (see Jer. 25:11-12). In later years, some of the exiles returned to rebuild Jerusalem under the leadership of men such as Nehemiah and Ezra. From this band is descended most of the Jewish race today.

How often the people had been warned of disaster by the voices of the prophets! Every prediction that told of God's judgments upon His people was fulfilled. "The LORD said, 'I will also remove Judah from My sight, as I have removed Israel, and will cast off this city Jerusalem which I have chosen, and the house of which I said, "My name shall be there"'" (2 Kings 23:27). Remember that God is faithful to fulfill His judgments as well as His gracious promises. People forget this too often!

The Messianic plans were bound up in Judah. Christ, the Messiah, the Savior of the world, was to be born of Judah. Judah was placed in Babylon to be punished. The sin of idolatry was purged. After she was chastened, she returned to her own land to prepare the way for the coming Messiah, who should arise in Palestine, not Babylon, Greece or Egypt.

Heed the Warnings of God

During all the time Israel was deliberately disobeying God and disregarding His commandments, He had been faithful in warning them. The voices of His prophets had never been silent. How faithful each one of them had been! Prophet after prophet had appealed in vain to people who had departed from the truth and had rejected God and put idols in His place. One after another had sounded the warning until God had no recourse—captivity was inevitable. This was an expression of divine displeasure and punishment.

The story of Israel is one of great sadness, but nothing happens by chance. The destruction of Israel was not sudden, because, as we have seen, she had been warned in one way or another from the very start. The people of Israel would not believe that the Lord would really punish them. They looked about them and saw that the people seemed to be happy. Everything seemed to be going well. It just did not appear possible that all this could change. But God's warnings are just as sure as His promises. That which He has said, He will do.

This is just as true for us as it was for the Israelites. Sometimes we think that we can get away with disobedience, but this is not true. The Bible says, "Be sure your sin will find you out" (Num. 32:23). Never play around with the love of God. Remember He is also a holy God and a God of justice. Live as He would have you to live, according to the commands that you find in the Bible. Take heed, "Do not be deceived, God is not mocked; for whatever a man sows, that he will also reap" (Gal. 6:7).

Daily Meditations

Sunday: Prophecy in Scripture—2 Peter 1:15-21

Monday: Scoffers of prophecy—2 Peter 3:1-14

Tuesday: God's promise to Abraham—Genesis 12:1-3; 13:14-18; 15:1-21; 17:4-8

Wednesday: The Israelites disobey—Leviticus 26:27-34; Nehemiah 9:26-29

Thursday: God remains faithful—Leviticus 26:40-46

Friday: Israel taken captive—2 Kings 17:5,21-33

Saturday: Judah taken captive—2 Kings 24:11–25:10

15

A King's Dream Reveals God's Plans

There is a God in heaven who reveals secrets, and He has made known to King Nebuchadnezzar what will be in the latter days.
DANIEL 2:28

God gives us His news in advance. We do not even have to wait for it to happen. God's children can be more than abreast of the times—they can be years ahead of the times!

God's children do not have to have their hearts failing them because of fear as to what is going to happen to this great world. God tells us. The prophecy of God's Word is the very mold into which the events of the future are being poured. Let us read His Word and find His plan and purpose.

Peter called the Bible the "prophetic word confirmed" (2 Pet. 1:19). Prophecy of all kinds has always captivated people's interest. If anybody claims to be able to prophesy in any direction, that person immediately attracts a crowd who will listen to him or her. Many prophesy, but most prophecies fail.

In Genesis, Joseph dreamed that he was to be a ruler and that his brothers would be in subjection to him. This dream came to fruition. In turn, another young man named Daniel, divinely guided, told the meaning of the dreams of others.

Daniel was one of the greatest prophets in biblical history. He was taken to Babylon as a captive when he was only 18 years of age. He arrived at the time that Nebuchadnezzar came to his throne and saw Assyria develop into a worldwide power under this new monarch.

Daniel lived in the midst of all the wonderful works that made Babylon famous. The great walls about the city of Babylon were about 300 feet high, and along the top ran a magnificent highway about 80 feet wide . . . wide enough for a chariot with four horses to turn about on it. The vast palace of the king was a city within the city—56 miles around. The gardens of the palace rose one above another to a height of 70 feet, on which stood full-grown trees.

It was into such surroundings that the captives of Judah were transported, but they were homesick for the hills and pastures of Palestine. They hung their harps on the willows and refused to join in the court festivities. Psalm 137:1 describes their distress: "By the rivers of Babylon, there we sat down, yea, we wept when we remembered Zion."

Daniel saw this universal empire rise, reach its peak of power and then pass away. He spent the years of captivity in exile in Babylon and saw the Jewish exiles freed by Cyrus. When he was about 90 years old, he was given an outstanding position of authority.

Daniel Knew God's Secrets

One of the ways in the Old Testament that God seemed to tell people what He was going to do was through their dreams. As we have seen, Nebuchadnezzar was the king of the world's greatest domain. One night he had a dream—a dream in which

God revealed to this heathen ruler the future of the gentile nations in God's plan of the ages. When the king awoke, he had forgotten what the dream was. So Nebuchadnezzar called his magicians, the wise men of that day, and asked them to tell him both his dream and the interpretation of it.

The wise men came before the king and said, "There is not a man on earth who can tell the king's matter; therefore no king, lord, or ruler has ever asked such things of any magician, astrologer, or Chaldean. It is a difficult thing that the king requests, and there is no other who can tell it to the king except the gods, whose dwelling is not with flesh" (Dan. 2:10-11). The king was angry at his magician's inability to tell him the answer. So he ordered that all the wise men in the kingdom be put to death.

Daniel lived in the palace of the king. Now, he and his friends were included in the number marked for execution. When Daniel heard of the decree, he went to the king and asked for time to find out the meaning of the dream. The king granted the request, and Daniel learned from the Lord God what the king had dreamed (read Daniel's prayer of thanksgiving to God for wisdom in Daniel 2:20-23).

Not a single magician in the land could tell the king what his dream meant. Only God could explain it, and He revealed the dream to Daniel. Daniel made sure that the king understood that the dream and the interpretation of it came from the one true God.

Nebuchadnezzar's Dream

The dream that Nebuchadnezzar had was a strange one. He dreamed that he saw a great image. The head of the image was fine gold, its chest and arms were silver, its belly and thighs were brass, its legs were iron, and its feet were part iron and part clay. In his dream, the king saw a stone, cut without hands, fall upon the feet of the image and break them.

The whole image was crushed so completely that the pieces were like the chaff left after grain is threshed. The wind blew the pieces away, and they were not to be found. However, the stone grew until it became a great mountain and filled the whole earth.

The image foretold a succession of four empires. Nebuchadnezzar's empire was first. His was the greatest and the richest of all the kingdoms. When Daniel spoke of Nebuchadnezzar's kingdom, he said, "You, O king, are a king of kings. For the God of heaven has given you a kingdom, power, strength, and glory; and wherever the children of men dwell, or the beasts of the field and the birds of the heaven, He has given them into your hand, and has made you ruler over them all—you are this head of gold." Indeed, the walls of the temples to Nebuchadnezzar's gods glistened like suns with gold and precious stones. It is true that in reality and in the memory of all peoples, Nebuchadnezzar eclipsed all other rulers. Gold symbolized the grandeur and glory of his kingdom, and it has never been equaled.

But the king of Babylon would soon be overthrown by the Medo-Persians, represented in the dream by the arms of silver. This would occur on the night of the feast of the wicked King Belshazzar, when Darius the Mede invaded and took the kingdom in 539 B.C. (see Dan. 5:1-31). The book of Esther tells us that the Persian monarchs ruled over all the earth. The prophet Isaiah, who lived 150 years before Cyrus, king of Persia, was born, had by the inspiration of the Holy Spirit referred to the nation and king of the Medes and Persians and called their king by name (see Isa. 44:28; 45:1). The very kingdom is again named in Daniel 5:28. We are told that the Medes and Persians would succeed Babylon.

Then came the belly and thighs of brass. In Daniel 8:21, we read that the united empire of the Medes and Persians would be replaced by the Grecian kingdom; this Medo-Persian dominion, after lasting for several hundred years, would be overthrown by a mighty Grecian warrior. This was fulfilled, as we know, by Alexander the Great, who conquered the Medo-Persians in 332 B.C.

The legs of iron typified the Roman kingdom, which would succeed the Grecian kingdom. This fourth kingdom that followed would be as strong as iron. This was the great world power that was in existence when Christ was born. "It came to pass in those days that a decree went out from Caesar Augustus that all the world should be registered" (Luke 2:1). The Roman Empire existed for some 500 years after Christ's death.

In Nebuchadnezzar's dream, the feet are iron and clay, which never mix or stay together. Some Bible students believe that the "10 toes" represent the division of the Roman Empire into 10 kingdoms that will be set up at the end of this age. Locate the boundaries of the Old Roman Empire and see what countries are found today within its limits. We believe that God's Word tells us that some day there will be 10 definite countries occupying this territory once known as the Old Roman Empire.

Both history and Scripture present these great empires in just this order. When Nebuchadnezzar dreamed this dream, the Persian kingdom did not exist. Persia was but a Babylonian province. A Grecian empire might have seemed an utter impossibility. The Hellenic states were warring tribes and kingdoms, giving little promise of their future greatness. The city of Rome was just being founded–an insignificant little village on the banks of the Tiber River. How did Daniel portray with such accuracy the future history of all these powers if unaided by the Holy Spirit of God?

The Stone

As we follow the account of the king's dream, we learn that Nebuchadnezzar beheld a "great stone" falling out of heaven. The climax of the dream tells what the stone will do to the image. It utterly destroys the whole structure, and then, in turn, it becomes a great mountain filling the whole earth.

This "stone" has great significance. It conclusively points to Christ as the Messianic King of the Jews. "The stone which the builders rejected Has become the chief cornerstone" (Ps. 118:22; see also Matt. 21:42; Mark 12:10; Luke 20:17-18). As Isaiah wrote, "Behold, I lay in Zion a stone for a foundation, a tried stone, a precious cornerstone, a sure foundation" (v. 16).

The falling of the stone from heaven represents the second coming of our Lord. All rebellion against God shall be put down, and Christ shall rule. Earthly rule will progress historically until, in a moment, a different power "not cut out with hands" will fall upon the whole thing and grind it to powder. Then this kingdom will become universal in the earth. All the nations of the earth will be brought under the glorious and peaceful rule of the Son of God (see Ps. 72:8). Christ's kingdom shall be everlasting and universal.

When we hear of peace conferences and the like, we know that there can be no lasting peace in this world until the Prince of Peace comes. He shall sway His scepter from sea to sea and from the rivers to the ends of the earth.

Times of the Gentiles

No other book in the Bible has been so attacked by scoffers as has the book of Daniel. People were determined to prove that this book that contained such predictions could not have been written before they happened. But the facts in the book of

Daniel have been fully supported by modern discoveries. For example, it has been shown through archaeological excavations that Belshazzar ruled jointly with his father, Nabonidus, and that he was the grandson of Nebuchadnezzar.

Other discoveries have brought to light inscriptions dealing with the time of Nebuchadnezzar, Nabonidus and Cyrus. Christ Himself, in Matthew 24:15, when He was telling about His coming again, quoted from Daniel. Thus we see our Lord putting His stamp of approval on Daniel's prophecy.

Daniel was distinctly the prophet of the times of the gentiles. He gives us a panorama of the four world empires. With the new Babylonian Empire began the long period of gentile rule. Daniel saw Nebuchadnezzar as the head of gold in the image of the king's dream. Notice that the image began with a head of gold and ended with feet of iron and clay. This gives a real picture of the course of human history. This vision really is basic to all the other visions of the book of Daniel.

This second chapter of Daniel has been called the "A B C" of prophecy. It contains the simplest yet most complete prophetic picture in all the Bible. Is it not strange that this prophecy was given as a dream to a pagan monarch? Nebuchadnezzar called in all the magicians and soothsayers of his kingdom to tell him the meaning of the dream, but they could not interpret it.

Nebuchadnezzar was the ruler of the greater part of the known world. He had taken the chosen people of the Lord into captivity because of their sin and disobedience. God was going to put aside Israel for a time and the Gentile nations of the earth were to rule. Nebuchadnezzar was the first of the gentile rulers whose power was to reach through 25 centuries.

To this same king God gave this dream that revealed His plan for the government of the earth. God has not left us in ignorance as to the future. He has given us His prophetic word to shed light on what is to come. All this was given to a man who did not know God, but it took a man of God to tell what it meant.

God's Word Is True

The words that Daniel spoke to King Nebuchadnezzar were true. Some of the prophecy Daniel himself lived to see fulfilled. He saw the city of Babylon fall to the army of Cyrus and then he lived under the rule of Darius the Mede.

Much more of the prophecy, we know from history, has occurred. The empires of Greece and Rome are historical facts. We are confident that the balance of the dream will also be fulfilled. The Lord Jesus Christ typified by the stone will triumph over all. The heathen kingdoms of the world will be judged by Him and will be crushed and destroyed.

Nations and individuals who neglect God and follow their own desires may be sure of God's justice and judgment. Remember, Daniel warned Belshazzar, who succeeded Nebuchadnezzar, that his disobedience was bringing his country to destruction (see Dan. 5:26-28). If you and I follow our own desires, we will also have to face God's judgment. Psalm 1:6 says, "For the Lord knows the way of the righteous, but the way of the ungodly shall perish."

Daily Meditations

Sunday: A king's dream—Daniel 2:1-18

Monday: The secret revealed—Daniel 2:19-30

Tuesday: The future foretold—Daniel 2:31-45

Wednesday: Daniel is promoted—Daniel 2:46-49

Thursday: The coming kingdom—Daniel 7:9-14; Revelation 19:11-16

Friday: The coming of the King in glory—Matthew 24:27-51

Saturday: The throne of David—2 Samuel 7:15-16; Luke 1:31-33

16

Four Hundred Years of Silence

Behold, the LORD's hand is not shortened, that it cannot save; nor His ear heavy, that it cannot hear. But your iniquities have separated you from your God; and your sins have hidden His face from you, so that He will not hear.

ISAIAH 59:1-2

By the time Old Testament history ended, a few of the Jews, chiefly of the tribe of Judah, had returned to Palestine under the leadership of a man named Zerubbabel, and about 80 years later, another company had returned with Ezra. The Temple had been rebuilt, and the religious ceremonies had been revived. Yet the greater part of the Jewish race was still scattered throughout the Persian Empire.

The last three history books of the Old Testament—Ezra, Nehemiah and Esther—give us the story of this time (the books that follow them are either poetry or the utterances of the prophets spoken before, during and after the exile). These three books give us the history for about 100 years following the decree of Cyrus that permitted the Jews to go back to their own land in 536–424 B.C.

We often speak of this period of time from Nehemiah to the beginning of the New Testament times as the "400 years of silence." No biblical prophet was recorded and no inspired writer gave us an account of what took place during this period. But even though the Bible is silent, religious and secular history is available to help us fill in the gaps. These 400 years deserve mention, because during this long period of time there were great happenings in the history of the world. The seat of power changed from Asia to Europe. Greece rose and fell, and Rome reached the zenith of her power. These and other great events intimately affected the Jewish people.

For the narration of these important events, we must rely upon secular sources, including the writings of Josephus, the books of the Apocrypha, and some of the Dead Sea Scrolls.

Alexander the Great

At the time of Nehemiah and Ezra, the first world empire, Babylon, had been brought under the rule of the Medes and Persians, and that part of Daniel's prophecy regarding the four great world empires had actually been fulfilled. As we have seen, the Persians were tolerant and permitted the Jews to carry on their own religious observances without persecution. Because of her geographical position, the Holy Land suffered keenly from the wars between Persia and Egypt.

In 331 B.C., a Greek named Alexander, at the age of 20, succeeded his father, Philip of Macedon, as king. During the next brief period of 13 years, he changed the entire course of human history. He conquered the Persian Empire and overran the world. At this point, the Holy Land became one of the subject states of

Greece. His was the third world empire of Daniel's vision, represented by the body and thighs of brass.

Josephus tells us that Alexander came down to Jerusalem and was met by Juddua, the high priest, with a procession of Jewish priests dressed in white, purple, scarlet and gold. Alexander bowed in reverence to them. His generals thought him mad, but he told them that he had seen the God of Juddua in a vision while in Macedonia and had been encouraged by this vision to conquer the world. Josephus states that Juddua read to Alexander from the book of Daniel, where the prophecy indicates that one of the Greeks would destroy the Persians (see Dan. 7:6; 8:3,20-22). Alexander, supposing this meant himself, went forth to conquer.

This young monarch had a ruling passion not only to conquer the world but also to plant everywhere the civilization of Greece. He was determined to bring the East under the cultural influence of the West. He was an ardent student of Aristotle and gave to the world a universal language into which the Old Testament was later translated at Alexandria, a city he founded. This translation was called the Septuagint, meaning "seventy," a name that comes from the tradition that the work was accomplished by seventy scholars. The Septuagint is an important work, because it represents the first major translation of the Scriptures.

Upon Alexander's death, following a life so brief but so remarkable in achievement, his kingdom was divided among his four generals, to whom he had assigned different parts of his vast dominion. Daniel had predicted this empire should be separated into four parts. In this division, Egypt and later Palestine fell to one of his generals, Ptolemy. Great numbers of the Jews settled in Egypt. Ptolemy treated them with kindness, and for about 150 years the relations between the Jews and their Greek conquerors were pleasant.

A Terrible King

After the death of Alexander, the Greek Empire began to decline. Conflicts erupted between Syria and Egypt, and in 198 B.C., Antiochus IV Epiphanes of Syria was able to conquer Palestine. Immediately, the Jews were bitterly persecuted.

This monarch was determined to stamp out all Jewish faith and to make everyone in his kingdom conform to the Greek customs. He did everything to defile the sacred Temple, even killing a herd of swine and spattering the blood of these unclean beasts upon the very altar of God! The Jews fled from such profanation of this most sacred spot. The daily offerings ceased, the golden candlesticks were no longer lighted, and the people were forced to eat the flesh of swine, which God through Moses had forbidden (see Lev. 11:1-8). Antiochus erected an altar to the Greek god Jupiter and forced the Jews to worship before them. Many refused, and a period of horrible massacre and martyrdom ensued. This "desolation" is considered a type of the final "abomination of desolation" (Matt. 24:15).

The people fled from Jerusalem in terror, and for more than three years worship in the Temple was abandoned. In addition to having an altar to Jupiter, the Temple was devoted to the worship of the Greek god Zeus. Antiochus used every conceivable torture to get the Jews to renounce their faith.

The Rise of the Maccabees

The cruelties of this terrible king soon brought about a revolt. In the small town of Modin, in the northern kingdom, a priest name Mattathias arose who showed the spirit of Gideon and Elisha. When Antiochus's officer came hunting for victims to sacrifice to Zeus, he went to Mattathias as the headman of the town. The old man killed him, destroyed the heathen altar, and called on his sons and the men of Modin to follow him.

Mattathias's five brave sons had each been given a special name: John, "The Lucky"; Simon, "The Jewel"; Elazar, "The Beast Sticker" (so named because he had killed one of the enemy's fighting elephants in battle); Jonathan, "The Cunning"; and Judas, "The Hammer," who was the most valiant of them all. From the Hebrew word for "hammer," *maccab,* comes the title by which this family was known: the Maccabees.

After destroying the altar in Modin, Mattathias, his five sons and all the men who dared follow him then ran into the wilderness and proclaimed war to the very death against this hideous persecutor. Aroused by the patriotism and religious ardor of Mattathias, a group of Jews soon gathered about him and began an insurrection that spread rapidly.

When the old priest died, his son Judas carried on. At first, the Jews' cause seemed hopeless, for they were untrained and unequipped. Opposing them was the army of Antiochus, led by generals skilled in world campaigns. This army outnumbered the Jews six to one, but the ragged little band was acquainted with the wilderness and won battle after battle against fearful odds. Eventually, this band of ragged but loyal Jews, inspired by an undying faith in God, came out victorious. Antiochus died of a loathsome disease, and Judas Maccabeus became governor of Palestine. Thus began the reign of the Hasmonean kings.

Judas was indeed the deliverer of the Jewish race and the Jewish faith. He purified the Temple, built a new altar to Jehovah, furnished new vessels and, on December 25, 165 B.C., rededicated the Temple. This memorable date became a national holiday for the Jewish people after that time. In our Lord's time, it was known as "The Feast of Dedication," but today is known as "The Feast of Lights."

Under the Maccabees, the religious life of the people was restored. This state continued even under Roman rule.

ROMAN RULE

In 63 B.C., the Roman general Pompey entered Jerusalem and placed Palestine under Roman rule. After Pompey, Julius Caesar rose to power and ultimately became the emperor of all Rome. When Julius Caesar was assassinated, the empire was divided and a man named Herod secured the kingship of Judea.

Fearful lest some member of the Maccabee family should endanger his position, Herod decided to destroy that family. There was a growing antagonism among the Jews, and he feared that they would appeal to Rome. So, in order to gain their favor, he promised them a new Temple. The second Temple, built by Zerubbabel, had been in existence for about 500 years at this time. Herod's Temple was a very beautiful structure that was built on the same site as Solomon's magnificent structure. It was in this Temple that Jesus came to worship.

The Jews had been given full political liberty under the Maccabees, but under the Romans they were required to pay a yearly tax to the government. It was for this reason that Mary and Joseph, some years later, went to Bethlehem to pay the tax and to be registered. The Messianic promise, given in the Garden of Eden (see Gen. 3:15), was fulfilled in the birth of Christ, the long-anticipated Messiah.

Herod's life was dominated by the fear that his throne was not secure. He even murdered his wife and his two sons. We can understand the terror that seized him when it was announced that the King of the Jews had been born. That was the reason he ordered all the baby boys of Bethlehem to be slain, so that in this way he might kill baby Jesus.

THE CANON OF THE OLD TESTAMENT

As we mentioned, one of the historical sources of this chapter is the Apocrypha, a Greek word meaning "secret" or "hidden."

The Apocrypha is comprised of 14 books: 1 and 2 Esdras, Tobit, Judith, Additions to Esther, Wisdom of Solomon, Ecclesiasticus, Baruch (chapter 6 of which is the Epistle of Jeremy), Song of the Three Holy Children, History of Susannah, Bel and the Dragon (chapters 9–11 of which are additions to the book of Daniel), Prayer of Manasses, and 1 and 2 Maccabees. The Protestant Church has always considered these books not to be divinely inspired and does not recognize them as Scripture.

What did the Jews consider the sacred canon? Josephus, their own historian, who was born about A.D. 37, surely may be considered an authority as to what books comprised the Old Testament canon of the Jews. He states positively that the very last writing of the Old Testament canon was completed during the reign of Artaxerxes, king of Persia (called Ahasuerus in the book of Esther). Read his statement: "Although so great an interval of time has now passed, not a soul has ventured to add or to remove or to alter a syllable, and it is the instinct of every Jew from the day of his birth to consider these Scriptures as the teaching of God; to abide by them and, if need be, cheerfully lay down his life in their behalf."

Josephus's list exactly coincides with that of the Protestant Old Testament of today. This was the Bible known in the days of Jesus, and He put His approval upon it when He stated that in the Law of Moses and the prophets were to be found the things that were fulfilled in Him (see Matt. 5:17-18). Nor did Jesus ever quote one sentence that can be ascribed to any book in the Apocrypha.

The bare fact that the apocryphal books were rejected by Josephus and never included in the Hebrew collection is reason enough for our rejecting them as sacred writings. However, these little books are of great value to us because it is within them that we find the history of the Maccabees and the persecution of the Jews by Antiochus IV Epiphanes. They carry the history of the 400 silent years down to the death of Simon Maccabeus in 135 B.C.

Daily Meditations

Sunday: Seventy years of exile–Jeremiah 25:8-14

Monday: The dispersion predicted–Leviticus 26:32-33; Deuteronomy 28:63-68

Tuesday: The exiled Jews return under Zerubbabel–Ezra 1:1–2:1

Wednesday: Under Ezra, 78 years later–Ezra 7:1-10,27-28

Thursday: Under Nehemiah, 14 years later–Nehemiah 2:1-20

Friday: The prophecy about Cyrus–Isaiah 44:28–45:4

Saturday: Israel's hope–Isaiah 9:1-7

17

God's Plan for Israel

He will set up a banner for the nations, and will assemble the outcasts of Israel, and gather together the dispersed of Judah from the four corners of the earth.

Isaiah 11:12

Have the Jews really a right to the land of Israel? This question is more pertinent today than ever. In Ezekiel 36:2, God put these words in the mouth of the prophet, telling him just what the enemy would say: "Because the enemy has said of you, 'Aha! The ancient heights have become our possession.'" For centuries, the Jews were indeed a conquered people, their lands held in the possession of other powerful nations. Now, the Jews are in control of their homeland. The nation of Israel occupies all of its beloved capital, Jerusalem.

For centuries, the Jewish problem could be expressed by the simple word "homeless." It is true that many individual Jews had homes, but they had no land to call their own. Their homes were theirs according to the whim of the country. At times they had peace and thrived. Then, almost without warning, the attitude toward them would change and persecution and often death would follow. When it did, there was no place for them to go.

The Jews who lived in countries around the world were known as the "Diaspora," or the "dispersion." Always their eyes turned toward the Land of Promise, and they dreamed of coming home.

The Return to Palestine

During World War I, a Jewish chemist, Dr. Chaim Weizmann, worked as the director of the British Admiralty laboratories. A specialist in the use of industrial fermentation, Dr. Weizmann developed the chemical acetone, a compound that was critical to the Allied war effort for the manufacture of explosives.

Dr. Weizmann could have asked a fabulous sum of the government for his research, but when he was asked his price, he is reported to have said that his only wish was that Britain's power could be used to free the land of Palestine from its oppressors and deliver it back to the Jewish people. Britain kept her word. On November 2, 1917, the British government issued the Balfour Declaration, a formal statement of policy on the partitioning of the Ottoman Empire after World War I. God used this Jewish man to help Great Britain in her crisis so that Britain could help the Jewish people in theirs.

The Balfour Declaration did not install the national Jewish home in a vacuum; it allowed it to be formed in what was in effect an Arab country. It did not install the Jewish national home in a territory remote from political contingencies but permitted it in a section of the world that for generations had been the focus of a fierce imperialist struggle. But Zionism could not have been realized anywhere else. The Holy Land is the Jewish national home.

Following the events of World War II, the State of Israel was proclaimed on May 14, 1948. Shortly thereafter, Egypt, Syria, Jordan, Lebanon and Iraq attacked Israel, initiating the Arab-

Israeli War. In 1967, Egypt, Jordan and Syria massed troops close to Israel's borders and blocked the nation's access to the Red Sea. The Israelis launched the Six-Day War, during which time they captured Old Jerusalem and the Arab-occupied land of Palestine surrounding it.

Amazing changes have taken place since the Six Day War of June 1967. When the troops of Israel moved into the Old City on June 7, 1967, and stood for prayer at the Wailing Wall, Rabbi Shlomo declared, "We have taken the city of God. We are entering the Messianic era for the Jewish people, and I promise to the Christian world that what we are responsible for we will take care of."

Remember, the Jews for centuries had been divorced from agricultural pursuits. They were petty traders and small manufacturers. Yet the Jews returned to the land. They planted vineyards and orchards, cultivated the soil and raised cattle and poultry. They did not turn their backs on the activities of the city life but instead concentrated on making their land productive. The prophet Micah said, "Everyone shall sit under his vine and under his fig tree, and no one shall make them afraid" (Mic. 4:4).

Zionism, a love and desire for a land, is as old as Moses. Even if Moses himself did not reach the Promised Land, he first emphasized the concrete political actuality of the need of the Jews to possess a land, to have for themselves that most essential of all things–a homeland.

Accompanying Zionism came a revival of the Hebrew language. As Jews from all countries began to return to Israel, a problem of language arose. The young nation faced the problem and decided to revive the ancient Hebrew. This is the first instance in history where an ancient language was brought back into use. Hebrew theaters were organized, and a living literature in Hebrew was developed. Schools were opened in considerable numbers, including a great Hebrew university on Mt. Scopus near the city of Jerusalem.

When the British issued the Balfour Declaration, there were some 55,000 Jews in Palestine. A considerable number of them were of the old religious world–men who had come to spend their last years in Palestine. The land to which the Jews came was impoverished by four centuries of Turkish neglect, and misrule had crippled it.

However, after the events of the Six Day War, the standard of living of the whole country was enormously elevated. Jewish capital entered the country in large amounts. The remarkable town of Tel Aviv arose on the sand dunes north of the ancient city of Joppa. Swamps were drained, malaria was controlled, irrigation and water prefects were outlined, and agriculture was promoted. The Jewish people built hospitals, welfare stations, libraries, clinics and laboratories for scientific research.

The Wailing Wall

The Wailing Wall, or Western Wall, in Jerusalem, is a stretch of wall about 164 feet long and about 65 feet high outside the walls of the Dome of the Rock. The blocks are enormous stones of brownish color. They are supposed to be the fragments of the foundation stones of Herod's Temple wall that the Roman emperor Titus did not destroy in A.D. 70. Here the Jews come day and night, but with renewed vigor every Friday at sunset, the beginning of their Sabbath day. They mourn over the departed glory of their nation. They have done this for years.

Constantine allowed the Jews, once a year, to weep on the Dome of the Rock, where Abraham offered up Isaac, the site of the Temple. But since the twelfth century, this part of the exterior wall has been allotted to the Jews for their particular place of prayer. It is a sight indeed to see some of them standing in front of the wall, rocking back and forth in prayer. Others stick prayers, written on small pieces of paper, in the cracks in the stones, for the Jews believe that the Shekinah glory has never deserted those stones. Prayers from Jews all over the world are offered at the Wailing Wall.

Remember, some day these persecuted and scattered people are going to be forgiven and restored (see Ezek. 36:24).

The Clock of Progress

On July 5, 1950, the law was passed: "Every Jew has the right to immigrate to Israel." With the passing of that edict, the Jewish people girded up their loins and poured into their ancient homeland by the hundreds of thousands. No wonder the Arab peoples complained and protested! They could see themselves swallowed up in this tide of Hebrews returning to the land God had given to their father Abraham.

Since the Six Day War of 1967, Jerusalem has been open to the Jews. Their other really great cities are Haifa, a seaport city located on the Mediterranean coastline in the Bay of Haifa, and Tel Aviv, the largest and most populous metropolitan area in Israel.

In Ezekiel 36:33-35, the prophet writes, "Thus says the Lord GOD: 'On the day that I cleanse you from all your iniquities, I will also enable you to dwell in the cities, and the ruins shall be rebuilt. The desolate land shall be tilled instead of lying desolate in the sight of all who pass by. So they will say, "This land that was desolate has become like the garden of Eden; and the wasted, desolate, and ruined cities are now fortified and inhabited."'"

As one drives over the fine highways of Israel, he or she can see how the land is being changed from a desert into a garden by modern methods and machinery. Swamplands have given place to fields of grain. The finest oranges in the world are being shipped put from the port of Haifa. Today, with irrigation and intensive cultivation, the desert is blossoming like a rose. Surely, it was only by divine inspiration that Ezekiel could have made his prophecy that describes what is going on in Israel today.

A great amount of water is necessary to make the soil of this land productive. Much water is taken from the Sea of Galilee and from the River Jordan and other streams for irrigation and domestic use. In addition, increased rainfall is supplying a considerable amount of this needed water. Modern methods of bringing water from distant places add more, and today fresh water is being produced at desalination plants from the salt water of the Mediterranean Sea. Ezekiel's prediction that the land would again be tilled and sown and that it would increase and bring fruit is already being fulfilled in all parts of Israel.

The Dead Sea

One always thinks of the Dead Sea as a scene of desolation. What a surprise to drive down from Beersheba and see the great salt plants stretching along the water's edge. But stranger still it is to see the resorts with umbrellas and eating places for the people of Jerusalem to enjoy. The climate is warm and balmy in the winter, and one can bathe all the year around. The water is so saturated with salt that swimmers cannot sink; they just lie back as they would on a couch, hold an umbrella over their heads and comfortably read a book!

Minerals in the Dead Sea are of tremendous importance. No one ever considered this body of water as valuable. It contains no living creatures except for a tiny shrimp that is not edible, and the water is too salty for any use. But now we know that in addition to salt, the sea contains minerals, the value of which is beyond computation. Potash for fertilizing is found in abundance, and the magnitude of the potash companies is astonishing. Great vats or artificial pools, each many acres in extent, are pumped full of water and allowed to evaporate in the hot desert sun, leaving a residue of valuable minerals.

Early in Genesis we find mention of "pitch," which many believe is the biblical name for petroleum and coal tar products. Noah used pitch to make the ark watertight. Pitch was found in the plains where Sodom and Gomorrah stood. In fact, geologists now know that a vast share of the land is underlain by oil deposits. What a source of wealth!

Fifteen hundred years before our Lord walked the earth, Moses foretold the future of various tribes of Israel. This was even before the children of Israel entered the land of Canaan. Here is his prophecy concerning the tribe of Asher: "Asher is most blessed of sons; Let him be favored by his brothers, and let him dip his foot in oil" (Deut. 33:24).

When the land was divided by lot among the 12 tribes, the portion of Canaan that fell to Asher lay along the Mediterranean Sea. It stretched north beyond Tyre and south beyond Haifa. In addition to her own deposits of oil, a gigantic pipeline stretches from Eliat in the south of Israel to Haifa, carrying more than 400,000 barrels of oil an hour. Is Moses' prophecy being fulfilled, that Asher shall dip his foot in oil? Think of God's telling this to Moses 3,500 years ago!

There is another remarkable development that we must mention: the building of the National Water Carrier. Water is taken from the Sea of Galilee and other sources and carried south to the Negev desert, where thousands of acres of desert are being cultivated. But let us not forget that the present land of Israel is only a small bit of the ground that God promised to Abraham and his seed. We have every reason to believe that some day this promise will also be fulfilled.

The Jewish People's Charter

One of the Jewish leaders made this startling, but incontrovertible, statement before the British Royal Commission: "Our claim to Palestine derives not from the Balfour Declaration, but the Hebrew Bible. The Hebrew Bible is the Jewish charter to Palestine. History supports this. Jewish need renews that charter. Jewish capacity will vindicate it. Our claim to Palestine is of divine gift."

For centuries, the Jews have closed their Passover service with the prayer, "Next year in Jerusalem." On the seventh of June, 1967, when the Israeli army conquered the Old City, the chief chaplain of the army spoke from the Western Wall. In part, he said:

> Your children have returned to their borders, our feet now stand within thy gates, Jerusalem: city bounded together once more with New Jerusalem; city that is perfect of beauty and joy of the whole earth, Capital City of the eternal state of Israel. In the name of the entire community of Jewry in Israel and in the Diaspora, and with joy sublime, I herewith pronounce the blessing: Blessed art Thou, O Lord our God, King of the universe, for having kept us alive and sustained us and brought us to this day. This year in rebuilt Jerusalem.

The rebirth of Israel is one of the miracles of modern times. This land has been called the navel of God's kingdom, the corridor of the world to come, the entrance to the mysteries of life. It gave birth to the three great religions of the world.

The sacred literature created on its soil gave direction and shaped the lives of many generations of men and women. It has been the most significant and fruitful of all lands in the changing history of the human race. But over it was heaped the dust of the desert and the heels of many conquerors that brought ruin and death. It seemed as dead as the ruins of Pompeii and the buried cities of Egypt.

Going Back to Unbelief

We must pause to remember the sad fact that with all this progress, the Jewish people returned to their homeland in unbelief, exactly as prophesied. But Zechariah 12:10 tells the glorious end of this story.

What a wonderful Lord we have! All that He has promised to do He will surely perform. "The Lord is not slack concerning His promise" (2 Pet. 3:9). God made promises to the Jews throughout the Old Testament; these promises He will keep. We are privileged to live in a day in which we can watch God perform.

We may be just as sure that each promise He has made to us He will bring to pass. "God is not a man, that He should lie, nor a son of man, that He should repent. Has He said, and will He not do? Or has He spoken, and will He not make it good?" (Num. 23:19).

God is fulfilling His promises to Israel, and He will also fulfill His promises to us. All we need do is to trust Him, secure in the knowledge that His way is perfect and that He will never make a mistake. Our part is to believe and obey; God's part is to perform.

Daily Meditations

Sunday: The title deed to Palestine—Genesis 13:14-17; 17:4-8

Monday: The Jews are punished—Zechariah 7:4-14

Tuesday: The Jews' future blessing—Zechariah 8:1-15

Wednesday: The Jews' future restoration—Ezekiel 36:16-38

Thursday: David's everlasting throne—Ezekiel 37:21-28

Friday: The King of the Jews is rejected—John 19:16-30

Saturday: The King of the Jews is triumphant—Revelation 1:7; 5:11-14; 11:15; 19:11-16

18

Christ, the Virgin-born Son of God

"Behold, the virgin shall be with child, and bear a Son, and they shall call His name Immanuel," which is translated, "God with us."
Matthew 1:23

Hector, a mythical warrior of olden times, stood outside the city walls, ready to depart on what would prove to be his last campaign. His wife and child had come out to say goodbye. Hector put out his arms to take his little boy. But when the baby saw his father's shining helmet flashing in the sun, he began to cry. The warrior then took off his helmet and again put out his hands. At once, the little one, recognizing him, laughed and sprang into his father's arms.

This is very much like our feelings about God, the Almighty Jehovah, the judge and avenger of sin. It may strike awe into our hearts and minds when He reveals His punishment of sin and the greatness of His power. But Christ came down to the earth and put aside His majesty and glory to become a man with feelings such as you and I have. Christ stretches out His loving arms to draw us to Himself.

The Messiah Prophesied

Christ is found everywhere in the Old Testament. Someone has said that He is the golden link that builds all of its parts together. "In the volume of the book it is written of Me," said our Lord Himself (Heb. 10:7). The nature of the Redeemer's work and even His history and character are described in such minute detail in the Old Testament that one could even compile a history of Christ from the prophecies. Prophecy captivates everyone. It helps to confirm our faith in God's Word.

The prophets told of the birth of Jesus Christ years before He came to Earth. They told many wonderful things about Him years in advance. Learn these facts and you will never doubt that Jesus was indeed God manifest in the flesh. These prophecies were made by many different men at different times throughout a period of 500 years–from 1000 B.C. to 500 B.C. They were all fulfilled at Jesus' birth.

Of the Jewish Race

The gospel of the Jews must be the fulfillment of prophecy. You remember that when God spoke to Abraham, He said, "In you [your seed] all the families of the earth shall be blessed" (Gen. 12:3). The Savior of the world was to be a Jew, a descendant of Abraham. He was to be born in one of the thousand little Jewish towns, and in Micah 5:2 we discover just which one it is: "But you, Bethlehem Ephrathah, though you are little among the thousands of Judah, yet out of you shall come forth to Me The One to be Ruler in Israel, whose goings forth are from of old, from everlasting."

Of the Seed of a Woman

The Messiah was to be the Seed of a woman, foretold in the first promise in Scripture, Genesis 3:15. Paul writes, "But when the fullness of the time had come, God sent forth His Son, born of a woman, born under the law" (Gal. 4:4). Someone has said that this is the germ of all prophecy that unfolds into the perfect, fragrant bloom of the Rose of Sharon and the Lily of the Valley.

Of the Tribe of Judah and House of David

Prophecy concerning the Messiah was narrowed down to a very definite person. The blessing of the earth was to come through *one man.* He was to be of the seed of Abraham, in the line of Isaac, then Jacob (see Gen. 28:13-14). He was to be of the tribe of *Judah* (see Gen. 49:10). In Isaiah 11:1 we read, "There shall come forth a Rod from the stem of Jesse, and a Branch shall grow out of his roots." The Messiah was to be a descendant of David, born of the royal house. The Lord God said to David, "Your house and your kingdom shall be established forever before you. Your throne shall be established forever" (2 Sam. 7:16).

Of Humble Birth

Although Christ was born of a royal house, it had been shorn of its splendor. There was nothing superior about His station or worldly wealth to commend Him to Israel. He was born in a stable, not in a palace. This was foretold in Isaiah 53:2. In fact, His condition was regarded with contempt. "Is not this the carpenter's son?" they asked (Matt. 13:55; see also the prophecy in Isa. 49:7). Indeed, He had no advantages. His knowledge was inexplicable to the men of His time. "And the Jews marveled, saying, 'How does this Man know letters, having never studied?'" (John 7:15).

The Messiah's Rejection and Death Foretold

In Isaiah 53:3, it was written, "He is despised and rejected by men, a Man of sorrows and acquainted with grief." In Isaiah 49:7,

He is the One "whom man despises . . . whom the nations abhor." Not only was He rejected by the Jews of His own day, but even to this present hour, Jewish people deny Him.

Daniel 9:26 says that He was "to be cut off," and again in Isaiah 53:8, by oppression and judgment, He was to be taken away: "He was cut off from the land of the living." Is it not strange that the Jews failed to recognize this suffering Messiah who was prophesied in Isaiah? He had to come first in humiliation and be led as a lamb to the slaughter. He had to be revealed as the Lamb of God before He could be presented as the Lion of the tribe of Judah.

The very manner of His death was foretold. "I am poured out like water, and all My bones are out of joint" (Ps. 22:14). "I gave My back to those who struck Me" (Isa. 50:6). "All those who see Me ridicule Me" (Ps. 22:7). How many times we have read these words but failed to realize that they were prophecies written centuries before the Lord Jesus came to this earth to live.

Isaiah furnishes us with the richest source of Messianic prophecy in all the Old Testament. From the fortieth to the sixty-sixth chapters, Isaiah's one continuous message concerns the Messiah. In the center of these chapters is his jewel, the fifty-third chapter, and the prophet's message is "Christ died to save sinners."

In Psalm 22:16-17, we find a real enigma unless we can leap the gulf of a thousand years and see Calvary, which is its solution: "For dogs have surrounded Me; the congregation of the wicked has enclosed Me. They pierced My hands and My feet; I can count all My bones." This all describes a man's death on a cross. The suffering described in this psalm is not the *Jewish* mode of punishment. The Jews did not hang men on a cross. It is a *Roman* form of execution, and it was at Roman hands that Jesus was nailed to the cross!

The Virgin Birth

The greatest point in all of the prophecy concerning the Messiah that we must take into consideration is the fact that Jesus was born of a virgin. If Christ was not born of a virgin, we must look for another Savior, for God said this should be so. If God was not His Father, then He was not God in the flesh.

Let us see what God declared in His promises in the Old Testament concerning this prophecy. The original promise is in Genesis 3:15: "I will put enmity between you and the woman, and between your seed and her Seed." The *Seed* of a woman refers to the virgin birth. Christ's birth was a biological miracle, because He had no earthly father. Isaiah prophesied this: "Therefore the Lord Himself will give you a sign: Behold, the virgin shall conceive and bear a Son, and shall call His name Immanuel" (Isa. 7:14).

This virgin-born child was to be a sign to Israel that God was with them, for that is what the name "Immanuel" means.

Witnesses of This Fact

God sent an angel from heaven with the tidings of this great fact. His name was Gabriel. He had been in heaven around the very throne and had seen the Lord Jesus Christ in His preincarnate glory. When Gabriel announced to Mary that she would give birth to the Messiah, he said, "Rejoice, highly favored one, the Lord is with you; blessed are you among women!" (Luke 1:28).

Mary was troubled by this saying, but Gabriel continued, "Do not be afraid, Mary, for you have found favor with God. And behold, you will conceive in your womb and bring forth a Son, and shall call His name Jesus. He will be great, and will be called the Son of the Highest; and the Lord God will give Him the throne of His father David. And He will reign over the house of Jacob forever, and of His kingdom there will be no end" (vv. 30-33).

How could this be? "The Holy Spirit will come upon you, and the power of the Highest will overshadow you; therefore, also, that Holy One who is to be born will be called the Son of God" (v. 35). Great is the mystery of godliness. Jesus was to be called the *Son of God.* He was not to be called the son *of Joseph,* according to the flesh.

Many people say that it does not matter whether Christ was Joseph's son or not. Do you think it matters? What about Joseph? He was a humble carpenter engaged to be married to a lovely Jewish girl when the angel came to him and said, "Do not be afraid to take to you Mary your wife, for that which is conceived in her is of the Holy Spirit" (Matt. 1:20). Joseph did as the angel of the Lord commanded him. With faith equal to Mary's, Joseph believed the message. He did not take Mary to be his wife until Jesus was born. He said that he was not the father of Jesus (read Matthew 1:18-25).

Gabriel's words to Mary were definite when he said that Jesus "will be called the Son of God" (Luke 1:35). The people crucified Jesus because He said that He was the Son of God. He declared that He had no father by the flesh. Certainly Mary knew whether or not this was true. If it was not, the only thing she had to do was to name His father, but she could not, for He had no father according to the flesh. Jesus was the very Son of God.

Luke, the historian of this event, was not a Jew but a gentile. He declares in the Gospel called by his name that Christ was virgin-born. Luke was a doctor living at the time when Jesus was born. He could talk with eyewitnesses who had known the mother and the husband who was the legal guardian of Jesus (see Luke 1:26-27).

Christ's own statements also reveal that He understood Himself to be the Son of God. At one point in His ministry, the Jews surrounded Him and said, "If you are the Christ, tell us plainly." Jesus replied, "I told you, and you do not believe.

The works that I do in My Father's name, they bear witness of Me . . . My Father, who has given them to Me, is greater than all; and no one is able to snatch them out of My Father's hand. I and My Father are one" (John 10:24-25,29-30).

Jesus' accusers demanded His crucifixion for this one claim. Read what they said: "We have a law, and according to our law He ought to die, because He made Himself the Son of God" (John 19:7). Ignatius, a companion of the apostle John, spoke these words: "Stop your ears when anyone speaks to you at variance with the truth that Jesus Christ was conceived by the virgin Mary, of the seed of David, but by the Holy Ghost."

All of these statements are important because they help us to understand the truth. But this testimony means nothing unless we add our voices to it.

Christ Is God

How truly human is the Jesus of the Bible! There He lay, a little child, helpless, in the manger. But who was it who lay helpless in the lowly cattle shed? The answer is given in God's Word: "In the beginning was the Word, and the Word was with God, and the Word was God. . . . And the Word became flesh and dwelt among us, and we beheld His glory, the glory as of the only begotten of the Father, full of grace and truth" (John 1:1,14; see also Phil. 2:5-8). That little babe of Bethlehem was like no other baby born upon the earth, for He was God in the flesh! He was the One who created this whole universe. Yes, He made everything that was made (see John 1:3).

What do you think of Christ? Whose Son do you believe Him to be? These questions require an answer from every individual. You probably are quick to answer, "I believe that He is the Son of God." That's a good answer; in fact, it is the only true answer. But what difference does it make in your everyday living?

You believe that Jesus Christ is the Son of God, and so you believe that He has saved you. That's good, but there is more. You believe that Jesus Christ is God, and so you believe that He keeps you from day to day. That's good, but there is still more. You believe that Jesus Christ is the Son of God, and so you should follow His leading. That's good, but do you really follow where He leads?

If Jesus Christ is your Lord, you can't question His wisdom concerning the paths into which He takes you. If He is the Lord of your life, you must be willing to accept without question His will in every circumstance. If He says, "Go to Africa as My missionary," you say, "Yes, Lord, I will go." If He says, "You can't go to Africa; you have to stay here at home and others will go in My place," you say, "Yes, Lord, I will stay." There is more to acknowledging that Jesus Christ is the Son of God than just saying the words. You must acknowledge His Lordship daily by your life.

Daily Meditations

Sunday: Born of a virgin—Isaiah 7:14; Matthew 1:23

Monday: Descendant of Shem—Genesis 9:26-27; Luke 3:36

Tuesday: Descendant of Abraham—Genesis 12:3; 18:18; Matthew 1:1-2

Wednesday: Descendant of Isaac—Genesis 17:19; 21:12; Luke 3:34

Thursday: Of the tribe of Judah—Genesis 49:10; Matthew 2:6; Revelation 5:5

Friday: Of the house of David—Isaiah 9:6-7; Luke 3:31

Saturday: Born in Bethlehem—Micah 5:2; Matthew 2:16; Luke 2:4,11

19

Christ, Our Great Foundation

For no other foundation can anyone lay than that which is laid, which is Jesus Christ.
1 Corinthians 3:11

A terrific storm was sweeping the northwest coast of America. The people in the town all said, "Surely the lighthouse has been destroyed in the storm." Three days later, however, the keeper of the lighthouse appeared on the streets. One of his friends said to him, "We heard that the lighthouse had gone down in the storm."

The old keeper looked at him in amazement and said, "Gone down! It is true that the storm was the fiercest I have ever seen, but in all the storm, she never shook! The lighthouse stood because of her solid foundation." The true foundation of our faith is Jesus Christ. Storms of temptation and trials may beat against us, but our foundation will always stand sure!

One of the most sublime facts in connection with this wondrous *person of Christ* is the hold He has upon millions of believers in this age. After 20 centuries have passed, a large portion of the human race joins with Peter to say of Christ, "Whom having not seen we love." Everything connected with His personal life on Earth has perished. We can only guess at the spot where He was born, the place where He lived, the site of the cross and the tomb. And yet millions are living for Him and would die for Him. His unseen presence is their faith, hope, love and life. With this unseen Savior they hold daily communion; they go through the valley of tears, leaning on His arm; and they fear not the shadow of death, cheered on by His smile.

This fact is absolutely without a parallel. It impressed the great Napoleon of France more deeply than anything else about this mysterious person. Napoleon looked back through the centuries and saw the blood of Christian martyrs flowing in torrents while they kissed the hand that, in slaying them, opened the door to their Lord.

"You speak," said Napoleon at St. Helena, "of Caesar and Alexander; of their conquests; of the enthusiasm they enkindled in the hearts of their soldiers; but can you conceive of a dead man making conquests with an army faithful and entirely devoted to His memory? My army has forgotten me while living. Alexander, Caesar, Charlemagne and myself, have each founded empires. But on what did we rest the creations of our genius? Upon force! Jesus Christ alone founded His empire upon love; and at this hour millions of men would die for Him."

The Son of God and Perfect Man

The story of the life of Jesus Christ is the story of the greatest man who ever lived. He was the God-man. He lived a public life for three and one-half years. It ended with a death of shame at the age of 33. Yet today, He sways the world's history and destiny! All the Christian world celebrates the day of His birth. He is even Lord of the Christian's calendar—we date our letters and papers A.D., *anno domini,* "the year of our Lord." More books have been written about Jesus by far than any of the greatest men who ever lived in the world.

Although Jesus was of royal blood, He was not the son of rich and distinguished parents. He was not born in a palace. This babe was born in a stable, and a manger was His cradle. He grew into the very flower of humanity. Luke 2:52 says, "Jesus increased in wisdom and stature, and in favor with God and men." This man represented humanity in ideal perfection.

We can see in Jesus what God really expected when He created man in His own image to be His companion. Think how far man has fallen from this ideal! Men's minds are not keen and alert; their bodies are deformed and in their hearts they hate their creator.

Luke, in his Gospel, presents the Lord Jesus Christ as the perfect man. Luke tells of Jesus' virgin birth, of His boyhood, and of His visit to the Temple when He was 12 years of age. Luke presents Him as the man "in all points tempted as we are, yet without sin" (Heb. 4:15). How carefully Luke guards the *deity* of our Lord. We never once lose sight of the fact that this One is God.

Jesus' life was such a beautiful one. He was gentle, yet stern. He was indeed the combination of the "lamb" and the "lion." He was "made like His brethren" (Heb. 2:17). He "became flesh, and dwelt among us" (John 1:14). After the test of centuries, with the closest scrutiny of carping critics, not one flaw has been found in His character! He ate with sinners, yet His garments were untouched. He associated with prostitutes, yet escaped the breath of calumny. The outcasts of society were drawn to Him and lavished tears and kisses upon Him, yet He remained unsullied and sinless.

He was a man loved by all. His friends were among the rich and among those whom poverty harassed. He was found in the feasts of rejoicing and at the gravesides of loved ones. He lived with people and was touched with the feeling of all their infirmities.

Jesus' Humanity

Jesus was a man tempted as we are, yet He was without sin. The devil challenged the first Adam and ruined the first man. When he came to challenge the last Adam, who was Christ Jesus, Jesus challenged His adversary. The works of the devil were destroyed by this wonderful man's life and death.

Christ came to destroy the works of the devil. The first Adam brought the whole race into sin by his yielding to Satan; the last Adam included the entire human race in His victory. "We are more than conquerors through him that loved us" (Rom. 8:37). The apostle Paul realized that he could have victory in Christ, and so he said, "For to me, to live is Christ" (Phil. 1:21). Christ is the only One who overcame the devil in His life.

We cannot go into the details and explanations involved in the temptation of our Lord in so short a treatise, but many facts have been written by careful students that will stand the closest scrutiny. The fact remains that He was tempted in the flesh and that He came out victorious. No one can doubt this! Jesus must have told His disciples about His temptation, for a careful account of it is given even though we know that He was tempted while out alone in the wilderness. On the authority of His own word, we must accept the fact.

Remember, this sinless One will make a way of escape for us in the hour of temptation (see 1 Cor. 10:13).

Jesus' Intellect

Not only was Jesus Christ a perfect man morally, but He was also a perfect man intellectually. He was the very ideal of manhood in body, soul (mind) and spirit. Surely, "No man ever spoke like this Man!" (John 7:46).

How wisely He answered the doctors in the Temple when He was but a lad of 12 years (see Luke 2:47). He heard and asked questions of the Jewish doctors and surprised them with His understanding. Never before had the doctors of the law encountered such a boy. Amazement possessed them. His answers confounded them. Thus we know that His earliest years were years of communion with God and diligent study of the law of God.

Remember, this child was reared in a godly home and instructed at the feet of pious parents, so His interest in religious matters was not as premature as we may think. It is surprising today the grasp a child may have on spiritual things. At this early age, the law of God was His delight. The truth of Psalm 1:2 is beautifully exemplified: "His delight is in the law of the LORD, and in His law he meditates day and night."

Jesus foiled every advance of the devil in His temptation by the very words He uttered (see Luke 4:1-13). Through convincing arguments, He won over Nicodemus, the ruler of the Jews (see John 3:1-21). He gave perfect illustrations to His humble hearers, which helped them to understand His message (see Matt. 5–7). He gave wise counsel to His disciples in the upper room on that night before He left them (see John 13–17).

When the Scribes and Pharisees came to catch and confuse Him with questions, He quickly trapped them in their own net. Yet He was always eager to offer gracious words to His loved ones. He handed down incredible words of wisdom to us in His first Sermon on the Mount—and what incredible prayers He uttered! (Read John 17; you will never know Christ Jesus, the God-man, until you have read this wonderful passage!)

Augustine once stated, "I have read in Plato and Cicero sayings that are very wise and very beautiful; but I never read in either of them 'Come unto Me all ye that labor and are heavy laden.'" Who could say, "Come unto me all ye" but this God-man?

We have every reason to believe that God's own Son did take upon Himself not only the form of a man but also the very nature of a man, yet He did so without sin. Everything about His life seems natural and beautiful. The account of it in the Gospels is limited. This is one of the proofs of the inspiration of the Word. Had man invented a history of the life of Christ, the tales would have been exaggerated, like the ancients told of their gods.

Jesus' Miracles

Jesus proved that He was the God-man not only through the words He spoke but also by the miracles He performed. People kept coming after Him, seeking after a "sign" that would prove who He was. What signs did He furnish the honest inquirer? He said, "The blind see and the lame walk; the lepers are cleansed and the deaf hear; the dead are raised up" (Matt. 11:5).

But in no way did He ever cater to the demands of idle curiosity, nor were any of His wonderful works ever done selfishly. When He was hungry, He could have commanded the stones to be bread, but He would not. When He was on the cross, He could have called the very angels from heaven to deliver Him, but He did not. One less than God would have thought this a marvelous chance to show his real power and to prove to the doubting world that he was God.

There were no grand displays of the power and authority of God. He only desired to show men that He was sufficient to meet their needs in body and spirit. When He fed the 5,000, He ministered to a real physical need, but He was also teaching the great lesson that He was the bread of life. He wanted men to know that He was the Christ.

Jesus' Deity

One day when Jesus was walking with His disciples, He turned to them and asked, "Who do men say that I, the Son of Man, am?" (Matt. 16:13). They told Him. Then Christ asked of them, "But who do you say that I am?" (v. 15). Peter's answer was most significant: "You are the Christ, the Son of the living God" (v. 16). Did Jesus rebuke Peter for such blasphemy? Did He modestly refuse to be called the Son of God? No, He permitted Peter to make this public confession of just who He was!

If you would say to a godly man or woman, "What a good person you are; you are absolutely perfect," his or her immediate answer would be, "Oh, don't say that. You don't know me. I am not good. I am only a sinner, saved by grace." Do you see the great significance in Jesus' allowing Peter to make his unique declaration? Jesus not only called Himself the Son of God, but He also allowed others to give Him that name. Every other part of Jesus' character that we know to be true would have compelled Him to quickly deny such a statement if it had been untrue.

Jesus came to this earth, born of a woman, and became a partaker of human nature so that sinners might become partakers of His divine nature by faith in Him. "But these are written that you may believe that Jesus is the Christ, the Son of God, and that believing you may have life in His name" (John 20:31).

The Lord went about doing good. We know that He spoke as no other man spoke, but He also did as no other man did. He was a man of *deeds* as well as *creeds*. The works He performed ever recommended His teaching. His life always tallied with His doctrine. He left us an example that we should follow in His steps (see 1 Pet. 2:21).

Our Decision

Jesus stands before us as a perfect example of all the graces of a Christian. He loved, He forgave, He overcame temptation,

He prayed, He was fearless, He was self-sacrificing, He was humble. He was the perfect One in word and in deed.

Although His words were simple, they moved the world, for behind His speeches stood the perfect man. Even after 2,000 years He says, "Follow Me," and merchants leave their goods and lawyers their courtroom to move in obedience to His will.

What shall we do with Jesus, who is called the Christ? There is no middle ground. We must either accept Him as Lord or reject Him as a blasphemer and liar. It sounds terrible, but terrible it is! What shall you do with this One? What *have* you done?

Daily Meditations

Sunday: The annunciation—Luke 1:26-38
Monday: Christ, born of a virgin—Luke 2:1-20
Tuesday: Tempted as we are—Matthew 4:1-11;
Luke 4:1-13; Hebrews 2:17-18
Wednesday: The God-man—John 11-14; Colossians 2:9; Hebrews 4:15
Thursday: Christ was a man—Matthew 8:24; 21:18;
Luke 2:52; John 4:6; 11:35; 19:28
Friday: Adoration of Simeon and Anna—Luke 2:25-38
Saturday: Jesus and His parents—Luke 2:41-52

20

Christ, the Stone That the Builders Rejected

He is despised and rejected by men, a Man of sorrows and acquainted with grief. And we hid, as it were, our faces from Him; He was despised, and we did not esteem Him.

Isaiah 53:3

In India, there was once a leper colony in Allahabad where 500 adults and as many children were housed and cared for. People often asked those in charge, "Why do you bury your lives in such a place as this? Are you not afraid to be here among these lepers?" Their answer was, "We would be afraid not to be where we know God wills us to be."

There is really nothing grander than unselfish sacrifice for others, yet many sneer at the very idea. People can easily see how an individual may take a great risk when he or she may rise to fame or make a vast fortune by so doing. The valor of a soldier in battle can be understood, but how a person can risk his or her own personal comfort and interest—and even life itself—for those who have no claim whatsoever upon him or her is beyond ordinary comprehension.

Christ said, "He who finds his life will lose it, and he who loses his life for My sake will find it" (Matt. 10-39). One of the taunts that men threw at Christ on the cross was that He could save others but could not save Himself. Unknowingly, they spoke the truth. If Christ had not died upon the cross but had saved His own life, He could not have saved those for whom He came to give His life a ransom.

"The Son of Man did not come to be served, but to serve, and to give His life a ransom for many" (Matt. 20:28). "You shall call His name Jesus, for He will save His people from their sins" (Matt. 1:21).

A Climactic Event

Now we come face to face with the greatest of all events, for which Christ came to Earth and took upon Himself the form of a man. *He came to die.* All the prophets of the Old Testament had pointed forward to this mountain peak of history, and we on the other side of the cross look back to that same lofty height. Jesus' death is the fulfillment not only of the very mission of Jesus Christ but also of the predictions of the prophets that turned the face of the chosen people expectantly toward the future.

The cross was the event of which the Old Testament ceremonies and sacrifices were but types—these all spoke of the atonement of Jesus Christ, the Lamb of God. The great Day of Atonement and the Passover lamb only spoke of the cross.

Often in cases of serious illness or accident, when a person is in danger of dying from loss of blood, a remedy is used as a last resort that demands a sacrifice on the part of someone else. This remedy is taking the healthy blood from the body of a well person and transfusing it into the sufferer's veins.

Blood transfusion requires the utmost skill and caution in order to keep out any infection. Care must be used that too much blood is not taken from the well person; death to either or both might follow. But life has been saved in this way, by the gift of blood, for "the life is in the blood." *The outpouring of the precious blood of Jesus Christ and the inflow of the actual life of Christ are the only salvation for people who are dying in sin.* This is the supreme act of sacrifice that Christ made for us.

There are two great reasons for the cross. The first reason Christ died was to bear the sin of the world. But there is still another and greater reason for the cross: so that Christ might show the love of God to the world, "For God so loved the world that He gave His only begotten Son, that whoever believes in Him should not perish but have everlasting life" (John 3:16). We never could have known God's love in any other way.

No Other Way

God had punished people for their sins and had warned them of their transgressions. The Lord God had tried to woo them to Himself, but humans turned their back upon every attempt. *Sin separated humans from God.* The cross was the greatest expression of the heart of God toward all humankind. Men and women would not return to God or respond to His heart of love.

People had done everything they could to grieve the heart of God. They had been disobedient and stiff-necked, they had broken His laws, they had stoned and killed His prophets, they had dethroned God as their King, and they had put human kings to reign over them. The last act of sin was to crucify the Lord Himself, and this they did on Calvary. In Christ's Parable of the Tenants in Luke 20:9-18, our Lord taught this truth to the people.

Christ was led to the cross in full possession of His senses. He could have stopped the proceedings at any moment by the exercise of His will. Yet He voluntarily yielded up His spirit. "No one takes it [My life] from Me, but I lay it down of Myself" were His own words (John 10:18). He did not lay down His life until He had finished His work. The sin of the world had to be borne by someone, for the whole world had been pronounced guilty before God. Man could not bear his sin alone, for if he did, he would be lost forever. So Christ took it upon Himself and was made "to be sin for us" (2 Cor. 5:21).

Sin separates us from God, "for the wages of sin is death" (Rom. 6:23). That is the reason Jesus came to pay the wages of sin with His own life—so that we might be brought into fellowship with the Father.

Humans were created to be companions of the Father, but *our sin separated us from God.* As you remember, when Adam and Eve sinned, they hid themselves from God. Before this time, they had walked and talked with God in the Garden. Isn't it strange how sin always breaks fellowship? Even a little child will run and hide from his mother when he knows he has done wrong. Disobedience makes him afraid.

Christ died on the cross to make a way back to God possible, for Jesus is "the way, the truth, and the life. No one comes to the Father except through Me" (John 14:6). This is the only way that an unholy people can approach a holy God. We can never in this life understand the full meaning of the crucifixion and of the atonement.

Someone asked a fine Christian young man one day, "What is your theory of the atonement?" He answered, "I have no theory of the atonement. I *have* the atonement, and that is best." To know that the blood of Jesus Christ, God's Son, covers and cleanses our sin is better than any theory about it, for "the blood of Jesus Christ His Son cleanses us from all sin" (1 John 1:7).

Often on the prairies of the frontier, the grass in the dry season would catch on fire and the great flames, 20 feet high, would roll over the land faster than a horse could run. Men were terrorized as they saw the fire coming. They knew that it meant death unless they could make an escape. So they set fire to a certain plot of ground, and there they stood, perfectly secure in that burned-over area. There was nothing to fear, for the fire had burned all that there was to burn.

This is like Calvary. When we identify ourselves with Christ on Calvary and say with the apostle Paul, "I am crucified with Christ" (Gal. 2:20), then we need fear no judgment, for Christ has borne the condemnation for the sin of the whole world (see John 5:24).

The Power of the Cross

Isn't it wonderful what drawing power the cross has! Wherever we see the cross lifted throughout the world and the story of the crucified One told, people are drawn to Him. "And I, if I am lifted up from the earth, will draw all peoples to Myself" (John 12:32).

The story of the Son of God giving His life to atone for the sin of people that they might live can break the hardest heart. "He was wounded for our transgressions, He was bruised for our iniquities" (Isa. 53:5). Repeat this verse to yourself and put "my" in for "our." This makes it very personal.

The cross was the triumphant goal of Christ's life. To be sure, there were other victories still ahead, but His crucifixion was the one triumph to which He had been looking forward—not from the beginning of His earthly life, but from the beginning of time itself. He was "the Lamb slain from the foundation of the world" (Rev. 13:8).

Because of humankind's sin, it was absolutely necessary that Christ go to the cross if He were to succeed in bringing them back to the knowledge of God that had been lost in the Garden of Eden. Humans had forfeited their lives; Christ was giving His life for humans.

If Jesus had heeded the taunt of His tormenters, the rulers of the Jews, and had come down from the cross to save Himself, it would have proven conclusively that He was not the Son of God. Here was the Son of God voluntarily pouring out His life on the cross because of people's sin, doing what only God could do, and by that act proving gloriously His divine sonship. He did all this for us. "All we like sheep have gone astray; we have turned, every one, to his own way; and the LORD has laid on Him the iniquity of us all" (Isa. 53:6).

A preacher found a little girl weeping after a service. "What's the matter, dear?" he said. She replied, "I never knew before that Jesus died for *me!*" Yes, it was for *you and me* that Christ died upon a tree. He loved *you and me* and gave Himself for *us* (see Gal. 2:20). Listen to His prayer from the cross: "Father, forgive them, for they know not what they do" (Luke 23:34).

Evangelist Dwight L. Moody once said, "I can imagine when Christ told His disciples to go and preach to all that Peter said, 'Lord, do You really mean that we are to go back to Jerusalem and preach to those men who murdered You?' 'Yes,' said Jesus, 'Go hunt up that man that spat in My face. Tell him that he may have a seat in My kingdom. Go find the man that made that cruel crown of thorns and tell him I have a crown made ready for him when he comes into My kingdom and there will be no thorns in it. Search for the man who drove the spear into My side and tell him there is a nearer way to My heart than that.' "

How many just stood and beheld the Savior. It is a terrible thing to keep looking at Christ and hearing about Him without accepting Him.

An old man died in 1836 on Staten Island at the home of a poor Scotch woman. He had once been the most brilliant lawyer in America and vice-president of the United States. He might have been president had he been true to the talents with which

God had endowed him and the light that had shone upon his early life.

At the age of 15, a revival swept over the institution in which he was a student. Christ was on trial before him. "Give Me your life," He said. But, Pilate-like, he played with his convictions and sought advice from those who mocked at religion. His life ended in failure, crime and misery. His duel with Alexander Hamilton, his trial for treason, his long wanderings in Europe as an outcast among men, were the results of his choice. Let Aaron Burr's life be a warning.

What Will You Do with Christ?

What are you doing about the Christ of Calvary (see Matt. 27:36)? Are you standing around like the soldiers, just waiting to cast lots for His garments? Many people want the garments of Christianity. They like the civilization that it brings, but they do not want the Christ.

Do you belong to the crowd of indifferent passersby who go to church to pass the time of day and see what is happening and then say, as you study this scene, "It is just another incident in the life of a good man. Many have died a martyr's death, and Christ's name is just added to this list"? Remember, Christ died on the cross for *you*.

Are you like some of the friends of Christ who stood by the cross and watched through the hours until His death? Probably all of those friends watched with a feeling of hopelessness and despair. The One in whom they had put their trust and hope was dying. They felt that everything was lost. If you fit this group—if you are a friend of Christ—then be sure you realize that the Lord is sufficient for all your needs. He will not fail you. You need never face anything alone. The Lord Jesus Christ is the answer to your every need.

When we look at the cross, we see two other crosses, one on each side of Christ. On one was a sinner, for whom Christ's death accomplished nothing. On the other was a sinner, too, but for him Christ's death was life and victory. His cross is the dividing line today between those who shall live and those who shall die. On which side are you?

Daily Meditations

Sunday: His suffering for others—Isaiah 53:4-6;
Matthew 8:17; 1 Corinthians 15:3

Monday: Death with the malefactors—Isaiah 53:9-12; Matthew 27:38

Tuesday: His hands and feet pierced—Psalm 22:16;
Zechariah 12:10; John 20:27

Wednesday: His insults—Psalms 22:6-8; 109:25;
Matthew 27:39; Mark 15:29-30

Thursday: Lots cast for vesture—Psalm 22:18;
Mark 15:24; John 19:24

Friday: Not a bone broken—Exodus 12:46;
Psalm 34:20; John 19:36

Saturday: Buried with the rich—Isaiah 53:9;
Matthew 27:57-60

21

The Miracles of Calvary

So when the centurion and those with him, who were guarding Jesus, saw the earthquake and the things that had happened, they feared greatly, saying, "Truly this was the Son of God!"
MATTHEW 27:54

Did Christ die as any other man dies? His birth was not like any other man's birth; His death was not like any other man's death. His birth attracts the attention of the world. If such interest gathers around His cradle, what shall be said of the interest around His cross? The cursed tree upon which Christ died has become a blessing.

That cross of shame has been transformed into the most glorious object in the word. A sinner can look upon it and become a saint through Christ who died. A saint can turn to it and from the same Christ find the power to live. It is the focal point of all history. Every line from creation converges toward it, and from it every line diverges and radiates until the world shall end. The Lord Jesus had a miraculous birth and a miraculous death. His death indeed proved that He was God.

A man cannot see what is in a little kernel of corn even if he is holding it in his hand and looking at it. He must put that kernel in the ground and let it die. Then it will bring forth the stalk, the blade and the full ear. All this was in that tiny seed, yet one could not see it until it died.

Still all has not been seen. Take the kernels off the ear, plant them again and let them die and bring forth fruit. Repeat this and soon a field of growing corn will reveal just a little of what was stored up in that kernel. Christ's death revealed who He truly was. People saw Him as He walked this earth, but they *did not see* Him in His power. His death was to bring forth life like unto Himself.

There were many evidences at the cross that prove Jesus was God. Let us look at these miracles that occurred at the cross: (1) the darkness that covered the earth; (2) the veil of the Temple that was torn in two; (3) the earthquake that split the rocks and opened the graves; (4) the graveclothes inside the tomb that were not disarranged; (5) the many saints who were resurrected.

All these happened in direct connection with the death of Christ. All heaven and Earth seemed to speak. Each miracle was a tremendous testimony of the truth of our redemption in His blood.

The Miracle of the Darkness

The first great miracle at the cross was the darkness that covered the land. "Now it was about the sixth hour, and there was darkness over all the earth until the ninth hour" (Luke 23:44). There were three hours of intense blackness in the middle of the day and no record of what happened during those three hours. Matthew tells us that the darkness was "over all the land" (Matt. 27:45).

At the time of this miracle, Christ had already hung on the cross for three hours. How long did the darkness continue when Christ was on the cross? Yes, three hours! Some people who do not want to believe in Christ try to explain away this miracle by saying this darkness was only an eclipse of the sun. However, this could not have been the case, for an eclipse of the sun can last only about seven minutes. Luke's Gospel also tells us that at the time of the crucifixion, the Jewish people were celebrating the Feast of Unleavened Bread (see Luke 22:1). This feast was always held at the time of the full moon. It is impossible for an eclipse of the sun and a full moon to occur in the same 24-hour period.

This strange phenomenon of darkness occurred at noontime. It was darkness in the presence of the sun. What cut off the light? This is the significant point: The darkness of Calvary darkened the sun at noon! It was in a dark hour that Christ bore the sin of the whole world.

Someone once said that it seemed as if God threw a mantle of darkness around His Son so that no one could look on His agony. Only His Father could see Him as He bore the sin of the world and gave His life a ransom for you and me. This was not a sight for human eyes to see. No taunt or insult was flung at Him now. The crowds were frightened. They stood still where they were. Even the Roman centurion feared greatly, and many people "beat their breasts" (Luke 23:48).

Who can change the order of nature? *Only God.* Therefore, He must have suspended the regular course of His own natural laws. That darkness tells us that God the Father was present. Jesus the Son of God was dying, and God the Father was there.

Jesus' disciples had forsaken Him and fled (see Matt. 26:56). The Lord Jesus had told His mother that she was to look on John as her son (see John 19:26-27). Thus, He separated Himself from her. And then came that awful moment when even God the Father turned from His Son. In that moment, the Lord Jesus paid the price of our redemption on the cross completely alone.

Not until the close of the three hours did Christ speak. It was a period of *silence* as well as *darkness.* Matthew tells us the words He spoke: "My God, My God, why have You forsaken Me?" (Matt. 27:46).

This is all we know about those three hours. What happened in those three hours was so terrible—and so awesome—that it cannot be fully described. God has not allowed anything concerning it to be told.

As Dr. G. Campbell Morgan says, "In the stream of human history, from its beginning to its close-hours, days, weeks, months, years, decades, centuries, millenniums—from heaven's standpoint, the most tremendous period in all the running millenniums were those three hours of darkness and of silence." Whatever was done, it was done in the darkness and the silence of those three hours.

The Miracle of the Torn Veil

Matthew 27:50-51 describes the next miracle: "Jesus cried out again with a loud voice, and yielded up His spirit. Then, behold, the veil of the temple was torn in two from top to bottom; and the earth quaked, and the rocks were split." It would seem that the last loud cry of the Lord was the cry that tore the veil that led into the Holy of Holies. The cry was probably that cry of triumph, "It is finished!" (John 19:30).

The veil of the Temple was 60 feet long and 30 feet wide. It was embroidered in blue, purple and scarlet and hung by hooks of gold. It was probably as thick as a man's hand. The veil was used to close the view of the most holy place from the eyes of every man, save the high priest. He could go into that place only once a year with the blood of sacrifice to make atonement for the sin of the people (see Lev. 16:12-17). In the past, the Ark of the Covenant had been placed there, overlaid with the mercy seat with its cherubim of gold. The Shekinah glory was there; here God met the people through their mediator, the high priest.

The veil was so heavy that 300 priests were needed to handle it. Notice that the veil was torn from top to bottom, not from the bottom to the top, as one would expect. God rent that veil, and He began from the top. The veil was now needed no longer, and that holiest place of all was open to the view of all. At that instant when Christ said, "It is finished!" and expired on the cross, the function of the veil ceased. Jesus' work was done! He had made atonement for our sins though His precious blood.

No priest now needs to go into the presence of God for us to answer for our sins. "Therefore, brethren, having boldness to enter the Holiest by the blood of Jesus, by a new and living way which He consecrated for us, through the veil, that is, His flesh" (Heb. 10:19-20). The torn veil was the broken body of Jesus Christ. His body was broken for you and me, and His precious blood was sprinkled upon the mercy seat of God for you and me.

Now every child of God can enter into God's presence at any time. We can look into His face and call Him, "Abba, Father, my own dear Father." Every child of God should know what the "rent veil" means. We have access to God the Father.

The Miracle of the Earthquake and Opened Graves

Even the earth responded to the death of Christ. "And the earth quaked, and the rocks were split, and the graves were opened; and many bodies of the saints who had fallen asleep were raised" (Matt. 27:51-52). It was as if Jesus' death spoke of His great power and victory. At His death, the bands of sin were shattered and the bonds were broken.

The earth shook so hard that even the rocks were split in pieces. The sin of man had brought a curse upon the earth (see Gen. 3:17-18). Thorns and thistles had come forth; beasts had become savage. If man's sin had affected the earth and brought a curse upon it, then surely man's redemption would affect the earth as well.

The earth shook with the power of God, and those who were standing about "feared greatly" (Matt. 27:54). The earthquake happened just at the time of Christ's death and coincided with His shout of victory on the cross. It did not touch the cross on which Christ was hanging, but it opened the graves at Golgotha.

When God gave the Law to Moses on Mt. Sinai, there was also an earthquake. Now Calvary answered Mt. Sinai. The Law given at Mt. Sinai had proclaimed, "Do this and you shall live." Calvary answered, "It is finished." "For the law was given through Moses, but grace and truth came through Jesus Christ" (John 1:17).

Sinai was the prophecy of Calvary; Calvary was the fulfillment of Sinai. Sinai spoke a word of condemnation; Calvary spoke a word of pardon and peace. At Mt. Sinai the earth shook with fear; at Calvary it shook with joy!

The graves opened by the mighty earthquake were those of the saints—of God's children. This would make people wonder what it all meant. The opening of the graves was a sign of the glorious resurrection of all believers at the second coming of Jesus Christ. Christ destroyed the power of death through His death and resurrection.

"The wages of sin is death" (Rom. 6:23), and Christ paid the "wages" that were demanded.

The Miracle of the Graveclothes

The next miracle concerns the undisturbed graveclothes of the risen Lord. In Jesus' time, it was customary to bury people in special graveclothes. These were long strips of linen cloth wrapped around and around the body. A special napkin-like piece of cloth was wrapped around the head.

"Then Simon Peter came, following him [John], and went into the tomb; and he saw the linen cloths lying there, and the handkerchief that had been around His head, not lying with the linen cloths, but folded together in a place by itself. Then the other disciple, who came to the tomb first, went in also; and he saw and believed" (John 20:6-8).

John thought this was of great significance, for he describes in detail the exact arrangement of the clothes. It made a great impression on him. It was this marvelous arrangement of the graveclothes that made him believe the resurrection. John knew that Jesus had died and was buried. Now he saw that the body was gone from the tomb, for he saw the clothes lying there.

John knew that the body could not have been stolen, for the arrangement and order of the clothes forbade that. Would any robber stop to unwind and then rewind the wrappings? He saw the arrangement of the clothes and believed immediately in the resurrection of his Lord, although, as the next verse adds, he "did not know the Scripture, that He [Jesus] must rise again from the dead" (John 20:9).

There are two kinds of resurrection in the Bible. The first is represented by Lazarus and the saints from the opened graves after the crucifixion being raised from the dead, but they died again. The other is Christ's rising from the dead, never to die again. When Jesus was in His risen, spiritual body, He passed into rooms through closed doors. Remember, there is a natural body and there is a spiritual body (see 1 Cor. 15:44).

The body of the Lord Jesus Christ had been changed, and He had emerged from the graveclothes. It was the sublime testimony of the graveclothes that made John a believer. It was a miraculous demonstration. Lazarus had come from his grave "bound hand and foot with graveclothes, and his face was wrapped with a cloth," but Jesus left behind Him the clothing of the sepulchre (John 11:44).

The Miracle of the Resurrection of the Saints

The last miracle took place *after* Christ's resurrection. "And many bodies of the saints who had fallen asleep were raised; and coming out of the graves after His resurrection, they went into the holy city and appeared to many" (Matt. 27:52-53). The graves of the saints had been opened on the day of the crucifixion. But after Christ's resurrection, the dead actually arose and came out of the graves, and they went into Jerusalem and appeared unto many! This was indeed a miracle! A tremendous miracle!

How do we know it is historically true? Because the Bible says it is so. If the Bible is true, then this must be true. If there is a document in history more absolutely historical than the Bible, it has yet to be discovered.

There are many examples of people coming back to life in the Bible: the raising of the son of the widow of Zarephath (1 Kings 17:17-24); the bringing back to life of the Shunammite's son (2 Kings 4:18-37); the resurrection caused by the bones of Elisha (2 Kings 13:20-21); the raising of the daughter of Jairus (Matt. 9:18-26); the resurrection of the son of the widow of Nain (Luke 7:11-17); the bringing back to life of Lazarus (John 14:19). All of these miracles were "resuscitations," or restorations to this present life. In each case, it was only a bringing back to life of the natural body, which must die again.

But Paul tells us of another resurrection: "We shall not all sleep, but we shall all be changed—in a moment, in the twinkling of an eye, at the last trumpet. For the trumpet will sound, and the dead will be raised incorruptible, and we shall be changed" (1 Cor. 15:42-45). The mortal shall put on immortality, and the vile body shall be changed into a glorious body (see also Phil. 3:20-21). It is thrilling indeed. This is the true rising from the dead. When is all this to be? Paul says only after Christ and only at His coming. Christ says, "Because I live, you will live also" (John 14:19).

This great miracle points to the great day when we shall be raised from the dead! Christ's death was our death, and His life is our life (see Gal. 2:20).

We Also Shall Live

How wonderful it is to know that the Lord Jesus died for us. God gave these miracles so that there could be no doubt in anyone's mind that the Lord Jesus was who He claimed to be—the Son of God, the Savior of the world.

Think back over the miracles of Calvary. There was great darkness on all the earth. The Lord Jesus gave His life so that we might never have to know darkness but walk in the light, as He is in the light (see 1 John 1:7).

Jesus died and the veil of the Temple was torn apart so that we might have a free and constant access to God. He fulfilled the Law, and now you and I can live by grace. He finished the work of our salvation so that we might have salvation by grace through faith and "not of works, lest anyone should boast" (Eph. 2:8-9).

The miracles of Calvary were great because they showed forth the fact that Christ is God. But greater still is the miracle that the Lord loves us and wants us to be with Him forever. He wants this so badly that He endured the cross with all of its shame to provide the only way by which we may live with Him.

Great, too, is the fact that the Lord has entrusted to people like you and me the task of taking the message of what He has done. He has given to us, His Church, the task of spreading the gospel to the ends of the world. What a responsibility we have! We have considered just a little of what it cost the Lord to provide salvation for us. Now we have this priceless salvation, and the spread of it depends upon how well you and I do the job!

Daily Meditations

Sunday: The darkness–Matthew 27:45-50;
Mark 15:33-37; Luke 23:44-45

Monday: The rent veil–Matthew 27:51;
Hebrews 9:1-8; 10:19-22

Tuesday: The earthquake–Matthew 27:51,54

Wednesday: The graves opened–Matthew 27:52

Thursday: The graveclothes–John 20:1-10;
1 Corinthians 15:51-53

Friday: The resurrection of the saints–Matthew 27:52-53;
1 Thessalonians 4:14-17

Saturday: The story of the cross–John 19:16-37

22

Christ's Victorious Resurrection

That if you confess with your mouth the Lord Jesus and believe in your heart that God has raised Him from the dead, you will be saved.
Romans 10:9

A missionary to China was telling his audience one night of the life and words and works of Christ. He told them that Christ died for their sins. He urged them to believe on Jesus as the Son of God and to give themselves to Him. "How do you know that Jesus did not die for His own sins?" a scholar called out. "How do you prove that He is the living Son of God as He claimed? Confucius was also a great teacher and a good man. He is the founder of our religion."

The answer is that Jesus did one thing that no other good man or leader has ever done: He rose from the dead. The founders of other religions—Mohammed, Confucius, Buddha, and the others—are dead and buried. Their bodies have decayed and their bones have crumbled to dust. Their followers make long pilgrimages to their tombs. The founder of Christianity alone could not be held in the grave. After having died for our sins, He arose from the dead as the *living Lord of life.*

Other men have died for a good cause, but for them the grave was the end. Jesus Christ rose again on the third day according to the Scriptures. This fact was a proof to Christ's disciples and is evidence to all people that He was the Christ. Jesus opened the door on the other side of the grave and gave us a glimpse of the glory beyond. Christians have a proof that no other religion possesses that death is not the end.

A Living Christ

The disciples had been thinking of a dead Christ and had lost their confidence in His Messiahship (see Mark 16:11,13; Luke 24:11,21; John 20:9). When Mary Magdalene went to the tomb to complete her loving service for her dear friend, her whole thought was that He was dead. You remember that later Jesus found her weeping. She never once thought of the resurrection. She had come to the tomb of a dead friend.

The grief of the other women must have been great also. They thought all was ended. The hope that had thrilled their hearts had been blasted.

As Mary drew near the tomb, her keen eyes detected even in the dusky light of the morning that the tomb had been opened. Did this make her happy? Did this prove to her that Jesus had risen from the dead? No, she thought that someone had stolen away her Lord. So she ran to the city to find Peter.

Peter got John, and off they started on a run. John, being younger, reached the tomb first and reverently paused. But Peter rushed in and saw how things really were.

It was no ordinary sight within the tomb on that first Easter morning. What they saw made John realize that this was different from any other rising that they had ever seen. Remember, they had been with Christ when He had brought people back from the dead. But this was not the same. To be sure, the tomb was empty, but that didn't prove anything, for the body of Jesus could have been removed.

What did John see? The linen clothes in which the body had been wrapped were still there. In Matthew 28:6, the angel said, "Come, see the place where the Lord lay," as if that sight would be a proof of His resurrection (see also Mark 16:6). The apostle John says that Peter saw the linen cloths that had covered Christ's body lying there and the piece of linen that had covered his head folded together in a place by itself. When John, who was with Peter, saw this, he believed (see John 20:6-8).

These linen wrappings were proof of the resurrection of Jesus. No human power could arrange them, as they lay in the shape of the human body they had enclosed, no fold disturbed. How had the body been removed, leaving the wrappings untouched? No wonder the angel called attention to it! No robber had stolen that body.

What did all this mean? Jesus did not merely rise from the dead like Lazarus, but, as Paul says, He was "the firstfruits of those who have fallen asleep" (1 Cor. 15:20). So also His loved ones will be changed (see 1 Cor. 15:23). Jesus' natural body was changed to a spiritual body. His mortal body—the "body that can die"—put on immortality. This changed body came out from the linen wrappings of the body taken from the cross.

We Also Shall Rise

God has not left us in doubt about His promises. He has proven by the resurrection of Christ that there will be a resurrection from the dead. In Paul's words in 1 Corinthians 15:20, "firstfruits" means the "first one." The first fruit on any tree tells us what the rest of the fruit is going to be.

If I should plant a fruit tree and did not know what kind of tree it was, but one day saw small apples forming on the tree, immediately I would know that it was an apple tree. I would also know, if the first fruit of the tree was an apple, that every other bit of fruit that tree would bear would be apples. I would not expect to see plums the next year, or figs. The "firstfruits" always determine what a tree shall always bear. So, if Christ was the "firstfruits of those who have fallen asleep," then we also shall rise.

How can human bodies that have turned to dust be raised again? The same God who created man out of the dust of the earth and breathed into his nostrils the breath of life can raise a body from the dust to which it has returned (see Gen. 2:7; 3:19). Remember, facts are not disproved simply because they are unknown to us. If that were true, half of the cities of the world would have to be blotted out of existence for most of us, because we have not seen them.

The resurrection of Christ is the chief truth of the Christian faith. What does Christ say we *must* believe to be saved? "Confess with your mouth the Lord Jesus and believe in your heart that God has raised Him from the dead . . . for with the heart one believes unto righteousness, and with the mouth confession is made unto salvation" (Rom. 10:9-10).

If Christ had not risen from the dead, everyone would live in fear of death, for everyone must die (see 1 Cor. 15:26). Death comes to rich and poor alike. But the resurrection of Christ and the promised resurrection of all who believe in Christ have lifted from us the fear of death. If we take away the resurrection, we destroy the very foundation of the gospel and our faith. A dead Christ could do nothing for us after 2,000 years. A *living* Christ saves us and keeps us day by day.

If Christ is not risen, our faith is in vain. It is like a sailor who plunges into the sea to rescue the man who has thrown himself overboard. If the sailor does not come back, then both are lost. If the sailor cannot save himself, he cannot save the life of the one he tries to rescue. If Christ did not rise from the grave, surely He could not bring anyone else from the grave. He brought back with Him from the grave the keys of death and of hell.

Christ's Spirit Did Not Die

What did Christ say on the cross? "Father, into Your hands I commit My spirit" (Luke 23:46). He lay down His life that He might take it again. It was *His body* that was bruised. It was *His hands* that were pierced; *His feet* that were nailed to the cross; *His side* that had the spear thrust into it (see Isa. 53:5).

There is only a resurrection of the body; *there is no resurrection of the spirit.* The spirit never dies. Christ proved to Thomas that His body was a resurrected body. What did Jesus say to Thomas? "Reach your finger here, and look at My hands; and reach your hand here, and put it into My side. Do not be unbelieving, but believing" (John 20:27).

With what kind of a body did Christ come? As Peter testified of Jesus in his sermon at Pentecost, "His [Jesus'] soul was not left in Hades, nor did His flesh see corruption. This Jesus God has raised up, of which we are all witnesses. . . . Therefore let all the house of Israel know assuredly that God has made this Jesus, whom you crucified, both Lord and Christ" (Acts 2:31-32,36).

If Christ is risen from the dead, then He is the very Son of God (see Rom. 1:4). If He is the Son of God, then He is the Lord—and every knee must bow to Him (see Phil. 2:9-11). His resurrection means the resurrection of all believers (see Rom. 8:10-11; 1 Thess. 4:13-18).

We do not know what we shall be—but we shall be like Jesus! John says, "Beloved, now we are children of God; and it has not yet been revealed what we shall be, but we know that when He is revealed, we shall be like Him, for we shall see Him as He is" (1 John 3:2). Paul told the Philippians, "For our citizenship is in heaven, from which we also eagerly wait for the Savior, the Lord Jesus Christ, who will transform our lowly body that it may be conformed to His glorious body, according to the working by which He is able even to subdue all things to Himself" (Phil. 3:20-21).

Witnesses to the Resurrection

The disciples and others who knew Christ were eyewitnesses to the facts of His resurrection. They lived with Jesus. They saw Him die and brought precious spices to anoint His body. They saw His tomb sealed and knew it was guarded. They came back to the grave to weep, expecting His body still to be there, but found the stone rolled away. They heard the testimony of the angels at the tomb and saw Jesus' graveclothes lying there.

Scripture tells us that after the resurrection, Jesus appeared to Mary Magdalene (see John 20:11-18), the "other women" (see Matt. 28:1,9-10), the apostle Peter (see 1 Cor. 15:5), and the disciples on the way to Emmaus (see Luke 24:13-35). John also tells us that as the disciples, behind closed doors, were talking over the strange and terrible experience of the last three days—the trial and crucifixion—Jesus suddenly appeared with them in the room (see John 20:19). His risen body was not subject to ordinary physical laws.

What effect did all these appearances finally have on the disciples? They now *knew* in whom they believed. They *knew* that Jesus had conquered death and that He was the risen Master, Lord and Savior. Thomas's five-word confession of belief sums it up: "My Lord and my God!" (John 20:28).

Why was Jesus so anxious to meet all the doubts of His disciples? He wanted to prepare them for the biggest commission that was ever given to man: "Go therefore and make disciples of all the nations, baptizing them in the name of the Father and of the Son and of the Holy Spirit, teaching them to observe all things that I have commanded you; and lo, I am with you always, even to the end of the age" (Matt. 28:19-20). Jesus commanded them to carry on His work so that the whole world might come to believe in Him just as loyally as they did.

Know in Whom You Have Believed

The resurrection of Jesus Christ is the greatest proof that He is God. Remember, Thomas had lived and worked with Christ for three years. He had seen His faultless life and His marvelous works, but it was not until he saw in the risen One the marks of the nails and the spear that he made his proclamation of belief in Christ's resurrection.

The Lord answered Thomas with these words: "Thomas, because you have seen Me, you have believed. Blessed are those who have not seen and yet have believed" (John 20:29). This group of believers includes you and me if we can believe that which we have not seen.

Are you sure, very sure, that the Lord Jesus Christ is alive? Do you know for certain that He rose from the dead? If you do, you know it by faith. You have not seen Him; you cannot talk to anyone who has seen Him. You just believe because the Bible says so and because you have the witness of the Holy Spirit in your heart that Christ dwells in you.

If you are waiting for a proof by a test-tube experiment, you will not receive it. You can't put a sunset into a test tube and prove that it is beautiful. You can't put the resurrection of Christ into a test tube for proof. You know that a sunset is beautiful because something in your love of beauty says it is. You know that Christ lives because you accept the Word of God by faith. Faith is the only way.

Daily Meditations

Sunday: The witness of the resurrection—1 Corinthians 15:1-11

Monday: The importance of the resurrection—1 Corinthians 15:12-20

Tuesday: The method of the resurrection—1 Corinthians 15:35-50

Wednesday: The great victory over death—1 Corinthians 15:51-58

Thursday: The Christian's hope—Romans 8:10-18

Friday: Christ arose—John 20:1-18

Saturday: A spiritual body—John 20:19-29

23

Christ, Our Ascended Lord

Therefore He is also able to save to the uttermost those who come to God through Him, since He always lives to make intercession for them.
Hebrews 7:25

A story has been told imagining what may have taken place when Jesus went back to heaven after His resurrection. The Master was met by some of the angels. They were talking of the work Christ had done on Earth. One of the angels said, "Master, You died for the whole world down there, did You not?"

"Yes," said Jesus.

"You must have suffered much," the angel said. There was amazement on his face.

"Yes," again came the answer in a wondrous voice, very quiet, but strangely full of deepest feeling.

"And do all the people on Earth know what You did?"

"Oh, no. Only a few in a little land know about it so far."

"Well, Master, what is Your plan? What have You done about telling the world that You have died for them? May I go and tell of Your work?"

"No," the Master answered. "I asked Peter, and James, and John, and Andrew, and some more of them down there, to make it the business of their lives to tell others, until the last man in the farthest circle of the earth has heard the story and has felt the thrilling, transforming power of it."

The angel thought for a minute. He remembered all the things that had happened in the world. Then he answered with a sort of hesitating reluctance, as though he could see difficulties in the working of the plan. "Yes . . . but suppose Peter fails. Suppose after a while John simply does not tell others. Suppose their descendants, their successors way off in the centuries to come, get so busy about things—some of them proper enough, some maybe not quite *so* proper—that they do not tell others. What then?"

The angel's eyes were big with the intenseness of his thought, for he was thinking of the suffering. And he was thinking, too, of the difference to the man who hasn't been told. "What then?"

Back came that quiet, wondrous voice of Jesus. "I haven't made any other plans. I'm counting on them!" The responsibility and privilege of letting the world know about the work of Jesus Christ rests upon you and me. Did you ever think of that before?

We have been studying about this gift of God, our Lord and Savior. Have we accepted this great gift for ourselves? Do we believe on the Lord Jesus Christ and that He is the Son of God? Have we confessed Him as our Savior?

If we have, is that enough? Is this the only duty Christ gives to a person? Remember His last command to His disciples: "You shall be witnesses to Me in Jerusalem, and in all Judea and Samaria, and to the end of the earth" (Acts 1:8). After Christ said these words, He was taken out of their sight. He ascended into heaven. Where is Christ now? Yes, in heaven, making intercession for us (see Heb. 7:25).

Joy to All People

When the angels heralded Jesus' birth, they said, "For there is born to you this day in the city of David a Savior, who is Christ the Lord" (Luke 2:11). That Christmas gift from our heavenly Father to all of us is a Savior, His Son.

What were the tidings of great joy on that first Christmas day? "I bring you good tidings of great joy which will be to all people" (Luke 2:10). But Jesus only taught about Himself as a Savior for three years, and to only a small part of His world. Only once did He go outside of His own land. How then could this wonderful message of a Savior reach *all* the people of *all* the world of *all* time?

Christ gave a great command to His disciples. Peter, James and John and all the rest must not only believe themselves but also tell others. Christ depended on them. But that is not all! He depends on each of us to tell others in our day about Him—that He is the Savior. Read the great commission in Matthew 28:18-20:

> And Jesus came and spoke to them, saying, "All authority has been given to Me in heaven and on earth. Go therefore and make disciples of all the nations, baptizing them in the name of the Father and of the Son and of the Holy Spirit, teaching them to observe all things that I have commanded you; and lo, I am with you always, even to the end of the age."

This is the task that we have to do if we truly want to obey the Lord.

Without the ascension, the Christmas joy of the angels at the birth of Jesus would only be a faint echo today, but instead it is a present fact. The disciples did their part; now it depends on us whether we shall make known the purpose of Christ's death for the world. He laid upon us a sacred privilege of carrying on the work that He had begun. He wants us to recognize the personal responsibility He has placed upon us.

Has Christ's Claim Been Proved?

A leader had been put to death as a malefactor by the rulers of His day, both civil and religious rulers. He had only a handful of followers who had been with Him the three years of His public ministry. Most of them were without education. They had no money and no influence. Their leader was taken and nailed to a cross. All of a sudden, He appeared again and claimed to have "*all* authority in heaven and earth." He commanded these few disciples of His to go out and make disciples of *all* nations. He didn't tell them simply to preach to them, but to make disciples of them. And He promised to be with them even to the end.

Even then, some who saw Him and heard Him speak must have doubted that this could ever be a reality. How preposterous this all seemed! A crucified leader commanding a few weak followers to do something great! Yet this is what Christ said!

Let us look at it today—after more than 2,000 years have passed. Has Christ's claim been proved? What name has such authority or power today as Jesus? He is worshiped and honored in every land. More than two billion people are called by His name: Christians.

The foremost rulers of the leading nations of the world pay tribute to His *authority*. Because of this *command* of Christ's, tens of thousands of Protestant missionaries are in foreign lands and hundreds of thousands work for His kingdom at home. His *power* is seen in the transformed lives of countless men and women and boys and girls who have been redeemed by His blood.

Has Christ's command been obeyed and His plan carried out? His messengers have gone into practically all of the world, though billions are still not His. Truly, the command to go is still in force, and enough remains to be done to drive every available Christian soldier into the field of battle.

Christ's Work

Has Christ fulfilled His promise that He will be with us? Ask any person who strives to spread the gospel, for only those who obey the command to witness for Christ have any right to claim the promise. The famous missionary David Livingstone said that his consciousness of the presence of Christ was the one thing that sustained him in his lonely home in Central Africa. This will be the witness of every true Christian who is obeying Christ's last command.

There is never a time when any child of God feels His Father's presence so much as when he is doing God's will. This fact of Christ's reality and nearness amid all discouragements and dangers and all trials is what gives Christ's servants heart. Their work is in vain; the victory is certain.

Christ is on high, for the Bible tells us that His disciples saw Him ascend (see Acts 1:9). The martyr Stephen saw Him (see Acts 7:55). Saul of Tarsus heard Him speak (see Acts 9:3-4). In Acts 1:9, we read, "While they watched, He was taken up, and a cloud received Him out of their sight." Not while they dreamed, but while they looked, *He was taken up.*

Christ did a great work *on Earth.* It was a work of salvation. On the cross, He said, "It is finished." But Christ has a work *in heaven,* and it is still going on (see Mark 16:19). "He is also able to save to the uttermost those who come to God through Him, since He always lives to make intercession for them" (Heb. 7:25). What does that mean?

Just as Aaron the high priest was the only one who could go into the Holy of Holies (that is, into the presence of God) to intercede for the people, so Christ is our high priest who intercedes on our behalf (see Heb. 8:1-2). But notice the differences.

Leviticus 16 describes the law governing the great Day of Atonement. The high priest offered two sacrifices, one for himself and one for the people. Our high priest offered only one sacrifice, and it was for us. Our high priest was perfect; He did not have to make Himself ready for God's presence.

The high priest of the Old Testament went into the Holy of Holies once every year with a sacrifice. Our high priest offered Himself once for all (see Heb. 10:10-12). The Old Testament priest went into an earthly Tabernacle, into a room in which the glory of God shone. Our high priest went into heaven itself, into the very presence of God. There He presented His own blood, which was "shed for many for the remission of sins" (Matt. 26:28). Our high priest is in the presence of God all the time, and we can go into God's presence by faith in Him at any time (see Heb. 4:14-16; 7:23-28).

Christ, Our Advocate

The Jews of old believed their coming Messiah would be a prophet, king and priest, all in one. Did Jesus meet this expectation? He came as *prophet* in His ministry on Earth. He was "a teacher come from God" (John 3:2). He came as a *king.* When will He reign as king? "When the Son of Man comes in His glory, and all the holy angels with Him, then He will sit on the throne of His glory" (Matt. 25:31). And, as we have seen, He came as a *priest* in His death, ascension and intercession.

We need no other priest, because our high priest is in heaven at the right hand of the Father, acting as our advocate. What is an advocate? An "advocate" is one who pleads the cause of another. It means one who defends, an intercessor. Why do we need an advocate? We need an advocate because we keep on sinning (see 1 John 1:8-10). Christ keeps cleansing us from our sins. His blood is sufficient to cleanse us from *all* sin—past, present and future.

A boyhood companion of Robert Lincoln, Abraham Lincoln's son, entered the Civil War and went to the front lines as a private soldier. When Robert Lincoln found this out, he said to a friend, "Write, and tell him to write to me and I will go to my father and get him something better." The young soldier later said, "I never took advantage of the offer, but you don't know how much it meant to me. Often after a weary march, I would say, 'If the going gets too hard, I can write to Robert Lincoln. I would rather have him speak for me than a member of the cabinet, because he is the president's son.' "

As Christians, we know that we have a wonderful friend in heaven, the Son of God, who ever makes intercession for us. We can run into the presence of God at any time and find help in time of need. If we do sin, we have an advocate ever making intercession for us. We have a way to the Father through which Christ has entered—absolute obedience to God (see Heb. 5:8-9). Jesus, our high priest, will give to us all the blessings we need. He wants to impart to us His life, for "to live is Christ" (Phil. 1:21). We never have to go about carrying any burden of sin. All we need to do is to confess it, and God is faithful and just to forgive and cleanse (see 1 John 1:9).

Freedom from Sin

Christ has redeemed us not only from the penalty of sin but also from the power of sin. Christ bore the wages of sin on the cross. "For the wages of sin is death" (Rom. 6:23). He died to save us from the penalty of our guilt, but He *lives* to keep us from the power of sin. Paul tells us, "For sin shall not have dominion over you, for you are not under law but under grace" (Rom. 6:14).

A little boy was flying a kite that had soared so high as to be almost out of sight. Seeing him looking so intently upward, a gentleman asked what he had there.

"A kite, sir," the boy replied.

"A kite," said the gentleman. "How can that be? I don't see it."

"Oh! I feel it pulling, sir," was the boy's sure reply.

This should be our evidence that our Savior is above. We should "feel Him pulling."

Remember, Christianity is the only religion in this world that has a *living* leader and Savior. Paul said, "I have been crucified with Christ; it is no longer I who live, but Christ lives in me; and the life which I now live in the flesh I live by faith in the Son of God, who loved me and gave Himself for me" (Gal. 2:20). Christ lives, and He lives in us! This gives us power to overcome sin.

A poor servant girl who had been wonderfully saved told the reason she had victory over sin. When she saw the devil coming to the door of her heart to tempt her, she just sent Jesus to the door. The devil would back away and say, "Oh, I guess I have the wrong house."

You try this. Remember, your Christian life is just "Christ living in you." Don't try to live your own life. Let Him live it through you.

Our Part

Look again at the Great Commission in Matthew 28:18-20. Notice especially the four "alls." The Lord says that "all power" is His. We have seen that in this chapter. We have also seen that He gives us His power through His work as our high priest and our intercessor, or advocate. The strength to do the task comes from the Lord Jesus Christ. In Him, we have "all power."

The goal of our lives as Christians is to lead others to a place in which they may know the Christ that we do. So our goal, too, is a comprehensive one. We are to teach "all nations." The message is complete. We are told that those we teach, and we who are teachers, are to observe "all things." Then, the Lord ends the commission with His promise that He will be with us "always."

This is God's great overall plan for everyone who is a Christian. Our strength, "all power"; our goal, "all nations"; our message, "all things"; God's promise, "always."

Daily Meditations

Sunday: Our high priest—Hebrews 9:1-14

Monday: His supreme sacrifice—Hebrews 10:11-25

Tuesday: The high priest of old—Leviticus 16:1-34

Wednesday: The rent veil—Matthew 27:45-56

Thursday: The perfect priest—Hebrews 7:11-28

Friday: Christ, the mediator—Ephesians 2:13-22

Saturday: Only one mediator—1 Timothy 2:1-6; 1 John 2:1

24

The Power of the Holy Spirit

However, when He, the Spirit of truth, has come, He will guide you into all truth; for He will not speak on His own authority, but whatever He hears He will speak; and He will tell you things to come.
John 16:13

We are living in an age of power. The space age has long been ushered in. Men are discovering the mighty power stored up in this universe. But this is not the greatest power. Christ says, "All authority has been given to Me in heaven and on earth." Our Christ is a God of power.

What is "power"? The dictionary definition suggests that power is that property of anything or anyone that shows itself in action and that is able to produce a change. In our natural world, this could be the power generated by water, steam, electricity, gasoline, the atom, and so forth. But there is another kind of power: The power that Jesus promised to send into the lives of His disciples.

We have all seen a daily newspaper. It is printed on a great printing press. The huge machine is just a big, unmoving mass of metal until something wonderful occurs. The paper cannot be printed and the cylinders of the press cannot turn at all until a hand turns a little lever and sends electric current into the press's motor to give power to the drive shaft and motion to the whole machine. Any child can set that big press in motion. The slightest touch does it. Power gets the work done.

The disciples needed power before they could do the great work Jesus Christ had sent them to do. That power was promised to them. Are we today beyond the need of such power as Jesus Christ promised? Then why do we not have the power that Jesus Christ promises through the Holy Spirit and live the most useful lives we can possibly live?

The Descent of the Spirit

Have you seen the wind? What color is it? Where does it come from? Where does it go? How do we know there is such a thing? We can feel the wind and see what it does, but we can't explain it. That was the way with Luke when he tried to write about the coming of the Holy Spirit in Acts 2.

It was *like* a mighty rushing wind, he said. That was the best way he could explain it. Then there seemed to appear tongues *like* fire. Fire was the best word he could use to explain the wonderful thing that happened. Fire burns and cleanses and sets men aflame for God. Matthew tells us that another form the Holy Spirit took was that of a dove (see Matt. 3:16).

The disciples of old had lived with Jesus and knew all about Him. They believed in Him. They had left everything they had to follow Him. Yet one of these same men betrayed Him, another denied Him, and all forsook Him when He was arrested. They all had the necessary knowledge about Christ to go out and tell the world, but Christ said, "Tarry in the city of Jerusalem until you are endued with power from on high" (Luke 24:49).

Why? Because the Holy Spirit would bring power into their powerless lives. Without Him, they would have been powerless, but with Him, they could go forth to the ends of the earth. "You shall receive power when the Holy Spirit has come upon you; and you shall be witnesses to Me in Jerusalem, and in all Judea and Samaria, and to the end of the earth" (Acts 1:8).

What effect did the coming of the Spirit have upon the disciples? They spoke in different languages (see Acts 2:7). These Galileans spoke in various languages, and each foreign Jew heard them in his or her own (foreign) language. How could the disciples speak in so many languages? We do not know. There is no explanation except that it was a miracle and a mystery and the power of the Holy Spirit.

A "miracle" is something a man cannot do, a supernatural act not possible by human means. Some people think that a miracle cannot be performed because it requires the alteration of fixed laws. Cannot God change the laws He made? Surely, He can change and suspend a law—cause it to cease to operate.

If an electric light is turned on and you turn it off, did you break any natural law or alter any law? No. What did you do? You interfered with the flow of electricity by using another law—the law of resistance.

Think of the laws in operation that none of us know as yet! Some things we do today would have been accounted as miracles in days past. The miracles recorded in the Bible are no more difficult to understand than the fact that God takes a sinful life, hardened by wickedness, and makes it new. That's what took place at Pentecost and is taking place every day right before our eyes.

A Great Day

In Leviticus 23:15-22, God gave the commandments concerning the keeping of this Feast of Pentecost. This was a day that had been a special one for the Jews ever since the time of Moses.

It commemorated the ingathering of the firstfruits of the wheat harvest. Thus, it was closely connected in the Jewish mind with the Feast of the Passover and the Feast of the Firstfruits. All three feasts followed one another closely.

The Passover spoke of sacrifice and was a picture of the sacrifice of the Lord Jesus Christ. The Feast of the Firstfruits was commemorated three days after the Passover. It typified the resurrection of Christ. Fifty days after Passover was the day of Pentecost, which typified the calling by the Lord, through His Holy Spirit, a people for His name's sake. The beginning of the Church was pictured in the ancient Feast of Pentecost.

The disciples were in the upper room in Jerusalem (see Acts 1:12-14). This must have been a great day. It was the day of Pentecost. As they prayed, there came the strange, mysterious sound like wind, and the wonderful sight of tongues like fire. They were filled with amazement and yet with joy, for the Comforter that the Lord Jesus had promised would take His place had come (see Acts 2:1-13).

The coming of the Spirit could not be kept secret. It never can. This time, the men and women of 15 countries or regions knew about it (see Acts 2:9-11). This list begins with four countries east of Judea, then names five provinces in Asia Minor, then passes to Africa and Rome, and closes with the mention of the Cretans and Arabians.

Some of the crowd mocked the disciples because they seemed so happy and joyful, saying, "They are full of new wine" (Acts 2:13). Who took the lead in telling the crowd just what had happened? It was Peter, who answered, "Men of Judea and all who dwell in Jerusalem, let this be known to you, and heed my words. For these are not drunk, as you suppose, since it is only the third hour of the day. But this is what was spoken by the prophet Joel: 'And it shall come to pass in the last days, says God, that I will pour out of My Spirit on all flesh; your sons and your daughters shall prophesy, your young men shall see visions, your old men shall dream dreams.' "

The Beginning of the Church

It was strange that Peter should be the first witness for Jesus Christ in the church in Jerusalem. He did not show up very well the last time he had an opportunity to witness for Christ (see John 18:25-27). But remember, something had happened. *Power* had been given to him. Now, the Holy Spirit had come to make him brave, strong and splendid.

What a wonderful witness he became! Instead of a weak coward, Peter became the "rock" that Jesus said he would be (see Acts 2:14). This is what the Holy Spirit does to men. He will do it for you and me if we will let Him. What was the result of Peter's sermon on that day? "Then those who gladly received his word were baptized; and that day about three thousand souls were added to them" (Acts 2:41).

Acts tells us the results of other experiences in this first church. "Many of those who heard the word believed; and the number of the men came to be about five thousand" (4:4). "And believers were increasingly added to the Lord, multitudes of both men and women" (5:14). "Then the word of God spread, and the number of the disciples multiplied greatly in Jerusalem, and a great many of the priests were obedient to the faith" (6:7).

How were these remarkable accessions in this first church possible? One way was through the preaching of Christ by the disciples, who gladly bore witness to Him. People saw a reality and longed to have it as well. Another way was through the power of Christ by the Holy Spirit, who blessed this testimony. Each of these were manifested in the church at Antioch of Syria: "But some of them were men from Cyprus and Cyrene, who, when they had come to Antioch, spoke to the Hellenists, preaching the Lord Jesus. And the hand of the Lord was with them, and a great number believed and turned to the Lord" (Acts 11:20-21).

Peter's address was the keynote of the new church. The church of the Lord Jesus Christ was born on that day—on Pentecost. Some people pray for a return of the day of Pentecost. Dr. Burdette said he would as soon think of praying for the crossing of the Red Sea or a second crucifixion. This may startle some, but it is worth thinking about. We have only to read the biographies of our heroic missionaries to know that the Holy Spirit is doing more wonderful things today than He did back then.

Let us go back for a moment to our definition of "power." What was it? It was that which showed itself in *action* and could produce change. Does this fit in with what we have seen of the coming of power to the disciples? Action? They had to *do* something about it, didn't they? They testified boldly for Christ. Change? They were already changed. They passed this power on to others, and their lives were also transformed.

Some people wonder how much of the Holy Spirit they can possess. Our concern should be how much of us the Holy Spirit possesses. All believers have the Spirit, but they are not all *filled* with the Spirit, which is the believer's privilege (see Acts 2:4; 4:92-31; Eph. 1:13-14; 5:18).

The Coming of the Holy Spirit

When Nansen started on his Arctic expedition, he took with him a carrier pigeon, strong and fleet of wing. After two years—two years in the desolation of the Arctic regions—he one day wrote a tiny little message and tied it under the pigeon's wing. Then he let it loose to travel 2,000 miles to Norway. Oh! What miles! What desolation! Not a living creature, just land filled with ice, ice, ice, snow and death. But Nansen took the trembling little bird and flung her up from the ship, up into the icy cold.

Three circles she made, and then, straight as an arrow she shot south. One thousand miles over ice, one thousand miles over the frozen wastes of ocean, and at last the pigeon dropped into the lap of the explorer's wife. She knew by the arrival of the bird that her husband was all right in the dark night of the Arctic regions.

So, with the coming of the Holy Spirit, the heavenly dove, the disciples knew that Christ was alive and was fulfilling His promise to send the Holy Spirit.

There is a great deal of confusion about the Holy Spirit in the minds of earnest Christians. Christ's birth was prophesied and promised, and in the fullness of time He came, born a little babe in Bethlehem. We are not looking for Him to be born again as a babe. That is a historical event that took place 2,000 years ago.

When Christ left the earth, He told the disciples that He would send the Spirit into the world, and that they were to tarry in Jerusalem until He came upon them. The disciples believed Christ's words to them, and they waited until the Spirit came. The Spirit came at a definite time and to a definite place.

Christ promised the Holy Spirit's coming. The Spirit was to come when Christ ascended (see John 16:7). Pentecost, therefore, began a new period, that of the Spirit, following the period of the Old Testament. Today, we do not have a visible Christ living and walking in our midst, but we do have the Holy Spirit with us to teach us all things (see John 14:26).

Filled by the Spirit

Think of how the Holy Spirit used Peter, the man who denied Christ, and made him the preacher on the day of Pentecost to bring 3,000 to salvation. The Holy Spirit not only filled men of old, but He fills each of us today.

We must not confuse the giving of the Holy Spirit with the fullness of the Holy Spirit. We are *baptized* by the Holy Spirit the moment we receive Jesus Christ as our Savior (see Rom. 8:9,14-17). We receive the Holy Spirit in His *fullness* the moment we yield wholly to the lordship of Christ and trust God in simple faith for that fullness.

We are baptized by the Holy Spirit just once (see 1 Cor. 12:13), but we should be filled by the Spirit for every task. Many people do not understand how the Holy Spirit can fill us more than once. He can fill us for every task God gives us to do if we desire Him to work through us. We must be willing to be filled and willing to be used (see Eph. 5:18).

People are like electrical appliances. There are vacuum cleaners, toasters, orange juicers, electric irons, fans, and so forth, but each is useless to accomplish what it is made for unless it is connected to the power source. So it is with us. God has made each one of us for a purpose, but if we are not filled with the power of His Spirit, we are useless (see Ezek. 36:27; John 16:13). Are we in touch with the Holy Spirit? Can He use us for the glory of God?

If we compare the filling of the Holy Spirit with the filling of a glass of water, we learn that the object filled has no room for anything else. If we are filled with the Holy Spirit, there is no room for our selfish desires and ambitions. Perhaps you have heard people exclaim, "He is filled with enthusiasm." What does this mean? It means he is spirited and dedicated. A Christian, filled with the Holy Spirit, is dedicated to Christ and wants to please Him. The Spirit controls him or her.

A Comforter and Guide

Think of your time back in school. Perhaps at some point you became discouraged as you worked over a problem and just could not solve it. Then, finally, the teacher suggested that you do it such-and-such a way. At that moment, you began to see! The teacher did not do the problem for you. He or she just gave the help necessary to show you the way out and let you have the pleasure of doing it yourself.

That is what "comforter" means. The Holy Spirit does just this in each of our lives. As Paul says, "Likewise the Spirit also helps in our weaknesses. For we do not know what we should pray for as we ought, but the Spirit Himself makes intercession for us with groanings which cannot be uttered."

There was once a guide in the deserts of Arabia who, it was said, never lost his way. He carried with him a homing pigeon with a very fine cord attached to one leg. When in any doubt as to which path to take, the guide threw the bird into the air. The pigeon quickly strained at the cord to fly in the direction of home, and so led his master. Men called that guide the "Dove Man."

The Holy Spirit, the heavenly dove, is willing and able to lead us if only we will allow Him to do so. God wants us to be led by the Spirit. As Jesus said, "When He, the Spirit of truth, has come, He will guide you into all truth" (John 16:13).

Daily Meditations

Sunday: The Holy Spirit foretold–Joel 2:25-32
Monday: The Holy Spirit promised–John 16:7-15
Tuesday: The Holy Spirit's coming–John 14:16-26
Wednesday: The Holy Spirit arrives–Acts 2:1-21
Thursday: The Holy Spirit and believers–
John 3:3,6; 16:13-14; Acts 2:4
Friday: Walk in the Spirit–Romans 8:1-10
Saturday: Be led by the Spirit–Romans 8:11-17

25

God's Grace

For by grace you have been saved through faith, and that not of yourselves; it is the gift of God, not of works, lest anyone should boast.

Ephesians 2:8-9

In *Down in Water Street,* author Samuel H. Hadley tells of a character known as the "Old Colonel" who wandered into one of the rooms of a mission one night. The man was more than 6 feet tall and 60 years of age, but he looked at least 100. His dirty gray beard was a foot long, and his hair of the same color hung a foot down his back.

The Old Colonel's eyes were bleary, and the hue of his face showed that he had long been a stranger to water. He wore an old ragged overcoat fastened with a nail. His trousers could hardly be called a part of his outfit, for they were little more than holes with rages tied around them. On his feet, in place of shoes, were rags tied up with strings. Whisky had brought him to this condition.

After graduating from college, he had studied law in the office of Lincoln's great war secretary, E. M. Stanton, but drink had ruined his prospects and reduced him to the level of the lowest beasts. But "down in Water Street," Jesus Christ took hold of him. On his knees, the Old Colonel cried out, "O Lord, if it is not too late, forgive this poor old sinner."

When he arose, he said to Hadley, who was standing nearby, "Brother Hadley, I am saved." From that instant, the old tramp hated whisky. God restored his intellect, and he became a dignified Christian gentleman, faithful to the day of his death. "Where sin abounded, grace abounded much more" (Rom. 5:20).

There are some great words in Scripture that we read often but really do not understand. Many of the wonderful words of our language have absolutely lost their force and power because of familiarity. This is true of the word "grace." Grace, in the Scriptures, tells of the boundless goodness and kindness of God toward humans. It tells us why God can save a sinner, and also why He does.

Grace Is Unmerited Favor

Do you know what it means when we say that grace is unmerited favor? It is showing love when it is not deserved. It does not take merit into account in any way. In school, you are given points of merit, and rewards are based on your accomplishments. If you do anything wrong, it means a demerit. Everything depends on what *you* do. God's grace is not withheld because of demerit. God's grace never expects a return, and it never incurs a debt.

When we turn to John 1:17, we read these words: "For the law was given through Moses, but grace and truth came through Jesus Christ." This does not mean that there is no Law since Christ or that there was no grace and truth before Christ. God manifested His grace from the very beginning. When Adam and Eve sinned and tried to make a covering for themselves and failed, God gave them a covering of skins. God in His grace made a way of escape for Noah and his family. How manifest was God's grace for Abraham!

We must remember that the Bible teaches that the "law was our tutor to bring us to Christ, that we might be justified by faith" (Gal. 3:24). The Law today shows us how far we fall short of the glory of God and the standard that He has set for us. The

Law cannot save us from sin, but it shows us our sin.

God cannot show His grace where there is the slightest degree of human merit to be recognized. Christ, the Lamb of God, has taken away the sin of the world through His death on the cross.

Salvation by Grace Alone

As we have seen, when Christ died upon the cross, He said, "It is finished." He had *done* it all. His work was to do the will of His Father, and we may be sure that our salvation is complete and that there is nothing left for us to *do*. If we try to do anything to a finished piece of work, we only mar it. All we can do is to accept this wonderful gift of salvation. We cannot work for a gift, for then we would earn it. We cannot pay for a gift, or else it is ours by purchase.

One of the greater statements of the apostle Paul concerning grace is found in Ephesians 2:8-9: "For by grace you have been saved through faith, and that not of yourselves; it is the gift of God, not of works, lest anyone should boast" (see also Gal. 3:18). We are *saved to serve,* but service is the expression of love to our Master and Savior, who has saved us by grace and grace alone.

Pause and meditate on this for a moment. Think of an omnipotent God not demanding a payment of any kind who offers us salvation full and *free* by an act of sovereign grace. Yes, it is the *gift* of God. We can do nothing to deserve it, nothing to earn it. We have no coin for that realm! "Nothing but the blood of Jesus."

If God would look for any merit in the sinner, then grace would fail, for Paul tells us in Romans that the whole race is guilty before God. We are all sinners by nature and by practice. "Therefore by the deeds of the law no flesh will be justified in His sight . . . for all have sinned and fall short of the glory of God, being justified freely by His grace through the redemption that is in Christ Jesus" (Rom. 3:20,23-24). Hence, all human merit has been laid aside as of no avail.

God Looks at Christ

Take a little piece of paper and let it represent you. Now put the paper in your Bible and close it. Can you see the paper? No. Why not? Because it is hidden in the Bible. All you can see is the book. In the same way, we are "hidden in Christ." When God looks at us, He can only see Christ. Is the paper still there? Yes, but it is hidden. This is grace.

It is almost impossible to comprehend fully what grace means. We want to mix *works* with *grace*. We cannot help but think that our salvation depends somewhat on what we do. We keep putting ourselves under the Law. We observe days and feasts and rules and regulations, hoping that some way, somehow, we will *deserve* a slight measure of grace.

Grace is neither treating others as they deserve nor treating them better than they deserve; it is treating others graciously without the slightest reference to what they deserve. "And if by grace, then it is no longer of works; otherwise grace is no longer grace. But if it is of works, it is no longer grace; otherwise work is no longer work" (Rom. 11:6).

How little we realize what grace is—a gift! We should never forget that this gift can come to us, without money and without price, because it was purchased by the giver, the Lord Jesus Christ. He paid for it absolutely and eternally with His own precious blood. How God's grace transforms us!

Transformed by Grace

Luther Burbank was rightly called the "plant wizard." He produced the Burbank potato, high gluten wheat, and a new and superior berry from the dewberry and raspberry. He changed the hard-shelled walnut into a soft-shelled one and improved the quality of the wood of the tree itself. He improved several species of apples and other fruit and procured new varieties. He produced wonderful roses and other flowers. He took the spines from the cactus and made it food for livestock.

In like manner, our divine Lord takes the bitter, thorny, unlovely lives of people and transforms them by His grace into beauty, fruitfulness and glorious usefulness. In His hands, even the most unpromising are made into His own likeness.

But there is more to grace than just salvation. There is grace that keeps us day by day. Christ says, "My grace is sufficient for you" (2 Cor. 12:9). He gives us strength each and every day.

When the children of Israel were in the wilderness, the manna fell from heaven every night. It was free for everybody, the good and the bad, whether they deserved it or not. All they had to do was to go out and take it. They didn't have to plant the heavenly food for a crop or cultivate it. God provided it there, ripe and ready for the taking.

So it is with the grace of God. We have nothing to do about it except to take it by faith. Each day, like the manna of old, we will find it sufficient for our needs. If we need much, we can have much. There's a boundless supply.

The Law constantly says "you shall not" (see Exod. 20). A penalty is attached to each for disobedience of these commands. But the gospel of grace is positive. It says, "Believe on the Lord Jesus Christ" (Acts 16:31). It says, "Come to Me, all you who labor and are heavy laden" (Matt. 11:28). It says, "Be dead indeed to sin, but alive to God in Christ Jesus our Lord" (Rom. 6:11). Each one of these commands brings an ultimate blessing.

The Law says "do this and you shall live," but the gospel of grace says "*live* and do." You remember the words of the apostle Paul: "For to me, to live is Christ, and to die is gain" (Phil. 1:21). "It is no longer I who live, but Christ lives in me" (Gal. 2:20).

THE LAW OF GOD IS PERFECT

We think that the Law is weak because we are weak and cannot keep it. But there is nothing wrong with the Law. There is something wrong with us. Consider the fact that we have traffic laws, but accidents still happen every day. We do not have accidents because we have no laws. We have accidents because people will not obey the laws.

The gospel of grace teaches us that instead of being weak through the flesh, we can have power over the flesh, for the Holy Spirit dwells within us and makes us more than conquerors through Jesus Christ. "For sin shall not have dominion over you" (Rom. 6:14).

We walk on the earth with no fear that we will fly off into space because we know that there is a force called gravity. This force acts according to a fixed law. By this law we live in absolute assurance. But what happens one day when we go to the airport and board a plane? Within a few minutes, the motors start and soon we are flying into space. Was the law of gravity broken in order for the plane to be able to rise from the earth? Of course not; a higher law was made operative. The law of gravity was still in force, but the force that gave the plane power to rise was greater than the pull of gravity. There is a similarity between this experience and what happened when we were made righteous in the sight of God.

We have seen the awful results of disobedience to the Law of God. In the Bible, the Israelites did not keep the perfect Law of God, and so they had to suffer the consequences of breaking the Law. Eventually, we find the people of God in captivity because they obeyed not the Lord (see Neh. 9:26-27).

God ordained certain spiritual laws by which His people should live. These laws, when disobeyed, held them down. But God, in His love and by His grace, sent the Lord Jesus Christ.

He was not held by the Law, for He kept the Law. Thus, resting in Him, we can be lifted into heavenly places in Christ Jesus.

Without the plane, you and I could never soar into space. Without Christ, we cannot be set free from the law of sin and death. The Law imposes a yoke of bondage, but grace sets us free by the power of Jesus Christ (see Gal. 5:1).

A Great Difference

The Law demands perfection; we are far from perfect. The Law sets forth what we shall do; we do not do it. The Law forbids certain things; we choose to do these things. The Lord Jesus said, "Most assuredly, I say to you, whoever commits sin is a slave of sin" (John 8:34). Thus, without Christ, we are servants of sin or in bondage to sin.

However, the Lord Jesus promises us in John 8:36 that "if the Son makes you free, you shall be free indeed." When the apostle Paul told the Romans that they were free from the bondage of sin—that the grace of God had been given to them and that they no longer were in bondage—they presumed they now could live any way they pleased (see Rom. 6:1). Paul forcefully instructed them that this was not true.

Paul often called himself a "bondservant of Jesus Christ." This seems to imply that we leave one life of bondage to take up another. Once, we were bound by the law of sin and death, but the Lord Jesus Christ has set us free by His grace. Now, we voluntarily follow Him. We are not forced to be bound—we *want* to be bound to Him. "The love of Christ compels us" (2 Cor. 5:14).

We never want to grieve a person we really love. "By this we know love, because He laid down His life for us. And we also ought to lay down our lives for the brethren" (1 John 3:16; see also Eph. 5:1-2,15-16; 1 John 2:6). The more we love the Lord, the more we will wish to please Him. We must not only say with our lips that we love God but also declare it by our lives (see Titus 1:16).

Do you see what it is to live a Christian life only in the power of Christ? Only Christ can live a Christ-life. "The life which I now live in the flesh I live by faith in the Son of God, who loved me and gave Himself for me" (Gal. 2:20).

Remember that every temptation we have has been allowed to come into our lives by God Himself in order to bring out strength and achievement in character. So many people think that grace is given for ease and not for work. They think that they can just sit down and dream and pray. But it is not in that way that real victory is won in the life of the Christian soldier. There is no victory unless a battle is fought. In the ordinary temptations and trials of life, we need to use the grace we have more than we need to pray for more grace.

A Christian never needs to be alarmed when a task seems difficult or a temptation too strong, for God says that His grace *is* sufficient. The apostle Paul found this to be true in his own life. In his second letter to the Corinthians, he says that there had been given to him a thorn in the flesh. He called it a "messenger of Satan." The apostle Paul prayed about this problem. In fact, he tells us that three times he asked the Lord to remove it. But each time Paul received this answer: "My grace is sufficient for you, for My strength is made perfect in weakness."

Paul had learned his lesson. He could say, "Therefore most gladly I will rather boast in my infirmities, that the power of Christ may rest on me" (2 Cor. 12:9).

Grace Is to Be Used

Remember that when we are tempted, we have the promise that he will provide a way of escape. Perhaps it will not be a pleasant way, and maybe it will not be the way we would choose for ourselves, but we have the assurance that it will be a sure and sufficient way.

The grace of God then comes to us as a gift of God's love. We do not earn it or deserve it, but God gives us His grace. By this grace we are saved through faith. By this grace we have strength to overcome temptations and trials. It is always available to us. God continues to pour out more grace upon us. "But He gives more grace. Therefore He says: 'God resists the proud, but gives grace to the humble'" (Jas. 4:6).

Daily Meditations

Sunday: Law and grace—John 1:17; Ephesians 2:8-9; Luke 10:25-28; 2 Corinthians 4:6

Monday: All are guilty under the Law—Romans 3:9-20

Tuesday: God's grace—Romans 3:21-31

Wednesday: Saved by Christ's death—Galatians 3:13; 1 Timothy 2:6; 1 Peter 1:18-19

Thursday: Kept by Christ's life—Romans 5:1-15

Friday: Reckon on His grace—Romans 6:11-23

Saturday: Go and sin no more—John 8:1-11

26

Faith: The Key for Our Lives

But without faith it is impossible to please Him: for he that cometh to God must believe that He is, and that He is a rewarder of them that diligently seek Him.

Hebrews 11:6

Have you ever wondered why Columbus dared to cross the great ocean with three small ships when others would not dare to make the journey? Columbus believed the world was round; many others didn't. He believed his three ships would safely take him across the great ocean. So he dared to go.

If Columbus had not had faith to go, he would not have discovered America in 1492. That seems like an important step of faith. But there are other steps of faith even more important for each one of us—steps that will count for all eternity. Faith is the key to God's plans for us.

Sometimes we think that faith is such a strange thing that we shrug our shoulders because it is beyond us. And yet we live most of our lives by faith. Not a day goes by but that we do not exercise faith in a hundred different ways.

Just this morning, for example, you got up at a certain time because you had faith that the clock was right or because you had faith in the person who called you and told you that it was time to get up. You ate breakfast without any fear that someone had put poison into the food. You flipped on the light and had faith there would be light. You turned a faucet, confident that you would have water. These were acts of faith. You believed that each was as it was represented, and you acted accordingly.

Is it not strange, then, that you and I have faith in everything but God? The One who never is untrue, we suspect of not doing what He has promised.

Saved by Faith

If you wish to open a lock, you must have the right key. You might have a whole bunch of keys, but unless you have the right one, they would all be useless. Faith is God's key for us to enjoy His wonderful plan for our lives. He has set forth the principle that if you and I are to be Christians—if we are to live a Christian life—we will do so by faith.

As you remember, Ephesians 2:8-9 says, "For by grace you have been saved through faith, and that not of yourselves; it is the gift of God." As we said, grace is God's gift to us. We cannot earn it and do not deserve it, but God gives it to us anyway. But there is another word that is interesting in these same verses: "faith." What is faith? Faith is taking God at His word. It is believing that what God says is so, *is so.* It involves a decision to believe God.

Some people say, "But I don't feel any different, so how can I be a Christian?" However, Jesus did not say, "By grace you are saved through feeling." He did not even say, "By grace you are saved through faith and feeling." Instead, Jesus Christ said over and over again that if anyone *believed* in Him, he or she would have eternal life (see John 3:16,36; 11:25).

One day during this year, you had a birthday. The day before you were one age, and then when you woke up the next morning you were another age. How did you know that you were a different age? Did you feel different? Older than the day before? I doubt it. You just looked at the calendar and recognized the fact that this was your birthday. You accepted that fact by faith. Your feelings were not important.

It is the same way with your spiritual birthday. The Lord Jesus Christ said, "He who hears My word and believes in Him who sent Me has everlasting life, and shall not come into judgment, but has passed from death into life" (John 5:24). These are the Lord's own words. You know that He would not lie. He knows what He is talking about. These words, you believe, are completely true.

You hear His words in the Bible. You believe that He has come from God to be the Savior of the world–your Savior. So, by faith, you accept the fact and know that you have everlasting life. Now, you don't know this because you feel like you have eternal life; you know it because God said so and you believe Him. Someone has said, "First there is the fact, which we accept by faith, then, perhaps, comes the feeling." But be sure that you keep these three *F*s in the right order: fact, faith, feeling.

When someone asks you how you know that you are a Christian, you do not say, "I feel like one." No, you say, "I am a Christian because God says so and I believe Him." By grace, we are saved through faith.

Walk by Faith

The apostle Paul says, "For we walk by faith, not by sight" (2 Cor. 5:7). In another place, he says, "As you therefore have received Christ Jesus the Lord, so walk in Him, rooted and built up in Him and established in the faith" (Col. 2:6-7). We received the

Lord Jesus by faith, now we must walk by faith. But what does it mean to live, or walk, by faith?

So many times, you and I wish that we might be able to see a few years into the future. If we could just see a little way ahead, we would know the way to go. We are not the only ones to feel like this. Just look at the number of people who go to fortunetellers, or try to read tea leaves, or play with Ouija boards. All these people want a look into the future. But God does not let us look into the future on many occasions, and He never gives a look through these means that people try. His Word tells us very definitely that we should walk by faith, not by sight. We trust Him for our salvation. We must also trust Him for our daily lives.

In the Old Testament, when Moses had died and the Israelites were worried how they would ever cross the river Jordan, God called Joshua to Him. The Lord told Joshua what the people were to do. The people had one command only: follow the Ark. They did not know yet how they were to cross the river, but they knew that they must follow the Ark. The priests who carried the Ark did not know how they were to get across the Jordan; they just knew that they were to start walking. Imagine being asked to stand still in the Jordan.

The Ark that the priests carried was heavy. It was wooden and covered with gold. On the top of it was the mercy seat, made of solid gold. Inside of it were the pot of manna, Aaron's rod that had budded, and the tablets of stone. This was a heavy object to hold in the midst of a swollen river. But that was God's command.

Do you suppose that those priests wanted to ask for the ability to see ahead? I think they did. But God was showing only one step at a time. In the end, the Lord provided the way across the Jordan in safety. But the provision was not made until the priests by faith walked into the midst of the river.

How many times we foolishly refuse to follow the Lord and so lose out on His blessing. We say, "I can't walk that way. I don't have that much faith." Let's put it like this: Do you have enough faith to trust the Lord for the next 30 seconds? Of course you do. Well, what about the next 30 seconds? And then what of the next? We can't see all the road ahead, but we can see one step ahead. By faith, take that step.

You and I don't know what the future holds, but we know who holds the future. Trust in God and walk by faith.

Serve by Faith

We are beginning to see just how important faith is. We are saved by faith, we walk by faith, and we serve by faith. God wants His people to do great exploits for Him. These can only be done when we have faith.

Paul certainly had to learn that his service in many instances would be by faith. He told the Corinthians, "I planted, Apollos watered, but God gave the increase" (1 Cor. 3:6). Oftentimes in our Christian service, we will not see the fruits of our labors. But God commands us to be faithful. We will probably never know until we get to heaven the effect that our lives have had on those around us.

We do not always understand what God intends for us to do, but we are assured that by faith He will guide us. Our service must be done in the power of the Lord. We trust Him to show us what to do, and then, in His power and by the guidance of the Holy Spirit, we perform that which He has commanded. That which we try to do for the Lord in our own strength is bound to fail.

In Galatians 2:20, the apostle Paul told the people, "I have been crucified with Christ; it is no longer I who live, but Christ lives in me; and the life which I now live in the flesh I live by faith in the Son of God, who loved me and gave Himself for me." Did you notice that last part? "The life I live," Paul says, "I live by faith." It is the life of Christ who lives within us. We know that He is within us, and we obey His commands and do as He says.

It takes great faith to serve God. Satan is a strong and clever foe, ever ready to lead us astray. He is our greatest enemy and sneaks up on us at every opportunity. He does not want us to serve God and will do all he can to stop us.

Paul likened the Christian life to warfare, and us to soldiers. Soldiers are under the direct command of their superiors. If they are commanded to move, they must move. If they are commanded to camp, they must obey.

You and I should be just as willing to follow our superior officer. If the Lord says, "Speak to this person," we should speak. If the Lord says, "Live for Me at home in front of your family," we should be a good witness for Him. A soldier does not question his orders or ask his superior why he has been asked to do a certain thing, and neither should we.

The Bible says that the most important piece of armor that we as Christians have is the "shield of faith" (Eph. 6:16). When Satan comes to tempt you, turn to God in faith and obedience. God is mightier than Satan. "Therefore submit to God. Resist the devil and he will flee from you" (Jas. 4:7).

Where Do We Get Faith?

Where does this faith come from? The Bible has the answer for us. In Romans 10:17, Paul writes, "So then faith comes by hearing, and hearing by the word of God." The Bible is the foundation of our faith. How much faith do we have to have? "If you have faith as a mustard seed" (Luke 17:6). Do you know how small a mustard seed is? It is very, very small—one of the smallest of the seeds. It doesn't take much faith.

Remember that our faith must be in God Himself. Faith in just anything is not what God requires. Faith in Him is what He asks for. I may have faith that my car will take me home after church, but if I don't put gas in it, my faith is useless. I can put faith in things that I can see, or in my own ability, or in my friends, or in anything in this world, and I will fail. My faith is useless. But faith in God never fails, for He never fails.

Every promise in God's Word is ours, but we must claim each one by faith. Jesus said, "All things are possible to him who believes" (Mark 9:23). Faith is taking God at His word.

Daily Meditations

Sunday: Instances of faith in the beginning—Hebrews 11:1-7

Monday: Faith of Abraham and Sarah—Hebrews 11:8-9

Tuesday: Faith of Moses—Hebrews 11:20-29

Wednesday: Roll call of heroes of the faith—Hebrews 11:30-40

Thursday: Source of faith—Romans 10:8-17

Friday: Faith in a Gentile woman—Matthew 15:21-28

Saturday: "Increase our faith"—Luke 17:1-6

Section Three:

God's Plan Completed

27

God's Greatest Plan: Salvation

For God so loved the world that He gave His only begotten Son, that whoever believes in Him should not perish but have everlasting life.
John 3:16

We often think of southern California as a beautiful garden filled with roses and oranges and waving palm branches. But do you realize that southern California is really a desert? Without water, not a thing in it could thrive.

As the city of Los Angeles kept growing, engineers realized that the need for water was a great problem. They began searching for a sufficient supply. They looked within 50 miles of the metropolis, then within 100 miles, then within 200 miles, and still enough water could not be found. Provision had to be made. It is impossible for any city to live and flourish without pure water. It is the greatest need of human life.

Finally, these searchers decided that the distant Colorado River was their only hope. It was more than 400 miles away. How to bring that water to the needy city of Los Angeles was the problem. The engineers sat down together in conference and realized that they had to make a careful investigation of every foot of the ground, from the source of the supply to the city itself. They laid out a careful plan for every inch of the way—over the mountains, across the desert and skirting the many little towns and villages along the way. Before a spade of ground was turned, the *plan* had to be perfected. The chief engineer would not think for a moment of attempting this great feat until every detail was on paper.

One day, work began on the great aqueduct. A corps of laborers started at each end and worked toward each other. For months and months they dug, and at the very time that was appointed—which had been accurately calculated by the chief engineer—the two corps of laborers met. The tunnels they had been boring merged into each other with hardly a fraction of an inch difference.

God's Plan Is Perfect

You say, "That's marvelous." It is, but wait a minute. Do you think that the Lord God Almighty, the chief engineer of this universe, does any less accurate planning? He knows exactly what is going to happen from the beginning. There isn't the fraction of an inch difference between His plan and its execution.

Do you see all the analogies that can be drawn from this illustration? The chief engineer is God Himself. The needy city in a desert land is this lost, sinful, hopeless world. The Los Angeles engineers planned for years how the life-giving water might be brought to the needy city, but God's plan to bring the water of life to a needy, dying world—a world of lost sinners—was perfected in the councils of heaven before the foundation of the world (see Rev. 13:8).

The carefully mapped-out plan for the aqueduct is God's own plan. The foreknowledge of the chief engineer corresponds to the foreknowledge of God. The engineer going so carefully over the ground is the Savior Himself treading the earth in the likeness of sinful flesh for one purpose alone—to bring the water of life. Just as the water brought to the city in the desert makes it bloom and blossom like a rose, so the water of life causes the parched sinful lives of men to bloom and blossom with the things of the Spirit.

Some people try to get rid of sin by denying its existence or making fun of it. This is dangerous. It is like trying to cure a terrible disease by saying you don't believe you have it. In 1 John 1:8,10, God says the following about denying sin: "If we say that we have no sin, we deceive ourselves, and the truth is not in us. If we say that we have not sinned, we make Him a liar, and His word is not in us." In Romans 3:19,23, Paul writes, "Now we know that whatever the law says, it says to those who are under the law, that every mouth may be stopped, and all the world may become guilty before God. For all have sinned and fall short of the glory of God."

We Are All Sinners

How did sin get into the world? "Therefore, just as through one man sin entered the world, and death through sin, and thus death spread to all men, because all sinned" (Rom. 5:12). This tells us why sin is in the world. Adam was made in the image of God (see Gen. 1:27), but Adam's children were in the image of their father (see Gen. 5:3). Their father was a sinner, and they in turn were sinners also by nature and by choice.

You know that even little babies can exhibit bad temper, rebellion, selfishness and disobedience. We sin because we are sinners, just as an apple tree bears apples because it is an apple tree. Our sins do not make us sinners; we sin because we are sinners.

First John 3:4 states, "Whoever commits sin also commits lawlessness, and sin is lawlessness." When anyone dashes through a stop signal at an intersection at 50 miles an hour, he or she is arrested. Why? That person has broken a law. When a person breaks God's Law, he or she is a sinner. How many sins did Adam have to commit before he was a sinner? How many times does a person have to steal before he or she is branded a thief and put in jail? How many laws do you think you have to break before you become guilty of sin? "For whoever shall keep the whole law, and yet stumble in one point, he is guilty of all" (Jas. 2:10).

Open your Bible to Exodus 20 and look at the commandments that God gave to the children of Israel. These Ten Commandments are God's standard. How many of them have you broken? Do you love the Lord your God with all your heart, all your soul and all your mind? Do you ever take the name of the Lord in vain? Do you always keep the Lord's day holy? Do you always honor your father and mother? Can you honestly say that you keep the *whole* Law?

We do not have to be old men and old women steeped in sin and lawlessness to be sinners, for God says that if we offend in only one point, we are guilty of all. We must be willing to admit to ourselves that we have done far worse than that. Each of us has sinned over and over again. We have been disobedient.

The Law is like a mirror; it shows us ourselves as we really are. Paul says, "By the law is the knowledge of sin" (Rom. 3:20). There has been only one person who could look into the truthful mirror of the Law and see an image of absolute perfection reflected back—Jesus Christ, our Lord.

We have come to the conclusion that we are all sinners for two reasons. First, because our own investigation indicates that we are guilty of breaking God's Law. Second, because we know that God's Word distinctly states that we are indeed sinners (see Rom. 3:23).

Provision of a Savior

Someone has said that sin is like fire, for it burns and destroys. It is also like rust, for it corrodes and eats. You remember all the things that sin did when Adam first sinned in the Garden of Eden. Sin separated him from God and caused him to be driven out of his beautiful home. He saw his beloved children stained by sin; his oldest son was a murderer and another was the victim of his brother's jealousy and anger.

God warns us all through His Word of the awful consequences of sin. The Bible is like an X-ray machine that reveals all the hidden things of the heart and life. Our great physician knows what sin is really doing in our lives and longs to give us the remedy. Not only does sin stain our souls and bodies, it also puts us under condemnation. If it is proved that a man is a thief, his sin puts him in prison. Likewise, we all have had to be placed in the prison house of sin. We cannot save ourselves, so God has planned out our salvation. *We must have a Savior.*

The chief engineer of heaven was working out this plan before the world's foundation and long before humans sinned or realized their need of the living water. "But when the fullness of the time had come, God sent forth His Son, born of a woman, born under the law, to redeem those who were under the law" (Gal. 4:4-5). The New Testament opens with the great fact that the Savior has come. The angel said to Mary, "[You] will bring forth a Son, and you shall call His name JESUS." Why? "For He will save His people from their sins" (Matt. 1:21).

The salvation that God planned, promised and provided was in a person—not in a new set of laws. Salvation is a complete and finished work of God for humankind. Nothing has been forgotten; nothing needs to be added. As Jesus said on the cross, "It is finished!" God's plan of the ages for the redemption of mankind was completely finished that moment!

By His death, we are saved from the penalty of sin, the power of sin and the presence of sin. We receive a new life and a new heart. We are made into new creatures, a new song is put into our mouths, we are given new minds, and a new service opens before us. The new commandment of *love* becomes the only commandment of our lives.

Religion is not salvation. People may be religious without being saved. Nicodemus, the ruler of the Jews, was a Pharisee, a member of the Sanhedrin *and* a religious man, but he was not saved until he came to know Christ. But Jesus said to him, "Most assuredly, I say to you, unless one is born again, he cannot see the kingdom of God" (John 3:3).

Saul of Tarsus was of the strictest sect–a Pharisee–and he tells us himself in Philippians 3:4-6 what a blameless life he had lived. But he was not saved until he met Christ on the road to Damascus. Religion does not save; it is Christ alone who saves. In fact, religion is often a great hindrance.

Why Are We Saved?

We have seen that we are saved from sin. We cannot help but realize that we need salvation. We know that we are saved and given eternal life through the Lord Jesus Christ. But why did God bother to save us in the first place? The Lord God must have had a good reason, for certainly our salvation was not simple to obtain. The Lord gives it to us as a free gift, but it was costly to God. It cost God the life of His Son. It cost Christ 33 years on this earth and then a shameful death. Because our salvation was so expensive, God must have had a good reason to purchase it for us.

Certainly, you and I cannot fathom the mind of God to determine all that He had in mind when He provided salvation for us. However, there are some indications in the Word of God that point to some of His reasons. We shall be concerned here only with three of them.

In John 14:2-3, we read the words of Christ to His disciples just before His death. He tells the disciples that He is going to leave them in order to prepare a place for them. Then follow these words: "And if I go and prepare a place for you, I will come again and receive you to Myself; that where I am, there you may be also" (v. 3). Here, then, is one reason from the lips of Christ as to why we are given salvation: So that we may be fit to be with Him forever. We know that heaven could never house sin, which means that we, with our sin, could never inherit heaven. God so wanted us to be with Him that He provided a way for us to be cleansed from our sin.

Turn in your Bible to John 17:23. This verse is in the middle of the prayer of Christ just before His crucifixion. The Lord prays, "I in them, and You in Me; that they may be made perfect in one, and that the world may know that You have sent Me, and have loved them as You have loved Me." What a wonderful verse to teach us the amazing truth that our lives are united with Christ through His work of salvation. What a wonderful place for the Lord to put us. Christ is in us. Because of this union we can serve the Lord God. Not because we are so good or because we have gained salvation for our souls, but because Christ is good and He has given us salvation. We are saved to serve, and the power for that service comes from the indwelling Christ.

The last phrase of John 17:23 tells us that God loves us even as He loves Christ. God saves us because He *loves* us. We did not and never will deserve the free salvation that He has given to us. But God loves us, so He provided salvation despite our unworthiness.

There are certainly many other reasons why God provided salvation to us, but these three should make us realize anew what a privilege we have to belong to God. He wants us to be with Him. He wants us to be one with Him that we might serve Him. He loves us.

Yield to the Savior

How can we do less than yield our lives to God so that He may use us according to His will? If you have never accepted Christ as your personal Savior and have not accepted the salvation that He provides, do so now. If you are a Christian, take a new look at why God has saved you and see if He can accomplish His service through you. How many people have you ever talked to about the Lord Jesus Christ? You may say that you love Him, but do you try to keep it a secret so that others will not know you are a Christian? Surely, salvation is God's greatest plan and His greatest miracle. We need to share the good news of God's salvation to the world.

Daily Meditations

Sunday: The Passover lamb—Exodus 12:1-23
Monday: Our Passover Lamb—John 1:29;
1 Corinthians 5:6-7; 1 Peter 1:18-19
Tuesday: Christ died for us—Isaiah 53:1-9
Wednesday: His blood cleanses—1 John 1:3-10
Thursday: God's Law—Exodus 20:1-17
Friday: Guilty before God—Romans 3:9-20
Saturday: Christ and the Law—Romans 10:4-15

28

THE CHURCH IN GOD'S PLAN

On this rock I will build My church, and the gates of Hades shall not prevail against it.

MATTHEW 16:18

Consider the human body. What a wonderful thing it is, with its torso containing all the vital organs, and then the arms and hands, the legs and feet. But of what value would these parts be without the head? It is in the brain in that head that all commands are given to every part of the body. If you touch something hot with your finger, a little message rushes to the brain, which directs the muscles in your hand to withdraw quickly from danger. If a cinder gets in your eye, your brain tells your eye to close.

The government of the body is centered in that amazing organ we know as the brain. How sad it is to see a body that is not governed by the mind. There is a terrible disease called locomotor ataxia in which the body refuses to obey the brain. Those afflicted with this disease throw themselves about with the utmost abandon. Their arms and legs are without control. What a terrible plight!

You must see a person's face to know who he or she is. In the face we see intelligence. The face in this wonderful head truly tells so much. The eyes, which flash with anger or sparkle with love, are the organs that see oncoming danger and send warnings to the brain to protect the body. The ears hear the cry of the needy and afflicted. They are also the entrance for the strains of beautiful melody.

The Head

Do you know that Christ is called the "head of the body, the church" (Col. 1:18)? Think of this great head of the Church possessing a spiritually undernourished and undeveloped body. This is the sight that the world too often sees. The Church is the hand through which Christ works, the voice through which He speaks, the heart through which Christ loves and the feet by which He carries the gospel to the ends of the earth!

Today, how is the Body of Christ obeying their great head? Are they withered with paralysis so that they cannot perform the functions for which God made them? Is the heart cold and indifferent to the cries of the unfortunate? Are the hands grasping for riches and the material possessions of this world? Is the body covered with beautiful garments, surrounded with luxury and stuffed with rich food while people almost on its doorstep are naked and poor and hungry?

Many people say that the Church is a failure, but few know what the Church of Jesus Christ really is. Whenever we hear the word "church," we often think of a building to which people go every Sunday morning to worship God. We picture its spire, its pews, its pulpit and its choir loft. But this is not the Church that God speaks of in His Word. Just as the clothing on the body is not a part of the body, so also the organization we call "a church" is not the Body of Christ.

The word "church" in the New Testament comes from the Greek word *ecclesia*, which means "called-out ones." Called out from what? From the world. How do these individuals differ from others? They differ *only* in the fact that they have accepted Christ as their Savior. We previously discussed how Christ became the Savior of the Church. He redeemed the "called-out ones," or bought them, with His precious blood. Therefore, if we are bought by Christ, we are not our own—that is, we do not belong to ourselves. You say, "This is my coat." What do you mean? "I bought it. It's mine." So Christ says, "I bought you. You belong to Me."

We need to remember that even though a person may call himself or herself a church member, it is not a true indication of whether that individual is a real member of the Body of Christ, the Church. No one is or can be a member of the Church of Jesus Christ who has not accepted the Lord Jesus Christ as his or her personal Savior. That is the way the first Church received members (see Acts 2:42-47). A person may be a member of a Methodist, Baptist, Congregational, Presbyterian, Lutheran or Episcopal church, but the important thing is to be a member of the Church of Jesus Christ.

Called-Out Ones

So, we see that as the Body of Christ, we are "called out." But called out for what? Evidently for a definite purpose. Whenever a person buys anything, he or she has a purpose in mind. Sometimes this purpose may not seem sensible to us. It may also seem very extravagant. For instance, some rich man may pay hundreds of thousands of dollars for an oil painting to hang in his drawing room. It is meant to hang on the wall, and not as a screen before the fireplace.

A man buys a beautiful car with 16 cylinders. Someone says, "Why not haul trunks in that car? It has so much power. Or why not use it for a delivery truck? There's plenty of room in it." But the owner says, "This car is reserved for the use for which I bought it. It's my car to ride around in."

The Church belongs to Jesus Christ. It is His very own. He bought it and paid for it, and it should be reserved to be used as He wants it. You are a part of that Church that belongs to Him. Can He use you? Paul even says, "Your body is the temple of the Holy Spirit who is in you" (1 Cor. 6:19). Would you defile the building in which you worship God? Should you not beware of defiling the body that He has given to you?

As the Temple is the dwelling of the Lord, so the body belongs to the head. We have brought out the intimate connection between the directions given by the mind and the actions of the members of the body. How alarmed you would be if someone passed you an apple and your mind told your hand to take it, but it did not respond. Or you were sitting in a chair and wanted to get up, and you found yourself helpless. You would immediately call a doctor to find out what was wrong. Do we feel alarmed when we, a part of the Body of Christ, do not respond when Christ tells us what to do? Don't you think we should be concerned?

The story is told of a man who had a clock that would not run. So he took off the hands and went to the jeweler. "Will you fix these hands?" he requested. "Something is wrong with them. They won't go."

"Where is the clock?" asked the jeweler.

"Oh, the clock is all right," replied the man. "It's just the hands that won't work."

"Well, I can't fix the hands unless I have the whole clock," answered the jeweler.

Likewise, the great jeweler in heaven can do so little with us when we only give Him a part of ourselves instead of our whole being.

The First Church

When was the true Church of Christ born? The account of this occasion is given in the second chapter of Acts. The Holy Spirit was given to the disciples of Christ as their Comforter to abide with them when the Lord went back to heaven. The Holy Spirit came upon the people at Pentecost.

After the miracle of the sound of a rushing wind, the tongues like fire and the unlocking of the mouths of the apostles so that they spoke in other languages, those who listened began to question what had taken place. Peter rose, and, as we mentioned earlier, preached a sermon to the people. When he had finished speaking, there were added about 3,000 to the few believers (see Acts 2:41).

The next six verses in Acts describe the actions of these new believers (see 2:42-47.) These people studied what the apostles taught them. They had fellowship with one another. They prayed. They broke bread together (which is thought by some Bible students to mean that they commemorated the Lord's Supper). Then, in the last verse of the chapter, the name "church" is given to this group. This was the first church, as described by Luke, the writer of the book of Acts. We would do well to follow their example in our church.

God's promises were first given to the Jewish race. He had made *all* of His promises and covenants with them and had committed His divine knowledge to them. As Paul wrote, "What advantage then has the Jew? . . . Much in every way! Chiefly because to them were committed the oracles of God" (Rom. 3:1-2). But when Christ came to this earth, to these chosen people, how did they receive Him? "He came to His own, and His own did not receive Him" (John 1:11).

Peter preached especially to the Jews. However, as we see in Acts, they were not always glad to receive his message: "Now as they spoke to the people, the priests, the captain of the temple, and the Sadducees came upon them, being greatly disturbed that they taught the people and preached in Jesus the resurrection from the dead. And they laid hands on them, and put them in custody until the next day, for it was already evening" (4:1-3). In fact, the Jewish authorities eventually seized Peter for preaching the gospel and threw him into prison (see Acts 12:1-5).

Peter was not particularly anxious to go and preach this wonderful gospel to the gentiles. To change his mind, God sent a vision to him of a great sheet with all kinds of four-footed animals of the earth descending from heaven. "And a voice came to him, 'Rise, Peter; kill and eat.' But Peter said, 'Not so, Lord! For I have never eaten anything common or unclean.' And a voice spoke to him again the second time, 'What God has cleansed you must not call common' " (Acts 12:13-15).

The Church was born on the Day of Pentecost, but the Church had been formed long before in the mind of God: "He chose us in Him before the foundation of the world, that we should be holy and without blame before Him in love" (Eph. 1:4). To proclaim this new message to the whole world, God chose a special apostle. His name was Paul, and the story of his miraculous conversion is told in Acts 9:1-18.

In Ephesians 3:3-5, Paul writes, "He made known to me the mystery (as I have briefly written already, by which, when you read, you may understand my knowledge in the mystery of Christ), which in other ages was not make known to the sons of men, as it has now been revealed by the Spirit to His holy apostles and prophets."

Paul tried to preach to the Jews first and tell them about this mystery that Christ revealed to him, but they stoned him and dragged him out of the city (see Acts 14:19). Paul's final conclusion was that "the salvation of God has been sent to the gentiles, and they will hear it!" (Acts 28:28).

Peter's gospel was to the Jew first and also to the Gentile, as he found through his vision. Paul's message was to everyone, for he was an ambassador of Jesus Christ to all the nations of the world. As he wrote to the Corinthian believers, "Now then, we are ambassadors for Christ, as though God were pleading through us: we implore you on Christ's behalf, be reconciled to God" (2 Cor. 5:20).

The first believers did not worship in a mighty temple built by the hands of men, but went from house to house, teaching and preaching the Lord Jesus. They had such perfect fellowship and were so sincere in their relationship one to the other, as well as to the Lord, that hypocrisy and lying were easily detected (see the story of Ananias and Sapphira in Acts 5:1-11). They faced persecution without fear and were glad to give their lives as a sacrifice. They started a great missionary enterprise, which was in direct response to the last command of the Lord Jesus in Acts 1:8.

How easy it is to see in this first Church that the head, which is Christ, was directing every act, deed and word of the Church, "which is His body."

The Victory of the Church

The Early Church, as it is described in the book of Acts, was a powerful witness of the resurrection of the Lord Jesus Christ and of what the Holy Spirit could accomplish in the lives of those who would yield themselves to the Holy Spirit.

Whenever those who believe in the Lord Jesus Christ depend wholly upon Him, they find the same power. The Lord promised that the coming of the Holy Spirit would bring power to those who receive Him (see Acts 1:8). That power is ours for the asking. As Christians, we, too, are a part of the Body of Christ. Our union with Him is as close as that of the Early Church. The problem is not that God has failed to provide the power to act; the problem is that we have failed to appropriate the power that is available.

The Church is the Body of Christ—that close union that only God makes possible—and we are members of that Body. That suggests a relationship between Christians. When Paul wrote to the church at Corinth, he had this to say about this relationship: "That there should be no schism [division] in the body, but that the members should have the same care for one another. And if one member suffers, all the members suffer with it; or if one member is honored, all the members rejoice with it. Now you are the body of Christ, and members individually" (1 Cor. 12:25-27).

This means that Christians should not be jealous of other Christians. They should not hurt them or belittle them. How well do you and I measure up to this standard? Remember, this is what God expects of us, not just what would be nice if we would like to be like this. The Church of Jesus Christ is a body of believers who have been united in Christ and who should act as He would act if He were on Earth today.

The Lord promised that He would build His Church. He will keep His promise, and the gates of hell will not prevail against it. The Church will triumph until Christ comes again. You and I can triumph as well if we will let the Lord work in our lives to make us better examples of the way in which the members of the Body of Christ should act, both toward Him and toward other members of His Body.

Daily Meditations

Sunday: The Church's birthday—Acts 2:1-21

Monday: The first church—Acts 2:42-47

Tuesday: Peter's first sermon—Acts 2:14-41

Wednesday: Peter's sermon to the gentiles—Acts 10:34-48

Thursday: Peter's call—Acts 9:1-25

Friday: Paul preaches to the Jews—Acts 13:3-5,14-17,44-45

Saturday: Paul turns to the gentiles—Acts 13:46-49; 28:25-31

29

The Mission of the Church

And Jesus came and spoke to them, saying, "All authority has been given to Me in heaven and on earth. Go therefore and make disciples of all the nations, baptizing them in the name of the Father and of the Son and of the Holy Spirit, teaching them to observe all things that I have commanded you; and lo, I am with you always, even to the end of the age."

MATTHEW 28:18-20

Are you easily discouraged? If you are, you certainly must look upon the difficulties of taking the message of Christ to the whole world as insurmountable. If you think back over centuries since the Lord was here on Earth, and then you look at the world conditions, you cannot help but realize that this old world is far from being populated by Christians. Of course, you also realize that each succeeding generation has to be introduced to Christ. Christianity is not inherited; every person must accept Christ for himself or herself. But if you think about this, you may still be discouraged in the task.

Suppose there were just 12 Christians in all the world today—just as many as there were disciples of Christ. If each one of those 12 people were to tell one person about Christ today, and then those 24 were to each tell 1 person tomorrow, do you know how long it would take for everyone on Earth to hear the message? Get a pencil and paper and figure it out. In less than a month, every person on Earth would know that the Lord Jesus Christ came to Earth to die for our sins.

It isn't such an impossible task. It is just that too many times you and I are not willing to accept the job.

Christ Commands the Church

Certainly, the Lord Himself has given an important task to His Church. If you or I had gone through as much as Jesus did to make salvation possible, we probably would have been tempted to assure the spread of our work by some supernatural means. We might have decided that we would like our work told in letters of fire in the sky. Or we might have decided that hosts of angels would come to Earth and proclaim what we had done. We might, if we could, have made the knowledge of our act innate in every person so that he or she would automatically know about it.

However, the Lord Jesus Christ in His infinite wisdom did none of these things. He left the gospel of His salvation with the people whom He died to save. You and I and all those who have partaken of His salvation are the only messengers that He has. Angels will not tell it, nor will people be able to find it for themselves. It is up to believers to make the gospel known.

The Lord Jesus knew that we would need the fellowship of others to give us courage and to keep us diligent, and so He provided that the Church would be formed. The Lord knew that we could not do the task in our own strength, and so He provided the power for the task in the presence of the Holy Spirit. We do not work in our own strength; we act through the power of the Holy Spirit. We do not win souls; the Lord wins them through us.

In the New Testament, the members of the Corinthian church were beginning to think that the messenger was more important than the message. So Paul told them, "Who then is Paul, and who is Apollos, but ministers through whom you believed, as the Lord gave to each one? I planted, Apollos watered, but God gave the increase. So then neither he who plants is anything, nor he who waters, but God who gives the increase" (1 Cor. 3:5-7).

The Lord gave us the fellowship of others, the power to do the task, and the knowledge of what He wanted to be done. Our job is clear. There can be no question in our minds as to what we are to do.

The Church Answers the Command

The Church through the years has likewise known what God expected it to do. From its very beginning, the members of the Church have been at work spreading the gospel of the Lord Jesus Christ.

In early apostolic times, the book of Acts tells us of the activity of the Christians. Almost immediately, the apostles went to work to spread the good news that Jesus Christ came to bring salvation and that anyone who accepted Him as his or her Savior would receive that salvation. As we have read, the Church began at Jerusalem on the Day of Pentecost, and "the Lord added to the church daily those who were being saved" (Acts 2:47).

A man named Philip was one of the first witnesses who took the gospel beyond Jerusalem. He went to Samaria, in central Palestine, and then south to Gaza, where he introduced an Ethiopian to the Lord (see Acts 8:5,26-27). This man went back to his own country, and thus Christianity spread into the continent of Africa.

Some witnesses of Christ were killed and others were persecuted, but this did not stop Christianity from spreading. In Acts 9, we learn that Saul of Tarsus, one of the most dreaded enemies of the Christians, was on his way to Damascus (which is in the northern part of the country) one day to arrest some believers when God spoke to him. From then on, Saul, now known as Paul, served the Lord and helped to spread the gospel and establish churches.

And so, the Church spread as the gospel of Christ was preached. One of the most important of the Early Churches was the one located in Antioch. This city is even farther north than Damascus. In Acts 11:26, we find that it was in Antioch that the believers were first called "Christians," and in Acts 13:1-2, we read that it was from this city that the first missionaries were sent. All the rest of the book of Acts describes the activities of these apostles, and especially the activities of the apostle Paul.

The activities of the Church, of course, did not end with the death of the apostles. The Church, through consecrated people, continued the work as commanded in the great commission. Throughout the first and second centuries, the Church was subjected to times of tremendous torture and persecution, but still its members remained faithful. During this period, as many as 500 Christians were put to death in a single day. The emperor Nero held a circus in his gardens one night and used Christians to supply the artificial light for the occasion. He took the Christians, dipped them in oil, fastened them to posts around his garden, and then set fire to them. What a terrible death this must have been! Yet these people remained faithful to their Christian belief.

On other occasions the Christians were thrown to lions in the arena of the Colosseum or were crucified, burned, stoned and killed in ways that are almost too horrible to tell. But through it all, the message of Christ continued to spread. In fact, the people were so faithful to their task that the second century is one of the great centuries of the Church. It is far more important to live for Christ than it is just to talk about Him.

After the emperor Constantine issued the Edict of Milan in A.D. 313, Christianity was legalized throughout the Roman Empire. Christians soon met together in great councils to determine by study and discussion what the Church should believe. Theology, the study of God, was formulated, and the Church became even more firmly established.

Many long and difficult years followed (A.D. 476–1517), which history calls the Dark Ages. At times, the Church seemed to neglect its task of witnessing for Christ. But toward the end of this thousand-year period, men such as John Wycliffe and William Tyndale realized the importance of studying the Bible and began work on translating the Word of God into the language of the common people. This met with tremendous opposition from those of the established Church organization, for by this time, the Church had become a politically powerful group and had forgotten the commands of Christ.

Finally, in 1517, Martin Luther, a Roman Catholic monk, revolted against the unscriptural teachings of the Church and set out to reform it. He was ousted from the Church, and so the Reformation came into being outside of the established Church. This awakening of interest in the Word of the Lord and in obedience to His commands spread from Germany, where Luther lived, to Switzerland, Scotland, England and the western world. Some years later, in 1740, this interest spread into North America in a movement known as the Great Awakening.

Down through the years, other believers picked up the work and went forth under the commission of Christ in the power of the Holy Spirit. In 1780, Robert Raikes began the first Sunday School in England. In 1792, William Carey went to India as a missionary and started his great work there. In 1815, the American Bible Society was formed. This organization has helped to translate the Bible into thousands and thousands of languages in the world. Today, there are hundreds of thousands of people who have answered the call of Christ for service and are serving Him in almost all the countries of the world.

The work of Christ continues in the steadfastness of His people and through the efforts of His Church.

Our Work in the Church

The Church is the organization the Lord has ordained to carry on His work. If people are to hear the message of Christ and to come to know Him as their Savior, they will learn it through the workings and testimony of the Lord's people. Throughout all of history, the Lord's people have with varying degrees of steadfastness continued this work. Now it is our turn.

The work of the apostle Paul, of the Early Church fathers, of Wycliffe, of Luther, of Carey and all the others will not be sufficient for people today to come to know Christ. Paul, in writing to the people at Rome, said these words: "For 'whoever calls on the name of the LORD shall be saved.' How then shall they call on Him in whom they have not believed? And how shall they believe in Him of whom they have not heard? And how shall they hear without a preacher? And how shall they preach unless they are sent? As it is written: 'How beautiful are the feet of those who preach the gospel of peace, who bring glad tidings of good things!' " (Rom. 10:13-15)!

J.B. Phillips translates Romans 10:14-15 like this: "Now how can they call on One in whom they have never believed? How can they believe in One of whom they have never heard? And how can they hear unless someone proclaims Him? And who will go to tell them unless he is sent?"

The whole process of evangelization boils down to one point of beginning. Someone must tell of the love of Christ and the need to accept Him as Lord and Savior, or else people cannot come to Him and be saved. Here is the point of beginning: Someone must proclaim Christ.

Of course, we should pray. That is required of every Christian. But we cannot really pray unless we are willing to put in the effort to make our prayers come true.

The story has been told of a rich man who spent hours praying that the Lord would answer the needs of a destitute family. A friend of the rich man was visiting him one day when one of the children of the poor family walked by the house. The rich man called his friend to the window. "See that little fellow?" the rich man said. "His family is so poor they never have enough food to go around. I have been praying that the Lord will supply their needs. Would you like to join me?"

"No," his friend answered. "I think I'll just take some food over to them."

That's a little like our praying that the Lord will convert unbelievers when we are not willing to let Him lead our lives. Perhaps He wants to these people to enter into His kingdom through the instrumentality of our lives. We must always remember to ask the Lord if there is any way in which He wants us to bring about the answer to our prayers for those in need.

What Will You Do for the Lord?

Perhaps you have yielded your life to the Lord Jesus Christ and are willing to go wherever He sends you. Perhaps you are a young person and you are waiting to see whether He will lead you to the mission field or into the ministry here at home. That's fine, but what are you doing now? Don't think, *In a few years I'll be a missionary*. Look around you now and see what you can do for the Lord through your church.

Perhaps you can help by teaching a Sunday School class or by assisting in the office or by doing some other work that the Lord has for you. Perhaps you could go and visit shut-ins of the church and read the Bible to them. Or maybe there are some improvements you could do at your church or some equipment that you could repair.

Don't forget that the office where you work or the campus where you attend school is a mission field. Be sure that your life helps others to want to know your Christ. Your home is another mission field. Do you act as a Christian should around the house? You don't have to wait until the Lord gives you a pulpit or a class to serve Him. Right now, you can continue the ministry of His Church that was begun so many years ago and continues through you today.

Daily Meditations

Sunday: A parable on service—Matthew 13:1-23

Monday: The call to service—John 4:35-38

Tuesday: An example of evangelism—Luke 10:1-12

Wednesday: The commission of Christ—Matthew 28:16-20

Thursday: A lesson in methods—Acts 8:29-35

Friday: The autobiography of a missionary—2 Corinthians 11:23-33

Saturday: The last words of a missionary—2 Timothy 4:1-8,16-18

30

THE SECOND COMING OF CHRIST

For the Lord Himself will descend from heaven with a shout, with the voice of an archangel, and with the trumpet of God. And the dead in Christ will rise first. Then we who are alive and remain shall be caught up together with them in the clouds to meet the Lord in the air. And thus we shall always be with the Lord.

1 THESSALONIANS 4:16-17

Have you ever been up in the beautiful mountains of northern California? The queen of them all is Mt. Shasta, a snow-covered peak the year round.

Early in the morning as you look out of the bus or car window, she can be seen rising in all her glory, colored by the rays of the sun. You are awed at the beauty of Mt. Shasta! On your ride, and from first one side and then the other she looms before you in all her grandeur and beauty with her snowcapped summit coming into plain view. On and on you ride, and at last you arrive at Shasta Springs. On the way, you had passed a myriad of lesser hills and mountains, but this majestic giant had loomed above them all and held your attention while the others had come and gone and left no impression whatever.

So it is with the mountain range of the world's history. There is one peak that seems to rise above them all in glory and splendor—the coming again of our Lord and Savior Jesus Christ, who will appear in power and great glory to rule this world and sway His scepter from sea to sea and to the uttermost part of the earth.

Before we begin, let us clearly understand that the Second Coming of our Lord has two distinct phases. First, Christ is to "descend from heaven with a shout, with the voice of an archangel, and with the trumpet of God" (1 Thess. 4:16). Two classes of people will meet Him there: "The dead in Christ will rise first. Then we who are alive and remain shall be caught up . . . to meet the Lord in the air" (v. 17). How long we are to stay in this heavenly place we are not told. It may be, as many believe, seven years.

Second, at the end of this period, the army of the raptured saints will return to the earth with our Lord and Savior. At this time, He will set up His kingdom, occupying the throne of His father David, according to many prophecies in the Old and New Testaments.

The Blessed Hope

In Old Testament times, the prophets often spoke of the coming of Christ, the Messiah. There seemed to be some contradiction in these prophecies, for in some places the prophet would speak of His coming as a suffering Savior (see Isa. 53:2-3), while others told of His coming in glory and great power (see Isa. 11:1-2). The Jews overlooked what the writers said about their Messiah coming *first* as a *lamb* to give His life. They looked for a king to sit on David's throne and restore them to the power of the nations.

And so, many of the Jews in Jesus' day refused to accept their lowly Messiah. They wanted a king, not a Savior (see John 1:11; 6:15). They had confused the prophecies in the Old Testament of the Messiah coming in power and glory with those of His first coming. Peter was not confused, however, for he says in 1 Peter 1:11, "He testified beforehand the sufferings of Christ and the glories that would follow." Notice that the glory of Christ is only shown *after* His death upon the cross.

Because this event was of such colossal proportions in comparison with all other events of history, the apostles could say 2,000 years ago that the Lord's coming was "at hand," just as when driving toward Shasta Springs you declare Mt. Shasta to be at hand, when in reality it is hours away. Doesn't it seem strange that this glorious truth of the Lord's return in power and majesty, of which the apostles so often spoke after His ascension, became hidden from people for many centuries? Only a little over 100 years ago did certain Bible students begin to emphasize this reappearance of our Lord and Savior.

When our Lord returns to this world to reign, it will become as He intended it to be. His throne will be established, all sin and unrighteousness will be overthrown, and He will be crowned King of kings and Lord of lords. No wonder we are told to look for His coming (see Titus 2:13), because the Lord might come at any moment. Sorrow will cease, and wars will be at an end. There will be no more death or sighing. Loved ones will be united. The desert shall bloom as the rose.

Where is our Lord and Savior now? What is He doing? If we turn to John 14:2-3, we hear the answer in His own words: "I go to prepare a place for you. And if I go and prepare a place for you, I will come again and receive you to Myself." First John 2:1 says, "We have an Advocate with the Father, Jesus Christ the righteous." Christ is in heaven at the right hand of the Father, making intercession for us now.

When the Lord Jesus ascended from the earth, two men appeared and said to the sorrowing disciples, "Men of Galilee, why do you stand gazing up into heaven? This same Jesus, who was taken up from you into heaven, will so come in like manner as you saw Him go into heaven" (Acts 1:11). I believe what the Bible says about Jesus Christ's coming the first time when it tells us that He would be born of a virgin in Bethlehem. Now, when Scripture tells me that He is coming again to receive me unto Himself, I believe that as well.

But questions naturally arise: How will He come? In what form will He come? When will He come?

How Will He Come?

When Jesus went from the Mount of Olives, He was taken up and a cloud received Him out of the disciples' sight (see Acts 1:9). Then, two angels appeared and told the disciples, "This same Jesus, who was taken up from you into heaven, will so come in like manner as you saw Him go into heaven" (v. 11).

Christ was in bodily form and visible to every eye. When He comes again, the Bible says, "every eye shall see Him" (Rev. 1:7). Kings shall cast their crowns before Him, and generals will forget their rank and authority. He will come in a spectacular manner—not as a babe—"for as the lightning comes from the east and flashes to the west, so also will the coming of the Son of Man be" (Matt. 24:27).

When Jesus comes, He will bring His saints and holy angels with Him. "When the Son of Man comes in His glory, and all the holy angels with Him, then He will sit on the throne of His glory" (Matt. 25:31). "Behold, the Lord comes with ten thousands of His saints" (Jude 14).

If we understand this language correctly, it means that Jesus will bring millions of His saints and the shining angels with Him when He returns. Think of the Son of God blazing as the noonday sun amid the shouts of the archangel and the trumpet of God, echoing and re-echoing through the corridors of heaven! People will either accept Him then as King of kings or cry in fear for the mountains and rocks to fall upon them and hide them from the wrath of the Lamb (see Rev. 6:16).

A cloud carried Jesus away, and He shall return with the clouds as a chariot. Just picture the Lord on the glorious clouds of sunset, within full view of the wondering multitudes of the earth. Or, if His appearing is at midnight, His presence will make it shine as the noonday sun.

Before He comes in such glory, He will take believers to be with Him. Paul says, "For the Lord Himself will descend from heaven with a shout, with the voice of an archangel, and with the trumpet of God. And the dead in Christ will rise first" (1 Thess. 4:16). This ought to be a blessed hope to us, because "everyone who has this hope in Him purifies himself, just as He is pure" (1 John 3:3).

When Will He Come?

A certain preacher tells this story about his own family when his children were small. They were spending the summer at their old farm in New England. One morning, the preacher had to tell his family that he had go to the city on important business. Observing their disappointment, he comforted them by adding that he was coming back again. He said, "I shall expect you to be at the station waiting for me."

The children had no sooner returned home from the train station than they began insisting that their mother wash them and comb their hair and put on clean clothes so that they might return to the station in the afternoon. Moreover, day after day, they repeated this until their father did return. Their mother said she never knew the children to be so interested in soap and water in all their lives as they were while waiting for their father's return.

If we are seeking a motive for holiness for every day and every hour, surely we have it in this warning: "Watch therefore, for you know neither the day nor the hour in which the Son of Man is coming" (Matt. 25:13). The very knowledge of our Lord's return should have a practical effect upon each of us. Here are some things that should be in our daily thought because of this glorious truth:

- *Salvation.* Christ delays His coming so that a few more may confess Him as Lord. "The Lord is not slack concerning His promise, as some count slackness, but is longsuffering toward us, not willing that any should perish but that all should come to repentance" (2 Pet. 3:9). Don't lose the opportunity of telling others about Christ.

- *Readiness.* Every morning, make yourself ready for the Lord's return, for He may come that day. Every night, ask yourself, *If Christ should come tonight, would I be ready?* Make it a rule to (1) do nothing that you would not like to be doing when the Lord Jesus comes; (2) go no place where you would not like to be found when the Lord Jesus comes; and (3) say nothing you would not like to be saying when the Lord Jesus comes.

- *Watchfulness.* "Blessed are those servants whom the master, when he comes, will find watching" (Luke 12:37). Are we wide awake and watching for our Lord? Would He find you watching?

- *Obedience.* "Behold, I am coming quickly! Blessed is he who keeps the words of the prophecy of this book" (Rev. 22:7). Are we living a life of obedience to the Lord?

- *Purity*. We shall grow like Him as we behold Him. "It has not yet been revealed what we shall be, but we know that when He is revealed, we shall be like Him, for we shall see Him as He is. And everyone who has this hope in Him purifies himself, just as He is pure" (1 John 3:2-3).

- *Comfort*. The blessed hope of the gospel is a comfort to us as we wait for our Lord's return. "Therefore comfort one another with these words. . . . comfort each other and edify one another, just as you also are doing" (1 Thess. 4:18; 5:11).

- *Hope*. "Now when these things begin to happen, look up and lift up your heads, because your redemption draws near" (Luke 21:28). Those who follow Christ look forward to the day of His return.

- *Joy*. "So it was, when Jesus returned, that the multitude welcomed Him, for they were all waiting for Him" (Luke 8:40). Do you look for a friend's coming with joy? Are you looking for Christ's coming with just as much anticipation?

In 1 Thessalonians 4:16-17, Paul tells us that the dead in Christ will be raised and those who are alive will be changed in a moment and be caught up to meet the Lord in the air! Christ's coming has been likened to a great magnet approaching a bed of iron and scraps. As it approaches, the iron begins to quiver and leap toward the magnet. The dirt and scraps remain. When Christ comes for believers, they, attracted by His power, will be "caught up" to meet Him in the air.

What Are the Signs of Christ's Coming?

Even during the time that our Lord was on this earth, people were asking the same three questions that are often asked today: "Tell us, when will these things be? And what will be the sign of Your coming, and of the end of the age?" (Matt. 24:3). The Bible tells us that there are going to be many events that shall take place before Christ's return, which will let us know that His return is near:

- *The Jewish return to Palestine.* In many places in Scripture, we are told that the Jews shall return to Israel, their ancient homeland, to occupy that land which was given to Abraham and his descendants. There is to be an end to the gentile rule in this world. The throne of David is to be occupied by Jesus Christ, the son of David, the son of Jesse.

- *God's favor returns to the Holy Land.* In the Old Testament, God told Jeremiah to speak to the people and tell them that because of their sin He would withhold from them the latter rain. This falls in the spring, for the Jewish year begins at the time of the autumn equinox, around September 21. For many years, the Holy Land was really a desert country, for the "former and the latter rains" had literally been withheld. Then the "former rains" started to fall. During the last few decades, the "latter rains" have begun falling, and today there is sufficient rainfall to bring forth abundant harvests. This is a sign of God's returning favor to this land, which has been the land of His promise for so many thousands of years.

- *The gospel will be preached to all the nations.* "This gospel of the kingdom will be preached in all the world as a witness to all the nations, and then the end will come" (Matt. 24:14). Every nation is to have its chance. Today, it can easily be shown that every nation has, at one time or another, heard the good news of salvation.

- *Men are lovers of pleasure rather than God.* In 2 Timothy 3:1-4, Paul gives us a glimpse of how people will be in the last days: "In the last days perilous times will come: For men will be lovers of themselves, lovers of money, boasters, proud, blasphemers, disobedient to parents, unthankful, unholy, unloving, unforgiving, slanderers, without self-control, brutal, despisers of good, traitors, headstrong, haughty, lovers of pleasure rather than lovers of God." You will find this convincing and a perfect description of many professing Christians today.

- *The are wars and rumors of wars.* In Matthew 24:6-7, Christ told His disciples of several signs that would indicate the coming of the last days: "You will hear of wars and rumors of wars. . . . For nation will rise against nation, and kingdom against kingdom. And there will be famines, pestilences, and earthquakes in various places."

- *False teachers rise up and deceive many.* "Then many false prophets will rise up and deceive many" (Matt. 24:11). This is the reason why we should know the voice of our Shepherd, by studying the Word of God, so that we are not deceived by any false teaching. "The sheep follow [the shepherd], for they know his voice. Yet they will by no means follow a stranger, but will flee from him, for they do not know the voice of strangers."

No one knows the day or the hour of Christ's return, and yet Jesus distinctly tells us not to be ignorant. We know that spring is approaching when we see the leaves bursting forth on the boughs of the tree. When the robins begin to sing and the flowers appear, we know that spring is at hand. As Christians, we should be watching for the signs of our Lord's return and look forward to that day with joy.

The Blessed Hope of the Church

The Second Coming of our Lord is referred to 318 times in the New Testament, and in almost every prediction in the Old Testament, He is spoken of as One who is coming to reign and sit upon the throne of David (see Isa. 9:6-7). What does all this wonderful truth mean to the Church of Jesus Christ, the invisible building that He is now erecting, that is composed of those who believe in Him and are looking for His return?

The Church of Jesus Christ is not a building for this earth alone. Its place is not here, but in heaven. The head, the risen Christ, is in glory, and all the members of His body must be united to the head. Some people who do not love the Lord speak of His second coming as "the end of the world." But for Christians, it is the beginning of a new relationship and the climax of God's purpose for the Church. When this begins, there will be no more darkness, nor death, nor sighing, nor crying.

What a wonderful hope the Lord has given us in this promise of His return. The Lord has promised to come for His Church and to take us out of this world before His wrath falls upon it. Before the tribulation begins on Earth, the Lord will take away His own children to be with Him forever.

With such a wonderful promise, we should be alert to do the work of the Lord in spreading His gospel to all the world so that others may enter into the blessed promise. How many people have you told about Christ this week? How much are you eagerly watching for the Lord's return? Are you sure that you have accepted Christ as your Savior so that you will be ready when He does come?

Daily Meditations

Sunday: The signs of His coming—Matthew 24:3-14
Monday: The course of this age—Luke 21:8-19
Tuesday: The times and seasons—1 Thessalonians 5:1-11
Wednesday: The blessed comfort—1 Thessalonians 4:13-18
Thursday: The blessed hope—John 14:1-3; Philippians 3:20-21; Titus 2:13
Friday: A reward—2 Timothy 4:1-8
Saturday: The time of His coming—Matthew 24:36-51

31

The Rule of the Antichrist

And then shall that Wicked be revealed, whom the Lord shall consume with the spirit of His mouth, and shall destroy with the brightness of His coming.
2 Thessalonians 2:8

A man was traveling in Iowa, and a friend said to him, "We are about half a mile from one of the largest dams in our country. Would you like to see it?"

The man agreed, passes were secured, and they visited the great Keokuk Dam, which spans the Mississippi. They were told of the tons and tons of cement that went into its construction. As they came to where the waters were dammed back by a vast concrete wall one mile long, the visitor asked, "How deep is it here?"

"Forty-nine feet," he was told.

"How far back do the waters extend?"

"Fifty-four miles," was the answer.

Millions and millions of gallons of water were pushing against the dam, trying to get through. On the other side was the bare riverbed. As they stood there taking in the scene, the man's imagination began to work. He thought, *Suppose some gigantic hand reached down and lifted that dam bodily from its foundation. What a catastrophe! Fifty-four miles of water, rushing and leaping, carrying death and destruction in its wake; nothing able to withstand it; nothing able to deter its course!*

Then the thought came to the visitor: *One of these days something like that is going to occur when the Lord Jesus Christ takes out of the world the only thing that is hindering and restraining all the powers of sin. When every man and woman who knows the Lord Jesus is instantly taken, "then the lawless one will be revealed, whom the Lord will consume with the breath of His mouth and destroy with the brightness of His coming"* (2 Thess. 2:8).

I wonder if we realize what a wicked world we are living in! Just to scan the headlines of almost any morning's paper or watch a news telecast will make your blood run cold. Murders! Accidents! Suicides! Strikes! Riots! Wars! Violence on campuses! Drunkenness! Drug addiction! Sin of every description! Sorrow without end! Everything seems wrong. Political troubles, financial depressions, domestic difficulties, children rising against parents and parents rising against their children.

The one great agent for righteousness in the world that seems to be holding back these tides of evil is the Church of Jesus Christ. The blessed hope of the Church, as we have learned, is the coming of the Lord Jesus Christ for His own. It is then that God's completed "building," His Church, will be translated–that is, be caught up into heaven "to meet the Lord in the air."

The Church in the world is like a dam that holds back a great body of water. Some years ago in California a great dam broke, and the next morning the papers were filled with the pictures and stories of the terrible destruction that the water had caused when it suddenly rushed over the land below. Bridges had been washed out, homes had been carried away, trees had been uprooted, and huge boulders had been swept along that acted as battering rams to beat down anything in their path.

When the Church is taken, the light of the world and the salt of the earth shall be removed. As Paul says in 1 Thessalonians 2:8, the withholding power will be taken away, and then "the lawless one"—the devil's superman, the antichrist—shall appear. But who is this "antichrist"?

Daniel Describes the Antichrist

In Daniel 11:36, we read, "Then the king shall do according to his own will: he shall exalt and magnify himself above every god, shall speak blasphemies against the God of gods, and shall prosper." This verse of Scripture represents a life-size picture of a man who has not yet appeared but who will one day show himself. He will be a man more powerful than Napoleon and greater than Alexander—a world ruler whose like the earth has never seen. The devil will give him power. He will not be a king, but, as Daniel says, the king.

We know that the devil is mighty. He gave the magicians of Egypt power to imitate everything that Moses did by God's help in the presence of Pharaoh (see Exod. 7:11). So this antichrist, to whom the devil will give his power, will be able to imitate the miracles of God, "to deceive, if possible, even the elect" (Matt. 24:24). But remember, the devil will exercise power only so long as God permits. One day the Lord Jesus Christ will rob Satan and his followers of all their power.

As soon as the Church is taken, this dreadful being will become the political ruler of all the nations—a world dictator. The Bible gives us a portrait of him, and we catch glimpses of him all through the Scriptures. Everyone who has rebelled against God—from Cain down through the ages—foreshadows the coming of the antichrist who will take his place as world ruler after the translation of God's people.

Notice in Daniel 11:36 that the antichrist "shall do according to his own will." Now, look at the "I wills" of Lucifer given in Isaiah 14:13-14: "I will ascend into heaven, I will exalt my throne above the stars of God; I will also sit on the mount of the congregation on the farthest sides of the north; I will ascend above the heights of the clouds, I will be like the Most High." Christ came to do the will of the Father in heaven (see John 6:38). The antichrist shall do according to his own will.

Remember, it was self-will that drove the devil out of heaven. It was self-will that brought the curse on Adam. The Jews would not come to Christ so that they might have life. The root of all unbelief is found in self-will. When God captures our will, He has us all. The antichrist *shall exalt himself.* How different this is from Jesus Christ! He humbled Himself, and God highly exalted Him far above all principalities and powers.

The god of the antichrist will be the "god of forces." How men worship force and power today! That seems to be their god. "Might makes right" seems to be the slogan.

The antichrist will honor with gold and silver and precious stones those who acknowledge him. It will pay to honor this great man. Those who do so will become rich indeed. They will receive glory and worldly honors. At first, his power will be great.

The antichrist will offer the nations of the world a solution for all their troubles. He will tell them how to solve their problems of wars and rumors of wars. The people will be deceived by him and will believe his "great and swelling words," and they will gladly accept him as dictator of world affairs. This man, unlike the kings we know about, will doubtless be elected by the people. He will usurp authority from the rightful rulers and take his place by sheer force of personality.

In Daniel 11, we are told that the antichrist shall exalt himself and shall honor the god of forces. He will demand the worship of himself. There will be neither buying nor selling in business transactions unless people have received "the mark of the beast" (see Rev. 13:16-17). Everyone must wear some outward sign to indicate his or her allegiance to this world ruler.

"He shall come in peaceably, and seize the kingdom by intrigue" (Dan. 11:21). The world will think that the antichrist is the Prince of Peace for whom they have long been waiting. He will make a covenant with the high priest of Israel, for the Jews will have reestablished their ancient religion in Jerusalem with the rebuilding of the Temple. But the antichrist shall forsake that agreement and set himself up in the most holy place, to be worshiped as God. This is "the abomination of desolation" in the Holy of Holies, spoken of by Daniel and also in Matthew (see Dan. 11:31; Matt. 24:15).

The Temple and the False Prophet

The historic site of the Temple has been sacred for centuries. The first time we hear of it in Genesis 22:2, it is called Mount Moriah. This was the sacred spot upon which Abraham went to offer his son Isaac. It was a huge flat stone, which for generations was used for a threshing floor. It finally came into the possession of a man named Araunah.

David came to this man and made him an offer to buy this spot upon which to erect an altar to the Lord, for a great plague had come upon the people (see 2 Sam. 24). Later, David's son Solomon built his wonderful Temple upon this very spot. This marvelous building, which would have cost billions of dollars today, was the most beautiful building that man had ever constructed.

Centuries later, after Solomon's Temple was destroyed, Herod rebuilt the Temple upon the very same site. It is interesting to note that Mount Calvary, lying outside of Jerusalem, was no doubt the northern end of Mount Moriah, which was cut through in building the new Temple. Hence, the cross stood on the same mount as did the Temple and the altar of sacrifice.

Jesus wept over Jerusalem and prophesied her capture and the destruction of Herod's Temple (see Luke 21:20-24). This event occurred 40 years later in A.D. 70 during the Jewish revolt against the Roman authorities. Not one stone of the Temple was left remaining upon one another.

Besides a world dictator, a great false prophet will also arise. He will show himself in Israel's land, Palestine, and will take a very prominent part in the Temple, the place of worship for the Jewish people. The false prophet will head up the apostasy that will be sweeping over all the world. "Apostasy" means a departure from the truth of God as revealed in His Word. You hear of "infidelity" and "atheism" and "modernism"—anything that is not the absolute truth.

The false prophet will lead many—the Jews especially—away from God, for even up to this time they will have been keeping their feasts, year in and year out, worshiping God under the Law. They will think this false prophet is the leader whom they have been looking for, and that he and the antichrist have come to help them. How mistaken and deceived they will be! Every covenant the antichrist and the false prophet make with them will be broken.

There are many so-called Christians today who do not believe that Jesus Christ is God or that His death and the shedding of His blood are necessary for our salvation. We are forbidden in the Scriptures to have any fellowship with such unbelief. "For many deceivers have gone out into the world who do not confess Jesus Christ as coming in the flesh. This is a deceiver and an antichrist. Look to yourselves, that we do not lose those things we worked for, but that we may receive a full reward" (2 John 1:7-11).

Paul Describes the Antichrist

In 2 Thessalonians 2:1-12, Paul gives us a picture of the world just before the Lord returns. He says that there will be a great "falling away" from the faith, or "apostasy." Many people speculate as to the interpretation of this passage, but if language means anything, it gives us a very vivid picture.

Paul says that when Christ comes, He will find "the man of sin," commonly known as the antichrist, carrying on his satanic operations and actually being worshiped in God's Temple as God Himself. This antichrist is opposed to everything Christlike (as his name signifies, he is "anti-Christ"). We have already mentioned the fact that since the very beginning there has always been a spirit in this world working against Christ, but in this passage Paul is now speaking of a particular person whom he calls "the man of sin." He is Satan's masterpiece, as Christ is God's masterpiece.

When the Lord Jesus Christ was on the earth, He claimed to be God manifest in the flesh; and He is God. Now, the antichrist will deny God and set himself up as God, and the people will be deceived and actually worship him. John describes this in Revelation 13.

We wonder how people can be so foolish as to believe this wicked creature, for the Bible tells us plainly that Jesus is coming back as He went into heaven (see Acts 1:11). Paul says, "I do not want you to be ignorant, brethren" (1 Thess. 4:13). If we study the Bible, we need never be taken in by any fake doctrine or false prophet.

It would seem that when such a stupendous event takes place as the removal of the Church—the taking away of every real Christian from the world—that the people who are left will be much concerned. It is possible that much of the remaining world would be bowing their knee to our Lord out of fear, unless the devil should produce a substitute. Even as it is, many will turn to Christ in spite of the appearance of the antichrist and will refuse the mark of the beast. Remember that Satan will start out with a desire not to be a fiend but to be like the most high God Himself.

We believe that Satan's only chance of doing this will be after the rapture of the Church; that is the reason he sends the antichrist in the last days. It would seem that the Jews will at first believe that the antichrist is their Messiah. Remember, this "man of sin" makes his entrance into the world when all the light of God has been taken away and the world is left in spiritual darkness and hopeless confusion.

Through the antichrist, Satan makes his last convulsive effort to gain the power for which he forfeited his high place in heaven. He has always wanted to have dominion and power over people and the homage and worship of humankind. As the Gospels relate, He even tried to persuade Jesus Christ to worship him! Now, Paul tells us that the antichrist will sit in the Temple of God and set himself forth as God.

If we go through the Bible and itemize the characteristics of this antichrist, we find that there are a number of things we know about him:

- He is a gentile, for he arises from the sea (see Rev. 13:1), and the sea represents gentile nations (see Rev. 17:15).
- He is worshiped by all nations (see Rev. 13:8).
- He shall come in peace (seed Dan. 11:21).
- People will follow him willingly (see Rev. 17:13).
- He rules with absolute authority (see Dan. 11:36).
- He sets himself up as God (see 2 Thess. 2:4).
- He makes war against the saints (see Rev. 13:7).
- His power will come to an end by the direct intervention of Christ (see Rev. 19:11).
- He is judged and thrown into the lake of fire (see Rev. 19:20).

Those of us who are Christians will never see the antichrist, for we will have been taken out of this world when Christ comes for His Church. But still, there is a need for us to realize that although we will not see *the* antichrist, we do see *many* antichrists in the world today who are pictures of what he will be like.

The Spirit of the Antichrist

In 1 John 4:1, the apostle tells us that we are not to believe every spirit but we are to try the spirits. This is a warning to us that not everyone who talks about religious things is necessarily telling the truth. Many cults talk about the Bible and God, but they do not speak the truth. Thus, we, as Christians, are to listen carefully to what is said falsely using the name "Christianity" so that we will not be fooled.

In 2 John 4:1, the apostle tells us how we can know the truth: "By this you know the Spirit of God: Every spirit that confesses that Jesus Christ has come in the flesh is of God." This is the test: Do the people who teach us believe that Jesus Christ is God, that He came to Earth in the form of man but without sin, and that He redeemed us unto Himself by His death and resurrection? The antichrist, when he comes, will not believe this. He will present himself as God and will deny the deity of our Lord Jesus Christ. Those who do not believe these facts about Christ are antichrists. As John states, "Every spirit that does not confess that Jesus Christ has come in the flesh is not of God. And this is the spirit of the Antichrist, which you have heard was coming, and is now already in the world" (v. 3).

We must be careful that we are not fooled. It is important for us to know who the Lord Jesus Christ is. He is God, the eternal God, and He is our Savior.

It is important to guard now against the antichrists in the world. We must be on guard to be sure that we will not be deceived by the talk of some who claim to be Christians but who deny the deity of Christ. After the Christians are gone from the world, the people will be fooled by the antichrist. Be sure that you are not fooled by the little antichrists that are in the world today.

Daily Meditations

Sunday: The man of sin—2 Thessalonians 2:1-12

Monday: The antichrist—Revelation 13:1-10

Tuesday: The false prophet—Revelation 13:11-18

Wednesday: Many antichrists—1 John 2:18-24

Thursday: The test for truth—1 John 4:1-6

Friday: Dangerous fellowship—2 John 1:7-11

Saturday: The real ruler—Revelation 19:11-16

32

THE GREAT TRIBULATION

For then there will be great tribulation, such as has not been since the beginning of the world until this time, no, nor ever shall be.
MATTHEW 24:21

As we have seen, when this part of God's plan for the future begins to unfold, the Lord will first of all come for His Church and take the Christians to be with Him. This is a swift, silent coming, of which the rest of the world will be unaware. Only the Christians will be affected by it. They will be taken from this world to be forever with the Lord.

Also as we discussed, when the Church has been taken out of the world, the hindrance to the forces of evil is removed and the Antichrist is revealed (see 2 Thess. 2:7). The antichrist will be an imitation of the true Christ that Satan will bring into power. Remember, he comes in peace but brings war. He comes with a message of freedom but puts his followers in bondage. Many people are fooled by his words and follow after him, but he will not be able to do any good thing for them. "For then there will be great tribulation, such as has not been since the beginning of the world until this time, no, nor ever shall be. And unless those days were shortened, no flesh would be saved" (Matt. 24:21-22).

There will be such a time as the great tribulation, for these are the very words of our Lord Jesus Christ. When He spoke in His messages to the seven churches in Revelation, He mentioned "the hour of trial" (see Rev. 3:10). On the Lord's authority, we believe that the greatest tribulation that will ever come upon the world will fall just before His coming in glory.

The Rapture of the Church

In a previous chapter, we referred to the time when the Lord is going to return to take His Church out of the world. This event is known among Bible students as "the rapture," and is a secret "catching away." The Lord describes it by saying that He will come "as a thief in the night."

In Luke 17:34-36, Jesus also says, "I tell you, in that night there will be two men in one bed: the one will be taken and the other will be left. Two women will be grinding together: the one will be taken and the other left. Two men will be in the field: the one will be taken and the other left." You will note that these events naturally would happen at different times of the day–morning, noon and night. Scholars take this to mean that His coming will be visible around the whole earth at the same time. The Lord then adds, "Therefore you also be ready, for the Son of Man is coming at an hour you do not expect" (Matt. 24:44).

This secret rapture will be followed by a time of fellowship with our Lord, before His final appearance in the earth with power and great glory. During this time, the children of the Lord will be rewarded for their deeds. Believers will not be judged for their sins, but only judged so that they might receive their crown and rewards. The judgment of the believers' sin was made on the cross when Jesus bore the sin of the whole world in His own body.

Then the believers will be appointed to various posts of usefulness in Christ's kingdom that is to be set up on the earth. It is during this wonderful time of rejoicing in heaven with Christ that the great tribulation will be raging on the earth. This tribulation will be directed by the devil himself, who has been cast down to earth (see Rev. 12:7-12).

Stop and think of all the terrible things that have happened in the world since its beginning. Remember the Flood during the time of Noah. Think of the fall of Jerusalem under Titus in A.D. 70, when the suffering of the Jewish people was indescribable. It is recorded that during the struggle, a mother, desperate with hunger, ate her own son, and a million inhabitants died in the siege.

Then there was the Black Plague, which swept through Europe in the Middle Ages and almost depopulated London in 1665. The great flu epidemic in the United States, in 1918, brought death to more people than those who perished in World War I. World War II and other conflicts around the world then followed, along with awful earthquakes, tidal waves and volcanic eruptions. Yet all of these will not compare with the events of the great tribulation. We shudder and our brains actually dizzy at the description.

The book of Revelation, chapter 6, gives us the picture of this terrible time. During these days, God will allow sin to work out its tragic results. God's hand will be lifted from man and beast. The earth will be filled with war, hunger, famine and pestilence. Isaiah 24:20 also describes this time: "The earth shall reel to and fro like a drunkard . . . its transgression shall be heavy upon it, and it will fall, and not rise again." Think of the great civilization built up by humans falling with a crash! Daniel 12:1 says of this horrible event, "And there shall be a time of trouble, such as never was since there was a nation."

Sin Must Be Dealt With

Let us find out the purpose of this terrible punishment. The prophet Isaiah writes, "For behold, the LORD comes out of His place to punish the inhabitants of the earth for their iniquity; the earth will also disclose her blood, and will no more cover her slain" (26:21). Keep in mind that the great tribulation is a chastisement from the Lord because people have disobeyed His laws. His laws are holy and righteous and good and just, and the nations of the earth have trodden them under foot. God is love, but He is also just.

We cannot blame God for what people have brought upon themselves. Humans will reap what they themselves have sown. Sin must be dealt with–both the sin of the individual and the sin of nations. There are only two ways, the Bible tells us, of dealing with sin: Either people confess their sins and know that He is faithful and just to forgive, or they are punished. The blood washes white, but never whitewashes. The anguish and horror of the tribulation will be the result of sin: human ambition, unbelief, hatred and cruelty.

The word "tribulation" itself comes from the Latin word *tribulum,* which means a flail, an instrument used in antiquity for beating out the grains of wheat from straw. It is a process of purification for removing the chaff from the wheat, much like the process of refining gold from dross. There are some kinds of impurities that cannot be washed out; they must be flailed out or burned out. You cannot wash the dross out of gold, as this separation requires a furnace. So, through the tribulation, God is going to beat out sin and show His judgment upon the earth.

The nations of the earth have not repented and confessed their sins, nor will they do so in the future. They do not think that they need to because they believe that they are rich and great. Therefore, God must punish them according to their sins. You remember that Jonah was sent to tell the wicked people in the city of Nineveh to repent of their sins or in 40 days the city would be destroyed. What did they do? "So the people of Nineveh believed God, proclaimed a fast, and put on sackcloth, from the greatest to the least of them" (Jon. 3:5). Did God hear their cry? "Then God saw their works, that they turned from their evil way; and God relented from the disaster that He had said He would bring upon them, and He did not do it" (v. 10).

Do you think that the Lord would do any less for the nations of the world today if they would repent? What did He do to the children of Israel because they did not heed their prophets? He allowed them to be carried into captivity by the Assyrians. The kingdom of Judah was captured later by Babylon (see 2 Kings 17: 25).

What will happen to the Jews, God's people, after the Church is taken away? Jeremiah 30:7 states, "Alas! For that day is great, so that none is like it; and it is the time of Jacob's trouble, but he shall be saved out of it." The time of terrible suffering is to follow. The whole of Jeremiah 30 is a most illuminating commentary upon the last days, and it ends with the phrase, "In the latter days you will understand this" (Jer. 30:24, *ESV*). How true!

Remember, God is "merciful and gracious, slow to anger, and abounding in mercy" (Ps. 103:8), but the time is coming when He will make a settlement with the nations (see Jer. 25:15-17). The nations have sown to the wind; the whirlwind will come.

We suggested in the last chapter that all the terrible and sinful passions of the human race will go unbridled and unpunished after the Church is taken away. Crime will run rampant; the finer feelings of civilized men and women will become dull. Although this day is one of reckoning, it will not be the final judgment. God will deal with men as individuals in the judgment day, but in the great tribulation He will deal with the nations. God created humans as free moral agents. They have been permitted to break all of God's laws with impunity. This will all come to an end, and a settlement will be made.

Two Witnesses

There will be one bright day during this terrible time of tribulation. Hell will be turned loose, but God will not forget the world. He will not leave it without a witness, for He will send two righteous men.

Some have speculated that these two witnesses might be Moses and the prophet Elijah who, you remember, left this world without dying (see 2 Kings 2:11). These two men will declare the love and justice of God in the midst of the tribulation. "I will give power to my two witnesses, and they will prophesy one thousand two hundred and sixty days, clothed in sackcloth. These are the two olive trees and the two lampstands standing before the God of the earth" (Rev. 11:3-4). Such power is given to these two men that "if anyone wants to harm them, fire proceeds from their mouth and devours their enemies" (v. 5).

Who do you suppose will seek salvation at such a time as this? No doubt there will be people on the earth who had just put off accepting Jesus Christ as their Lord and Savior, and when all these terrible things come upon the world, like the children of Israel in slavery, they will cry unto the Lord. He will hear their cry, for salvation is never beyond the reach of anyone who really seeks it. Nevertheless, even those who cry for salvation at that time must go through the great tribulation (see Rev. 7:13-14).

There will be such a hatred of God at this time that anyone who dares to call upon His name will lose his life. Martyrdom will be the result of taking a stand for Christ during the tribulation. The "beast," the antichrist who is Satan's ruler, will be the master of all these murderous ceremonies. "I saw a beast rising up out of the sea, having seven heads and ten horns, and on his horns ten crowns, and on his heads a blasphemous name. . . . He was granted power to give breath to the image of the beast, that the image of the beast should both speak and cause as many as would not worship the image of the beast to be killed" (Rev. 13:1,15).

What a terrible time this will be! If people would only believe God's Word now and accept Him as their personal Savior, they could escape all this awful experience that is coming upon the earth. No wonder the writer of Hebrews says, "Today, if you will hear His voice, do not harden your hearts as in the rebellion" (Heb. 3:15)!

What Should We Be Doing?

When the time of the tribulation comes, the day of grace will then be over. Then it will be the day of wrath. We deserve punishment right now, but God's grace (unmerited favor) is holding the punishment back and giving man every chance to turn to Christ.

As we think about the coming of the great tribulation and the only way of escape, does it not behoove us to examine ourselves before the Lord? All who escape must be washed in the blood of the Lamb and be ready for His coming. When He comes as a thief, there will be no time to pray for forgiveness. This must be done now.

The first thing that we certainly must do in the light of this terrible time that is coming is to take a good look at ourselves. We must ask ourselves if we are sure that we will not have to go through the tribulation. There is only one way that we can be sure of this, and that is by knowing that we belong to the Lord Jesus Christ.

When you are sure of your own destiny, think about the souls of your friends. How many people do you know who are not Christians? What about your own family? What about your friends at school or the people at your workplace? What about the people who live around you? What have you done to introduce them to the Lord Jesus Christ?

If someone gave us a ticket to some place in this world that we have been wanting to go, and if this person told us that all of our expenses were paid and that the trip was ours, could you imagine not telling anybody about it? We could hardly wait to begin telling the wonderful thing that was going to happen to us. But for some reason, we are more likely to keep the gift of Christ to ourselves. He has given us a free ticket to heaven, all of our expenses are paid, and we are to spend eternity with Him in a place that the God who made all things has prepared for us. What's more, salvation was expensive—it cost Him His life on a cross!

There is still more! The Lord has not only given us an access to heaven but also provided it for all of our friends. Yet we keep the news to ourselves. Suppose, along with that vacation that person told us about, that we were also told that he would give us an all-expense-paid trip to anyone else who wanted it. We would go about telling all our friends where they could meet this benefactor. We would want to take all of them with us.

Why, do you suppose, do we then not want to take them with us to heaven? There is only one way that people are to find out about that which the Lord Jesus Christ has provided for them, and that is when you and I tell them.

We have been learning about the terrible events that are going to happen to everyone who is left here on Earth after the Lord has taken His children to be with Him. So you see, there is a double reason to tell everyone we know about the Lord. We have a wonderful salvation story to tell and eternal life in Christ to offer as a gift from God, and we also have the only means by which they can escape the wrath of God that is sure to come upon a disobedient world.

Daily Meditations

Sunday: Daniel's description of the antichrist—Daniel 11:36-45

Monday: The great tribulation—Psalm 2:5; Jeremiah 30:7; Daniel 12:1

Tuesday: The dragon cast down—Revelation 12:7-12

Wednesday: The day of the Lord—Joel 2:1-10

Thursday: The doom of the antichrist and the devil—Revelation 19:20; 20:1-3

Friday: Collapse of civilization—Revelation 6:12-17

Saturday: The judgment of the nations—Zechariah 14:1-9; Matthew 25:31-46

33

The Battle of Armageddon

For they are spirits of demons, performing signs, which go out to the kings of the earth and of the whole world, to gather them to the battle of that great day of God Almighty. And they gathered them together to the place called in Hebrew, Armageddon.

Revelation 16:14,16

It is very evident that the people in the world are becoming more and more defiant of God's authority. The world is becoming very proud and overconfident of its own genius and strength. People feel that they are entirely sufficient unto themselves and that they do not need God. This blasphemous challenge to God's authority is going to come to a head in a last terrible struggle called the battle of Armageddon.

God has often given divine warnings regarding this most awful tragedy of the ages. In Isaiah 34, we find one such description of this day in which the wrath of Almighty God is to come upon humankind: "The indignation of the Lord is against all nations, and His fury against all their armies; He has utterly destroyed them, He has given them over to the slaughter.

Also their slain shall be thrown out; their stench shall rise from their corpses, and the mountains shall be melted with their blood" (vv. 2-3).

As the terrible description goes on, the passage says that all this is to happen in "the day of the LORD's vengeance" (v. 8). As we read what Isaiah says, we see that it all belongs to the time of the Lord's appearing as described in Revelation 19.

The Day of Divine Wrath

There are other descriptions, which are no less terrible, of what is to come upon the world at this time. For the people of the earth, it is to be the day of divine wrath. For more than 2,000 years, God has been offering salvation full and free through His Son to all people, but God's invitation to the marriage feast of His Son has been spurned and rejected. People harden their hearts, and the nations of the earth will gather together with the beast to make war against God's anointed One.

There have been "wars and rumors of wars," but Armageddon is to be the last battle when Jesus Christ, who was one time rejected as King, shall come in glory and completely overthrow His enemies who will be drawn up in battle array against Him. The head of this great army will be none other than the antichrist, of whom we have been studying in the last two chapters.

We have already seen great gatherings of world armies in our modern conflicts, but this gathering will be greater still. It will not be any earthly ruler that will bring together so vast a combination. Satan, we are told, will be the organizer behind this mighty movement. He has great power over men and can gather a mighty army. The beast, or the antichrist, will be the devil's commander-in-chief. The nations will all be there, gathered in one place, to fight against God and His anointed One. *There will be no mercy.* The day of grace will be past.

"Then the beast was captured, and with him the false prophet who worked signs in his presence" (Rev. 19:20). Their day is over. They are to be cast into the lake of fire. *There is a lake of fire,* but remember, it is prepared for the devil and his angels.

Those who are led by the beast are all dead. The strength and the pride of the greatest armies the world has ever known are gone. They are slain, but not by a sword. They are slain by the sword out of the mouth of Him that sat upon the white horse (see Rev. 19:11,15). This will be the doom of all who refuse the mercy of a loving God and Father. After this, there will only be judgment (see Ps. 2:1-4,9; Ezek. 38:1-6,22-23; Zech. 14:1-3; Rev. 16:13-16; 19:11-19).

Where, When and How?

There is much guesswork about where, when and how this battle will be fought. Many people think the battle of Armageddon only symbolizes a great final struggle between good and evil. However, Armageddon is to be a real battle, with God on one side and Satan and his host and his army of 200 million out of the nations on the other (see Rev. 9:16). The devil is going to make his last attempt to become the ruler of the world.

Armageddon is a place that can be located as definitely as New York or London or Los Angeles. From the earliest days, this plain of Esdraelon was a famous battlefield for the Assyrians and Egyptians. Barak and Deborah won a victory there over the Canaanites (see Judg. 4–5). Gideon fought his great battle with the Midianites at this place (see Judg. 7). It was also here that King Saul fought his last battle and was slain (see 1 Sam. 31:8), Ahaziah was slain by Jehu (see 2 Kings 9:27), and Josiah was slain during an Egyptian invasion (see 2 Kings 23:29-30). Judas Maccabeus put to flight the pagan hosts on this plain and set the poor stricken city of Jerusalem free. The Crusaders warred with the Mohammedan forces on this battlefield. In more modern times, Napoleon stood at this spot before the battle that would thwart his attempt to conquer the East and rebuild the great Roman Empire.

The word "Armageddon" means "Hill of Megiddo" or "Mount of Slaughter." The field is west of the river Jordan, just south of Mt. Carmel, and about 40 miles north of Jerusalem. It covers a piece of ground triangular in shape, about 20 miles by 15 miles by 15 miles. It is a fertile plain filled with vineyards and orchards. Wheat, corn, barley and alfalfa fields are everywhere. In the springtime it is covered with flowers, like the rose of Sharon and the lily of the valley so often mentioned by the poets of the Bible.

All of these facts about Armageddon in the past make it very interesting. Remember that Canaanites, Philistines, Jews, Egyptians, Greeks, Romans, Moslems and Christians, down to our very own day, have fought, bled and died on this historic ground. Now we are wondering what the future will bring forth. Many people thought that the World War of 1914-1918 was the Armageddon prophesied in Scripture. But Bible students knew that it could not possibly be, for Armageddon was not to have its center around Berlin or Paris or London, but Jerusalem. Furthermore, this last great battle will not be fought until the world ruler, the antichrist, appears and the Church of Jesus Christ has been taken away.

Many newspapermen called the first World War "Armageddon." That name was associated with the most terrible conflict the world could imagine, and people thought, as they saw almost the whole world thrown into the holocaust of war followed by plagues and famine, that this surely must be the realization of this prophecy. People were told that this was a "war to end wars," not knowing, poor things, that an even greater world war would soon follow. There will never be lasting peace on this earth until the Prince of Peace Himself sits on the throne of the world empire.

Revelation 9:16 tells us that 200 million soldiers will be mobilized at Armageddon under satanic leadership. Many people wonder how so great an army can be mobilized in so small an area, but remember the battle line will extend from Esdraelon down to Bozrah (see Rev. 19:21). They will all gather around the land of Palestine—from the north, the south, the east and the west—and the city of Jerusalem will be like a nut in a nutcracker. God has said that in that day, all the armies of the earth shall be gathered around this city (see Zech. 14:1-2).

The influence and power of Satan will be beyond imagination during those "last days." The antichrist will be able to rally this great worldwide army to do his bidding. He will stir up hatred for God and blasphemy against His Son. Wickedness will envelop the earth and lead to Satan-worship. Finally, Satan's ambitions and rebellion against God will dare him to challenge Almighty God and His power. And on that day, "He who sits upon the heavens shall laugh; the LORD shall hold them in derision" (Ps. 2:4).

Who Shall Wear the Crown?

This last great war is to be fought for world supremacy. Armageddon will decide who shall wear the crown, Christ or the antichrist. Although the nations of the world will be lined up, they will be led by the God-defying, devil-incarnated antichrist. This superhuman leader will dare to meet in battle array the forces of Jesus Christ, who is to descend from heaven. The artillery will be the fire of divine wrath, proceeding from the presence of Him who comes to wrest the scepter of universal empire from the usurper-prince. His very presence will consume all the nations of the earth and their leadership.

History has been filled with many religious wars. But this is to be a new kind of religious war. It will be a mobilization of all false religions and all political powers under the leadership of this political genius, the antichrist, who claims the worship of humanity and offers himself to be worshiped as God.

We must comprehend the purpose of this final conflict. The earthly participants will be carrying out Satan's final scheme for world control. The devil has never given up his idea of someday conquering this world once for all. What conceit! We think he is very foolish, knowing (as he doubtless does) the numberless legions of the hosts of heaven, but he seems determined to make this one last attempt. We have seen his spirit in men in our own day—dictators who have imagined they could conquer the world. Some have actually tried it, with what awful results, not only to themselves and their countries but also to every other nation of the globe!

We do not have to look only at rulers to find such egotism. Individuals by the scores—yes, by the thousands—think that they can live and run their own lives in open defiance of the Lord God of the universe. When the time of judgment comes, they will realize just how false their assumptions have been.

Great Resources

We may wonder why tiny Israel is to be the center of this great conflict. If there is one thing the world wants, it is money and the resources that make money. We have heard of the astounding riches of the Dead Sea. It seems as if God has been pouring into that small body of water the wealth of the earth for centuries upon centuries so that His people might use it in the last days.

The Jews were always historically the richest people of the world; they were the bankers of the nations. When they finally gather in Israel, every nation of the world will be compelled to acknowledge Jerusalem as the capital city of the world, in business and in religion. God has foretold that the armies of the earth will in that day be brought around Jerusalem. "Behold, the day of the LORD is coming, and your spoil will be divided in your midst. For I will gather all the nations to battle against Jerusalem" (Zech. 14:1-2).

Heaven will then take part in the struggle, and "at that time Michael shall stand up . . . and there shall be a time of trouble, such as never was" (Dan. 12:1). And again, "Then the LORD will go forth and fight against those nations, as He fights in the day of battle. And in that day His feet will stand on the Mount of Olives, which faces Jerusalem on the east" (Zech. 14:3-4). Jehovah shall be made the King of the whole earth. Israel shall look upon Him whom they have pierced. "And the LORD shall be King over all the earth. In that day it shall be—'The LORD is one,' and His name one" (Zech. 14:9).

The last phase of this battle is unusual. Not a gun will be fired! How strange! In Psalm 2:9, we read that Jesus Christ will break His enemies "with a rod of iron" and will "dash them to pieces like a potter's vessel." In this battle of Armageddon, we find that the "swords and spears" of the enemy will be unable to combat the rider of the white horse, and His heavenly hosts, who fights with a sword that issues out of His mouth. The battle is referred to in the "vintage" of Revelation 14:17-20, where the enemy's battle line is compared to a long trough into which the grapes are poured and the blood to the juice that is trampled out by foot (see also Isa. 34:1-17). According to the prophecies, Israel will be seven months in burying the dead after that awful time.

The Antichrist Doomed

What is the doom of the antichrist and the false prophet? They are taken and thrust into the lake of fire. In addition, an angel will be sent from heaven to bind Satan for 1,000 years. "And he cast him into the bottomless pit, and shut him up, and set a seal on him, so that he should deceive the nations no more till the thousand years were finished" (Rev. 20:3).

The pride and strength of the mightiest armies of the world will be silenced forever at the battle of Armageddon. Even though the dragon's fiercest wrath is poured out at this great uprising against God, Jesus' glorious triumph assures us that no matter what Satan may do, or how powerful he may be, the children of God will always be safe. The great conflict of Armageddon will also fulfill the Scriptures written hundreds of years ago concerning the Jews, God's chosen people. By the wonderful and supernatural intervention of Jesus Christ, Israel is to be delivered from her enemies. Unbelief is to drop as scales from her eyes, and they will recognize this One as the Lamb that was slain for their sins. As Paul writes, "At the name of Jesus every knee [shall] bow . . . and every tongue [shall] confess that Jesus Christ is Lord" (Phil. 2:10-11).

This will end the "times of the Gentiles" and will usher in the actual power and glory of the descendants of Abraham that were promised to him and to his seed forever some 4,000 years ago. Israel had often been disobedient and rebellious. God had to allow them to go into captivity. Then Christ came and offered Himself to be their King, but they rejected Him. This time, they will receive their Messiah, and He will sit upon the throne of David and reign over them for 1,000 years.

Daily Meditations

Sunday: The reign of the Lord—Zechariah 14:1-21

Monday: A great battle of the Lord—Revelation 19:11-21

Tuesday: Satan's doom by the Lord—Revelation 20:1-15

Wednesday: The winepress of the Lord—Revelation 14:14-20

Thursday: The judgment of the Lord—Joel 3:1-21

Friday: Final dealings of the Lord—Psalm 2:1-12

Saturday: The mercy of God today—Psalm 103:1-22

34

The Millennium

Blessed and holy is he who has part in the first resurrection. Over such the second death has no power, but they shall be priests of God and of Christ, and shall reign with Him a thousand years.
Revelation 20:6

What is the trouble with this old world? Why is there so much wickedness? Why is there such widespread use of drugs and so much crime? Why are the courtrooms crowded with those who have broken the law? Why are the prisons full? Why do we need a policeman on every corner? Why? The reason is because Satan, that old deceiver, lives and influences men to sin and disobey God, just as he influenced Adam and Eve. He makes people believe that they can enjoy sin and then escape the punishment of sin. What a lie that is!

You can't end sin and trouble until the one who causes it is removed. In Revelation 20:1-3, we are distinctly told that this will occur. An angel shall come down from heaven and lay hold on the dragon, which is the devil, and bind him for 1,000 years. He shall be cast into the bottomless pit and a seal shall be set upon him so that he can deceive the nations of the world no more until that period of time has been fulfilled. How wonderful it will be to have this awful promoter of evil shut up!

Although this may be figurative language and there will be no "chain" or "lock" or "key" used, we do not doubt for a minute what these words mean. Satan is removed and his power is checked for 1,000 years. There can be no peace on Earth until this is an accomplished fact. But let us remember that the devil is not almighty. Satan may be mighty, but only God is almighty. One angel can bind the devil. We do not have to be bound by the power of this evil one. Christ says, "All authority has been given to Me in heaven and on earth. . . . and lo, I am with you always" (Matt. 2:18, 20).

The God of this Age

There never has been any necessity for human failure. With every temptation, God has made a way of escape for everyone. But humans have been the "chore boy" of the devil. They have been made into brutes by this archenemy. Satan schemes to dethrone Christ in the hearts of people and enthrone himself. He is the god of this age.

But something more is going to happen in this old world besides the removal of Satan: Christ is going to reappear. His manifestation will be a glorious one, for He is "Far above all principality and power and might and dominion, and every name that is named" (Eph. 1:21). He has all power in heaven and Earth. His are the crown rights over all the world.

Today, this mighty victor over Satan, sin and death is seated at the right hand of God in heaven. At one point in the past, this One came to live upon this earth for 33 years and then died on the cross to save us. Some day He is coming again, but this time in might and power. His coming will be the most wonderful and the most startling event of the future. All will be changed when Christ comes to reign.

The Bible tells us about it. You know that it is impossible to forecast future events. No one can predict for certain what any present ruler's power will continue to be. Everything in the future is shrouded in mystery. But there is one way in which we *can* know the future. We can read news long before it happens. Who writes this news? The Lord God Almighty by His Holy Spirit writes this in advance for us, and it is found in the Bible, the Word of God.

The Bible forecasts the future, and it is "the prophetic word confirmed" (2 Pet. 1:19). How do we know? Because history has proved it. Because it is the Word of God.

When someone wanted to travel across the country in the days before the highways were as clearly marked as they are now, he procured a good map. It had to be very detailed and show him just how far to go each stretch, just where to turn, and just what direction to travel. It had to show him exactly the towns that would be reached when the speedometer gave a certain reading. After he had traveled for 200 miles and found out that every direction on that map was absolutely correct, did he doubt for a minute that all the rest of the directions were true? He knew that someone had gone over that road before him.

God knows all in advance. God's Word told of certain empires that would come into existence and what would happen to them hundreds of years before the events came to take place. We found these when we studied the "image" of Nebuchadnezzar's dream. Other prophets foretold the utter ruin of Babylon at a time when she was at the zenith of her power. The history of the great nation of Egypt was all prewritten in God's Word, and the events all came to pass. The history of the children of Israel was all recorded, and even today prophecy is being fulfilled. Now God's Word tells of another great kingdom and a coming King.

The greatest of all the prophecies was the one concerning the Messiah who was promised to Israel. For centuries the prophets had told of His coming. At last, "when the fullness of the time had come, God sent forth His Son, born of a woman, born under the law" (Gal. 4:4). His birth, His life, His sufferings, His death, His resurrection and His ascension all fulfilled what the prophets had spoken. Yet there is one event that the prophets tell us that has not yet come to pass: Christ, or the Messiah, is to come again a second time in power and great glory. He is to sit upon the throne of David as King and reign as the Prince of Peace.

The Millennium

Many people have an idea that the word "millennium" means a time of great happiness, and so it does, but we need to look at the Latin term from whence this word came and discover what it literally means. The word *mille* means "one thousand" (the *M* in Latin numerals on public buildings and cornerstones is the abbreviation for *mille*). The word *annum* means "year." Hence, "millennium" means one thousand years. The word "millennium" does not appear in Scripture, although it is from the book of Revelation that we get the term "one thousand years" (see Rev. 20:6).

Will this literally be a period of 1,000 years? In Revelation 20, the term "thousand years" occurs six times. Why should God say "a thousand years" if He did not mean that length of time? Three times it is mentioned in regard to Satan, twice it is mentioned in connection with the reign of the saints with Christ, and once it describes the length of time between the resurrection of believers and that of the wicked dead (vv. 4- 5). Christ is to reign over the whole earth during this millennium.

In the Old Testament days, the Jews looked forward to the coming of their Messiah. They looked for only one advent, and that to them was to be a glorious one, bringing in a time of wonderful happiness and prosperity. He who came to die would one day come to reign.

We, too, are looking for such an advent. What wonderful peace and joy will cover the earth (see Ps. 72:3; Isa. 33:24; 35:5-10; 55:13; Mic. 4:2-4). All creation is going to share in this glorious time. You remember that the earth was cursed in Adam's day because of his sin. The ground brought forth thorns and thistles. You know today that if any piece of land is neglected, weeds spring up immediately and flourish, crowding out the crop that has been planted. But when our Lord returns, the earth and the "desert shall rejoice and blossom as the rose" (Isa. 35:1).

When we read these wonderful descriptions of these golden days to come, we say, "How can this be?" The answer is simple. Remember who causes sorrow, sighing, sickness and sadness—the devil! Get him out of the way and you do away with all the misery that exists today. This is just what will happen.

Peace and Judgment

Christians are to be taken out of the world before the tribulation comes upon the earth. But the unbelieving dead shall remain in their graves until the end of the 1,000 years (see Rev. 20:5). Then, Christ will reign over the whole world. All people will be His subjects, although many will be unwilling subjects (see Isa. 9:6-7; 24:23). In these wonderful days, "the earth will be filled with the knowledge of the glory of the LORD, as the waters cover the sea" (Hab. 2:14).

What a wonderful thing it will be when all the kingdoms of the earth are under one perfect ruler! There will be no disputes over boundary lines to bring about wars and no petty jealousies between rulers. No one need misunderstand his neighbor, and one part of the world cannot oppress another. All the world will be one big family. The Lord Jesus Christ will rule with a rod of iron and with justice. This will be the glorious day that is promised when the Son of Man "shall have dominion also from sea to sea, and from the river to the ends of the earth" (Ps. 72:8).

People will be given one supreme chance of seeing what a glorious life is possible if only Christ is King! But do you know there will still be rebellious hearts? As we mentioned, it will be during this millennial reign that the living nations will be judged. This must not be confused with the great white throne of judgment (see Matt. 25:31-46). There is no mention of a "resurrection" or "books being opened." The nations will be judged by their treatment of the Jews—a judgment based on works.

The Final Battle

But all this time of glorious happiness and prosperity is to come to an end. When the thousand years are ended, the devil will be set free from his prison. "Now when the thousand years have expired, Satan will be released from his prison and will go out to deceive the nations which are in the four corners of the earth, Gog and Magog, to gather them together to battle, whose number is as the sand of the sea" (Rev. 20:7-8). Satan will still have a multitude of people who are deceived by him. Think of his attempting another assault against the Almighty!

Satan gathers the nations together for battle. They come from the four corners of the earth. They are compared to the sand of the seashore for number. You remember that 1,000 years before this time, there had been a similar gathering of nations against God's earthly people, Israel, at the battle of Armageddon. This final struggle under the personal leadership of Satan is to be gathered against the camp of the saints and against the beloved city.

Once again, Satan's forces will besiege Jerusalem. What is the outcome of the battle? "They went up on the breadth of the earth and surrounded the camp of the saints and the beloved city. And fire came down from God out of heaven and devoured them" (Rev. 20:9). The armies of the devil are completely destroyed.

Satan is now finally dealt with. His judgment has come. First he was cast out of heaven, then into the bottomless pit, and now he is thrown into the lake of fire. Many people question whether this means real fire or whether it is merely symbolic. After all, if the symbol is so terrible, how much more the reality must be!

Is your heart full of gratitude for your wonderful salvation? Are you praising the Lord that He has delivered you from the penalty of sin?

Daily Meditations

Sunday: The thousand years—Revelation 20:2-4,7

Monday: The kingdom age—Isaiah 11:4-11

Tuesday: The Prince of Peace—Psalm 72:8-9; Isaiah 9:6

Wednesday: Resurrection of the just—1 Corinthians 15:51-58; 1 Thessalonians 4:13-18

Thursday: The great transformation—Isaiah 35:1-10; 55:12-13

Friday: Satan's doom—Revelation 20:1-15

Saturday: The return of the King—Matthew 24:27-31; Mark 13:24-27; Luke 21:25-36

35

THE GREAT WHITE THRONE

And I saw the dead, small and great, standing before God, and books were opened. And another book was opened, which is the Book of Life. And the dead were judged according to their works, by the things which were written in the books.

REVELATION 20:12

The first great event in God's calendar of the second coming of Christ is the removal of the Church by the rapture. This is described by Paul in 1 Thessalonians. Next follows the revelation of the antichrist and his rule on Earth. It is from Daniel and 2 Thessalonians that we learn most of this matter. The wrath of God comes next upon the world with the great tribulation. Matthew 24 and the book of Revelation are the main sources of information about this horrible time. The tribulation is brought to a close by the battle of Armageddon, which John also describes in Revelation. Then comes the reign of Christ during the 1,000 years of the millennial kingdom.

Now the millennium, or the "thousand years," has come to an end. The rebellious nations are destroyed and the old adversary, the devil, is in the lake of fire. What is to come next? "Then I saw a great white throne and Him who sat on it, from whose face the earth and the heaven fled away. And there was found no place for them. And I saw the dead, small and great, standing before God, and books were opened" (Rev. 20:11). We are not told when this event happens, but it is after the thousand years. We are given a picture of the great white throne as the final scene before the new heaven and the new earth are introduced.

Many people are seized with fear when they think of a great judgment seat and the Lord who knows everything sitting upon it to judge them. But we know this: Not a single child of God will ever have to stand before this judgment throne. The great white throne is not a big "general judgment" at the end of the world, as many suppose, but just the judgment of the wicked who, during Christ's reign for the thousand years on the earth, have been left in their graves.

Two Resurrections

Every person in this world who has died will be raised at some time. In John 5:28-29, Our Lord spoke of two resurrections: "Do not marvel at this; for the hour is coming in which all who are in the graves will hear His voice and come forth—those who have done good, to the resurrection of life, and those who have done evil, to the resurrection of condemnation." The *first* resurrection occurs before the millennium. All those who are God's children because they believe on His Son shall be raised to reign with Christ. "But the rest of the dead did not live again until the thousand years were finished. This is the first resurrection" (Rev. 20:5).

The righteous will stand before the judgment seat of Christ to be rewarded according to their service in the world (see 2 Cor. 5:10). But the wicked dead will be raised at the end of the millennium to be judged according to their works. Every person who dies without Christ will be condemned because he or she rejected Jesus Christ. Remember, God's Word tells us, "The wages of sin is death, but the gift of God is eternal life in Jesus Christ our Lord" (Rom. 6:23).

The description of that great crowd who shall stand before the throne is solemn indeed. As John tells us, "The dead were judged according to their works, by the things which were written in the books. The sea gave up the dead who were in it, and Death and Hades delivered up the dead who were in them. And they were judged, each one according to his works . . . anyone not found written in the Book of Life was cast into the lake of fire" (Rev. 20:12-13,15).

The Judge

Who is this One who sits upon the throne to judge people for their sins? Not God the Father, but God the Son. The Lord Jesus Himself shall sit upon the great white throne. "For the Father judges no one, but has committed all judgment to the Son" (John 5:22). He who once hung on the cross is now to be the judge.

A boy was about to drown in the river in which he was swimming. He frantically cried for help. A man on the shore jumped in and rescued the drowning boy. He had been his "savior" from death. Some years later, this same boy, who now was a young man, was brought before a judge to answer for a crime that he had committed. Much to his relief, he saw that the judge was none other than the man who had saved him from drowning.

Surely he will free me again, the young man thought. But instead, the judge rose in the courtroom and pronounced a sentence of "guilty." The young man pled with the judge on the grounds that he had once saved his life.

"No," said the judge. "Then I was your savior; now I am your judge. You are guilty, and in all justice I must pronounce your condemnation."

God keeps a perfect record of the acts of everyone who has not had his or her sins washed away by the blood of Jesus Christ. God will recall every sin, and the sinner must face his or her own record. "But I say to you that for every idle word men may speak, they will give account of it in the day of judgment" (Matt. 12:36). "Now 'If the righteous one is scarcely saved, where will the ungodly and the sinner appear?' " (1 Pet. 4:18).

Notice that there are no white robes of righteousness, no palms of victory, no crowns of power. There is only the nakedness of sin. Only the unsaved are here. Even though their bodies have been buried for centuries or hid in the depths of the sea, on this day, their body, soul and spirit will be reunited and they will stand trembling before the judgment seat. All from Adam who have died without Christ will be there. Remember, every child of God has been raised 1,000 years before on what was definitely called the "first resurrection." These have been living and reigning with Christ for 1,000 years. The multitudes that now stand before the judgment throne are the rest of the dead who believed not on Christ.

The Books Opened for Judgment

"Books were opened. And another book was opened, which is the Book of Life. And the dead were judged according to their works" (Rev. 20:12). What was first opened? "The books." What do these books evidently stand for? God's remembrance (see Mal. 3:16).

The "books" probably contain an exact record of all that has happened in each person's life. Every unbeliever will be judged according to his or her works. All that a person has done or thought or said will come before him or her. Think! Even the thoughts of a person's mind will be judged. The psalmist says, "There is not a word on my tongue, but behold, O Lord, You know it altogether" (Ps. 139:4).

There will be the book of conscience. How the conscience keeps a record of our actions! People resuscitated from drowning have said that in one moment the events of a whole lifetime marched before their eyes. Think! If the conscience of a person can make a record of these sins, what may not God's memory be able to recall? The sinner must face his own record. The sad part of it all is that people will know that this judgment is a fair and just one. "Shall not the Judge of all the earth do right?" (Gen. 18:25). Yet men will accuse God of injustice.

The Word of God will be opened, too, for Jesus declared that His words would judge men in the last day (see John 12:48). The book of life will be opened. Many will take for granted that their names are there because they have been listed on some church roll. Does being a church member give one salvation? Our names will only find a place in the book of life by our sincere acceptance of the Lord Jesus Christ as our Savior. The book of life must contain the names only of those who have life (see John 3:36). People may be very moral and kind without having their names in that book.

"And anyone not found written in the Book of Life was cast into the lake of fire" (Rev. 20:15). The lake of fire is the symbol of sorrow and torment. It is a picture God has given to make us shrink with dread as we think of its awfulness. It is terrible to disobey God and turn aside from His peace and mercy. If we will not accept that, there is only His wrath to meet. Read what the divinely inspired writer said in Hebrews 10:31: "It is a fearful thing to fall into the hands of the living God."

Christ Bore the Condemnation for Our Sins

How about those who believe in Christ? Will they have no judgment for their sins? Know this, once and for all: Christ died for our sins (see 1 Pet. 2:24; 3:18; Gal. 3:13; 2 Cor. 5:21; John 5:24).

The word "condemnation" means judgment. The sins of the believer *have been judged.* That is why Christ died.

You know that it is a person's sin that condemns him or her in court. If it is proved that a person has committed murder, that sin condemns him to death. He or she must die because of his sin. Now Christ takes our sin on Himself. He takes it away from us and bears it Himself. Who then must be judged? The One who bears the sin, who is Christ. That is why He had to die.

This is why we do not have to come under condemnation. At the great white throne of judgment, all who appear there have not put their sins on the Lord by confessing Him as their Savior. And so, they must suffer for each sin.

Daily Meditations

Sunday: The two resurrections–John 5:28-29; Revelation 20:5
Monday: The resurrection of life at Christ's coming–Romans 8:23; 1 Corinthians 15:23; Ephesians 1:13-14; 1 Thessalonians 4:16-17; Revelation 20:4
Tuesday: The resurrected body–1 Corinthians 15:37-38,42-44; Philippians 3:20-21
Wednesday: The wicked dead–Revelation 20:11-15
Thursday: The judgments of believers' works–2 Corinthians 5:10
Friday: Administered by Christ–John 5:22,27; Acts 10:42; Romans 14:10
Saturday: Judgment of actions–Ecclesiastes 11:9; 12:14; Revelation 20:13

A New Heaven and a New Earth

There shall be no night there: They need no lamp nor light of the sun, for the Lord God gives them light. And they shall reign forever and ever.
Revelation 22:5

Many people think that heaven is just a place people talk about and imagine exists, but that there really is no such place. Some think it is outside our knowledge, and anyone even talking about it is just speculating. Others think that the world is to be entirely destroyed—that it is "coming to an end." What does the Bible say about these things?

You know that this old earth was once destroyed by flood (see Gen. 7), but God promised Noah never to destroy the world that way again. "This is the sign of the covenant which I make between Me and you, and every living creature that is with you, for perpetual generations: I set My rainbow in the cloud, and it shall be for the sign of the covenant between Me and the earth" (Gen. 9:12-13).

Peter tells us that the present heavens and earth are a storehouse of fire. They will pass away with a great noise, and the elements will melt with fervent heat (see 2 Pet. 3:7,10). The language could not be clearer as to how all this is to happen—that the heavens and the earth that now are will pass away (see also Matt. 24; 25; Isa. 51:6; Mic. 1:4).

Some people think the destruction of the entire earth is impossible, but modern science admits that it can occur. Geologists tell us that we are living on a cooled crust of the earth. Should one of the forces that now often shake whole continents break up the bed of the ocean and let down the great body of water upon the fire beneath, the conflagration that the Bible describes could quickly happen.

The prominent nineteenth-century physicist John Tyndall said that if the earth were to be stopped in its orbit, it would generate heat enough to change it all into vapor. Michael Faraday, an English chemist and physicist, said that there is as much latent electricity in a single drop of water as there is in the lightning's flash that fills the heavens. Experiments in nuclear fission have revealed hitherto unknown sources of tremendous power, almost too dangerous for man to know about. Great scientists have misgivings that the world itself might be destroyed in some such manner.

The modern scientist has discovered that, in the end, the earth and even the heavens are likely to be consumed by fire. But thousands of years before our day, the prophets foretold that just such things were going to happen. How did they know? God told them. As the great fisherman apostle said in 2 Peter 3:13, "Nevertheless we, according to His promise, look for new heavens and a new earth in which righteousness dwells."

A Wonderful Vision

The destruction of Satan will finally end his attempts, through sin, to separate man from fellowship with God. His efforts have been constant, from his meeting of the first man and woman in the Garden of Eden, and he will persist until he is cast into the lake of fire. Then the fellowship between God and His children will be restored forever.

In Revelation 21:1, we are given a description of a wonderful vision that John saw in advance: "Now I saw a new heaven and a new earth, for the first heaven and the first earth had passed away. Also there was no more sea." A new earth, without the curse of sin and with its inhabitants purified from all sin, will take the place of our present earth. "Nevertheless we, according to His promise, look for new heavens and a new earth in which righteousness dwells" (2 Pet. 3:13).

John pulls back the curtain and we look into the future. What a sight is there! The best is kept till the last!

What is going to happen to the sea? In this new earth, no more sea will be needed (see Rev. 21:1). The sea is essential for life now, and we cannot imagine living without it. But the inhabitants of the "new earth" will not die. Death and hell have passed away (see Rev. 20:14). In our earth, the sea also separates people, but there will be no separation between the inhabitants of this "new earth."

"Then I, John, saw the holy city, New Jerusalem, coming down out of heaven from God, prepared as a bride adorned for her husband" (Rev. 21:2). This city "out of heaven" has been "prepared." What did Christ say in the upper room before His death? "I go to prepare a place for you. And if I go and prepare a place for you, I will come again and receive you to Myself; that where I am, there you may be also" (John 14:2-3). This city appears, a finished entity. A place is awaiting us in heaven, set in order and furnished for us by none other than the King Himself, who knows all our tastes and preferences, for our personal comfort and happiness.

Many who do not own a foot of ground on this earth will own a mansion in heaven. This is a place of *rest* from our labors, but it is also a place of quest. It will be filled with glorious activity. The Lord distinctly tells us we shall be satisfied (see Ps. 17:15). Christ said it in another way in John 16:23: "And in that day you will ask Me nothing." We will find countless new and unimaginable delights breaking out before us on every side. How wonderfully this fits in with what Jesus said.

The glories of the New Jerusalem are beyond human comprehension. We cannot even begin to image the wonderful things in that city that God is now preparing for those who love Him. The Bible tells us that this holy city will be extraordinary in size, measuring 1,500 miles in width, length and height (see Rev. 21:11,23).

Consider the incredible dimensions of this city and see how groundless is such a feat. Ancient Babylon, with its wonderful thoroughfares, its splendid palaces, and its famous hanging gardens, was the grandest city this world has ever known. We are told that it was furlongs on each side. The New Jerusalem is 12,000 furlongs! In height, in breadth and in length, it is a cube measuring 1,500 miles in each direction! Roughly speaking, its base would cover about one-half the entire United States.

The New Jerusalem

This wonderful city of such enormous proportions descends *out of heaven from God* (see Rev. 21:10). The city reflects the very glory of God. "Her light was like a most precious stone, like a jasper stone, clear as crystal" (Rev. 21:11).

The walls surrounding the city are of jasper (see Rev. 21:18). In these great walls are 12 gates, and on the gates are written the names of the 12 tribes of the children of Israel. Seven times the number "12" is found in the description of the city:

1. There are 12 gates in the wall (see Rev. 12:12).
2. There are 12 angels at the gates (see Rev. 12:12).
3. The names of the 12 tribes of Israel are written on the gates (see Rev. 12:12).
4. The wall has 12 foundations (see Rev. 21:18,20).
5. The measurement of the wall is 12 by 12 cubits (see Rev. 21:17).
6. On the foundations are the names of the 12 apostles (see Rev. 21:14).
7. The 12 gates are 12 pearls (see Rev. 21:21).

It is believed that 12 is the number in Scripture that expresses government. In this heavenly city, we may be sure there will be perfect government.

Notice where the gates are located–three on each side, and opened for all the redeemed of the earth to come in every direction. At the gates are 12 angels, divine messengers. They will be doing what angels are always doing–ministering.

Notice that the names of the 12 tribes of Israel are written on the gates and that the 12 names of the apostles are written on the foundations (see Rev. 21:12,14). Turn to Ephesians 2:19-20 and hear what Paul says: "Now, therefore, you are no longer strangers and foreigners, but fellow citizens with the saints and members of the household of God, having built on the foundation of the apostles and prophets, Jesus Christ Himself being the chief cornerstone." In Revelation 21:14, it speaks of "the apostles of the Lamb," for the Lamb is the foundation of all.

The foundations are all adorned by precious stones, and each one of these tells of the divine glory. I wonder what the deeper meaning of all these precious stones must be. When we think of the Tabernacle in which every color, every metal, every piece of wood and every fabric was symbolic, it must surely mean the jewels in this city have significance. What wonderful and unspeakable glory is ahead of us!

The city itself, which John saw, was of pure gold. Gold always typifies a symbol of perfection that is found only in God and His Son, Jesus Christ. The 12 gates are of 12 pearls, which bring to our remembrance at every gate the thought of the one "pearl of great price" for which the Lord gave all that He had (see Matt. 13:46).

"And the street of the city was pure gold, like transparent glass" (Rev. 21:21). No doubt this means that the pavement of the city is to be pure gold, so refined as to be clear as glass. This is a typical heavenly street. Some of our Bible teachers have pictured this city built foursquare with tiers of boulevards. They could be miles apart, each of them 1,500 miles long.

On this earth, the place where we worship is the church. In that day, there will be no temple seen, "for the Lord God Almighty and the Lamb are its temple" (Rev. 21:22). We go to church to worship God and to draw near to Him. In that wonderful day in the New Jerusalem, we shall all be near to the Lord our God. Nothing shall keep us from Him. In the Old Testament, a veil separated God's people from the Holy of Holies where He met His people, but there will be no veil between us and our heavenly Father in that glad day.

The Light of the World

The city will have no need of light, such as sun and moon. These are for this world, not for the world to come. In this new city, God is the light (see Rev. 21:23; Isa. 60:19).

Our Lord called Himself "the light of the world" (John 8:12). He is the light that has shone into our darkened hearts. Just think of this eternal day! Scientists tell us that the sun is likely to die out and grow cold, and then, of course, the moon will be dark, but as long as God lives, the eternal city will never know darkness.

We cannot finish the description of the New Jerusalem without considering the happy inhabitants who will dwell there. In that city of beauty, no unclean thing shall ever enter to defile it. The old deceiver, the father of lies, will never molest that joyful place. Only those who are washed in the blood of the Lamb and made clean shall enter those pearly gates and throng those golden streets. And a multitude it will be: "A great multitude which no one could number, of all nations, tribes, peoples, and tongues" (Rev. 7:9).

There will be no distinction or color line, and no crying, for "God will wipe away every tear from their eyes; there shall be no more death, nor sorrow, nor crying. There shall be no more pain" (Rev. 21:4). We can hardly imagine such a state of affairs. We are so accustomed to sin, sickness, sorrow and misery that we cannot picture a place where not one of these dares intrude.

How will we look? First John 3:2 says, "It has not yet been revealed what we shall be, but we know that when He is revealed, we shall be like Him, for we shall see Him as He is." Shall we know our loved ones in heaven? If we thought we were not to know each other in heaven, it would lose much of its attractiveness for us.

All these things the Lord God has promised to those who love Him and who have accepted His offer of salvation. We know, of course, that the Bible does not give us a complete picture of all that life will be like in heaven. We do not comprehend what He gives us now and surely do not understand what He has planned for us for the future. But there are glimpses of the Lord's plan given to us in the Bible:

- We shall be with Christ (see John 14:3).
- We shall serve Christ (see Rev. 22:3).

- We shall be glorified by Christ (see Col. 3:4).
- We shall worship God forever (see Rev. 19:1).
- We shall be like Christ (see 1 John 3:2).
- We shall have a body like Christ's (Phil. 3:21).
- We shall better understand (see 1 Cor. 13:12).
- We will have access to the water of life (see Rev. 21:6).
- We shall receive our inheritance prepared by Christ and given to us by Him (see 1 Pet. 1:4).
- It will be a time of rest from work (see Rev. 14:13).
- It will be a place without sin (see Rev. 21:27).
- It will be a place of joy (see Rev. 21:4).
- It will be a place of no night (Rev. 21:25).

Heaven is a glorious, wonderful, real place that Christ is now preparing for us. How terrible it would be to miss it!

There is only one way to this place. We cannot earn it, we cannot attain to it in any way, and we cannot even help to earn it. We may enter heaven only through the acceptance of Jesus Christ as our Lord and Savior. Remember the words of Christ in John 10:9: "I am the door. If anyone enters by Me, he will be saved."

Don't become impatient about Jesus' coming back to Earth. He is preparing a place for you. The great architect and the builder of the universe is planning a city full of *homes,* a place for our dwelling. It is to be a city of mansions.

Daily Meditations

Sunday: A new heaven and a new earth—Revelation 21:1-8

Monday: The New Jerusalem—Revelation 21:9-27

Tuesday: The new paradise—Revelation 22:1-17

Wednesday: A prepared place—John 14:1-11

Thursday: The old earth destroyed by fire—Isaiah 51:5; Micah 1:4; 2 Peter 3:4-15

Friday: A description of the new earth—Isaiah 65:17-25

Saturday: The eternal throne of God—1 Corinthians 15:20-28; Revelation 22:1

37

Understanding God's Plan for Our Lives

Not everyone who says to Me, "Lord, Lord," shall enter the kingdom of heaven, but he who does the will of My Father in heaven.

MATTHEW 7:21

When an architect draws a plan or blueprint for a building, he carefully sets forth exactly what he wants. Every detail is covered and all specifications are clearly marked. So it is with God, the great architect of the universe. He has a plan for the world. His plan covers all the ages from before the creation of the world into the eternity after the second coming of Christ. "From everlasting to everlasting, You are God" (Ps. 90:2).

God not only has a plan for the universe throughout all the ages but also a plan for your life today. Every good builder tries to build according to the architect's blueprint so that the finished construction might be perfect. To do this, he or she must study the plans carefully and *know* exactly what the architect wants. So we, too, must *know* what God's plan is and then be willing to follow it in every detail if we would build strong, worthwhile Christian lives.

Isn't it a thrill to know that God has a special plan for your life? The most important aspect of your life as a Christian is to know God's will and what part He has for you in His great plan. When you know God's will, your life is no longer a hit-and-miss affair. You have direction and know where you are going. You have a purpose and know what you are living for.

Seeking God's Will

Of course, we should know God's will at all times. But it is not always necessary to seek to find that will. Frequently, we will know God's will without asking Him what He would have us to do, because we know in our hearts what God says about some actions. Thus, in many instances, we do not need a special enlightenment.

Jim and Bob, two friends, met together one day. "Let's go to a certain place," Jim said.

"No," replied Bob. "That would not be right. I know my father does not approve of my going."

"How do you know? Has he ever refused to let you go?"

"No, but I know my father."

That is exactly the way that Christians often feel. They know what God's will is on certain questions, not because there is as definite a command (as concerning stealing), but because they know God, their Father. There are times when the Holy Spirit speaks to us like this in our hearts.

Yet there are also many times when we have to seek to know God's will. We have to find the answer to questions such as what church we should attend, what friends we should cultivate, what career we should pursue, or what we should make of our leisure time. These questions are not answered by direct commands in the Bible. Neither are they completely answered by knowledge of what God is like. So, how can we know the will of God in these instances?

Guidance of the Holy Spirit

A pilot, while flying his plane, hears a voice giving information and instructions. He sees no one and has contact with no one; he only hears a voice. So, if you are to be in line with God's will, there must first be the "still small voice" of the Holy Spirit speaking to you (1 Kings 19:12). God thus gives you an inward desire to do His will for you. This is the voice of conscience.

God's Word

The pilot must also consult his compass to determine what course he should follow. It is possible that there has been a jamming of the airways, and he may misunderstand the directions that are given him. As Christians we dare not trust our impulses or our conscience alone. It is possible that we may misunderstand. It may be that our own desires have so jammed the airways that God cannot speak to us at all. We must check our compass, God's written Word, to make certain that it is God through His Holy Spirit speaking to our heart.

We know that God's will for our lives will agree with the Scriptures, for the Bible is the inspired and infallible revelation of God to us (see 2 Pet. 1:21). So it is important when seeking to find the will of God to see how our personal desire lines up with God's clear declarations in His Word.

Let's see how this works. You think that you would like to be a missionary (see Mark 16:15). This desire is certainly in line with Bible teaching. But not all people are called to be missionaries, so there must be another test.

What about associating with a bad crowd? The answer is very clear: "You shall not follow a crowd to do evil; nor shall you testify in a dispute so as to turn aside after many to pervert justice" (Exod. 23:2). What about marrying a non-Christian? "Do not be unequally yoked together with unbelievers" (2 Cor. 6:14). Since these desires do not line up with God's Word, you do not have to look any further. You know God's will in regard to these problems.

How utterly foolhardy and dangerous it would be for a pilot to go where he wanted without a compass! Yet it is far more dangerous for you to do what you want without the compass of God's Word. You, like a pilot, must never rely upon your own ability to determine your course but always consult and trust your compass. Put your faith in the Word of God. It cannot fail!

Providential Circumstances

There are times when the voice speaking to the pilot and his compass agree absolutely, but he flies into bad weather and he cannot proceed in the direction that has been indicated to him. In the same way, sometimes a Christian has the desire to do something that the Bible does not forbid—such as being a missionary—and yet circumstances indicate that it is not God's will for that person to do that task. God often arranges circumstances so as to make a certain course obvious.

Sometimes the pilot is not equipped, capable or qualified to fly through the bad weather. In the same way, if some circumstance stops you from doing what you believe is God's will, it may be that God is using this method to keep you from doing that which you are not qualified to do. For instance, you might want to be a missionary, but your health will not permit you to go to a foreign country. Or maybe you have responsibilities at home that make it impossible for you to leave. These may be indications of God's will that He gives through circumstances.

Sometimes God works out, or changes, the circumstances that appear to block the way. In such cases, God's will for you to proceed is obvious. Regardless, the strong inner assurance, the Word of God and providential circumstances should all agree. When all of these harmonize, it is safe to say that God has spoken and that you know His will.

Do God's Will

When you know God's will and are convinced that you know what He wants you to do, then dare to act. Take God at His Word and step forth by faith. Yield your will to God's will.

Yield to the Lord

The first step requires the dedication of your will. God gave you a free will, and now you surrender it back to Him. This surrender is of a voluntary nature. You yield yourself to God because you want to do so. David said it like this: "I delight to do Your will, O my God, and Your law is within my heart" (Ps. 40:8). The surrender must be unconditional. "Not with eyeservice, as men-pleasers, but as bondservants of Christ, doing the will of God from the heart" (Eph. 6:6).

Pray

To hear God speak to your heart, to understand His Word, to evaluate circumstances and to make certain that these three are in agreement, prayer is essential. Pray with the sincere desire that the Lord answer in accordance with His will. "Now this is the confidence that we have in Him, that if we ask anything according to His will, He hears us. And if we know that He hears us, whatever we ask, we know that we have the petitions that we have asked of Him" (John 5:14-15).

We must be ready to do God's will when He reveals it to us. Can you pray, "Not my will, but Yours be done"? It is necessary if you really want to know God's leading. Preface your prayers with the words, "If it be Your will," and then pray in faith, believing that the Lord hears and will answer (see Mark 11:24; Jas. 1:6-7). After we know the will of God, we need to be taught to do His will. Then, too, we must pray for courage and strength to do what He would have us do.

Trust

"Commit your way to the LORD, trust also in Him, and He shall bring it to pass" (Ps. 37:5). Trust the Lord to guide you and give you the ability to do His will. Remember, you need the strength of the Lord to accomplish anything for Him. Without Christ, you can do nothing (see John 15:5). But with Christ, you can do anything (see Phil. 4:13).

No matter how hard or seemingly impossible something seems, if it is God's will, you can do it through Christ. It will not be you doing God's will by yourself, but rather the Lord working in you and through you. It will be the Holy Spirit controlling and guiding you, with God's almighty power at your disposal.

Act

Are you ready to do whatever the Lord asks of you? Will you do it in whatever place He sends you? Remember, it will not always be the easy road or place. Sometimes, you will be laughed at. Sometimes, you may be lonely, but the Lord will be with you. You will never go alone, for He has promised, "I will never leave you nor forsake you. So we may boldly say: 'The LORD is my helper; I will not fear. What can man do to me?' " (Heb. 13:5-6).

If we obey the Lord, we will do His will whenever He asks us to it. God's clock keeps perfect time; His timetable is accurate. We may get impatient, but God will always lead us at just the right time. Remember the story of Philip in Acts 8:26-40? Here is an example of the leading of the Lord. God called Philip out to a desert place—a place that he surely would not have chosen to go to himself—because it was His will for Philip at this particular time. And so, Philip went to the desert south of Gaza.

"Then the Spirit said to Philip, 'Go near and overtake this chariot.' So Philip ran to him, and heard him reading the prophet Isaiah" (Acts 8:29-30). God continued to lead Philip.

There must have been many chariots on the road that day, but God picked just one that Philip should go and join. Just think for a minute how important the timing was—if Philip had delayed just a few minutes, the chariot would have disappeared in the dust. If Philip had picked another chariot, the man inside might not have been reading from Isaiah 53.

There was just one chariot on the road that God had picked out for Philip to follow. There was just one man among all the people who traveled that road whose heart God had prepared for Philip's message. Philip had to obey the will of God completely and act at just the right time.

Set Out in Faith

Philip must have wondered why he had to go out to the desert, but God knew. Philip must have wondered why he had to join himself to one particular chariot, but God knew. So many times we cannot understand why God leads us in a particular way, but He knows. We cannot understand why certain things happen to us, but God knows. And we can be sure that whatever God does for us, it will be right.

Remember the words of Psalm 18:30: "As for God, His way is perfect." Set out in faith and do what the Lord has shown you that He wants you to do. Dare to act! Trust yourself to the care of the One who never makes mistakes.

Daily Meditations

Sunday: Find God's will in what you do—John 7:10-21

Monday: The Bible reveals God's will—2 Timothy 3:14-17

Tuesday: Consider God's will first—James 4:13-17

Wednesday: The command to obey God's will—Deuteronomy 6:17-25

Thursday: A parable about doing God's will—Matthew 25:14-30

Friday: The importance of doing God's will—Matthew 7:21-29

Saturday: An example of knowing God's will—Acts 16:1-11

38

The Bible: God's Blueprint for Our Lives

Some years ago, a New Testament was sent to a notorious criminal while he was awaiting execution for murder. Although he refused to read it, he was nevertheless curious about what was in it. One day as he was looking over his gift, he happened to read Luke 9:56: "The Son of Man did not come to destroy men's lives but to save them."

Evidently these are the words of someone who wants to teach men the way to live a good life, he said to himself. On another occasion, the criminal read the Bible again and described his feelings in this way: "I read the story of the crucifixion, and at the words, 'Father, forgive them, for they know not what they do' (Luke 23:34), I stopped. I was stabbed to the heart. It revealed to me the love of God, and with a grateful heart I believed. Through that simple sentence, I was led to become a Christian. I knew that a man who prayed like that must be the Son of God, for such an act is not possible to an ordinary man."

This kind of story reveals to us the mighty power of the Word of God. Just a short sentence was enough to bring a notorious criminal out of spiritual darkness and into the marvelous light. If the Bible is a book that has this much spiritual dynamite, do you wonder that God urges each of us to read it and study it that He might bring life to us and to others?

God's Word Reveals God's Will

The Bible, the source of Christian truth, is the most important textbook that we can ever study. It is the written Word of God. God is the author (see 2 Tim. 3:16; 2 Pet. 1:21). The beauty and majesty of its language; the agreement of all its parts; the absolute perfection of Scripture with its songs, stories, poems, parables, orations, history and letters gives us abundant evidence that the Bible is the inspired Word of God.

Other books are soon outdated, "but the word of our God stands forever" (Isa. 40:8). The Bible will endure forever, and it is completely trustworthy. "Heaven and earth will pass away, but My words will by no means pass away" (Luke 21:33).

We can see how essential the Bible is in our lives in order for us to know and understand God's will, but think of the Bible in still another way. It is the will of your Father, which reveals to you your inheritance and your riches and your promises. It is the letter from your best friend. How one waits for the mail to come to bring a letter from an absent friend! You know the joy with which one tears the envelope open. The person cannot wait to read the contents. He or she is not reading a series of events like a history book, but is reading the things that concern a person he or she loves.

You no doubt have seen the kind of ink used for secret writing. It fades away the minute it is used, and the paper seems to be blank. If the sheet of paper is held over a fire, the writing comes out and can be read easily. Now, to a great many people, the pages of the Bible (especially the Old Testament) seem to be blank. Such people need to be shown what is taught in the Bible. Christ said that the Holy Spirit enables us to understand God's Word, for He shows the truth of the Scriptures (see John 16:13). A person may have a most brilliant mind, but without the illumination of the Holy Spirit, the pages of the Bible are as blank sheets of paper.

A young lady threw down the book that she had just finished and said, "That's the dullest story I've ever read." In the course of time, she became engaged to a young man. One night she said to him, "On one of the books in my library, the author's name and even his initials are precisely the same as yours. Isn't that a singular coincidence?"

"I don't think so," he replied.

"Why not?" she said.

"For the simple reason that I wrote the book."

That night, the young lady sat up until two o'clock reading the book again. This time, it seemed to be the most interesting story she had ever read. The once dull book was now fascinating because she knew and loved the author. In the same way, when we know and love the author of the Bible, we will find it interesting because it reveals aspects of His character and His purpose for our lives.

Of course, just reading the Bible alone is not sufficient. Some people have this strange idea about the Word of God. In fact, the Bible is more like a signboard. Suppose I am traveling to Yellowstone Park in an automobile. All of a sudden, I see a big sign that says, "Yellowstone Park," with a big arrow pointing in a direction. Imagine my getting out of the car, climbing up on the sign and sitting on it.

The next tourist would come along and say, "What are you doing?"

I would answer, "I am going to Yellowstone Park, and here I am." You could not conceive of anyone being so absolutely foolish. The signboard only points the way. We must go in the direction that it says. It is a very foolish traveler who will not follow directions. The Bible tells us which way to go all through life. We just have to follow the directions and do what God says. "Be doers of the word, and not hearers only, deceiving yourselves" (Jas. 1:22).

Commitment in Studying God's Word

A minister once asked one of the members of his church how she was getting along in her Christian life. "Very poorly," she replied. "My life is a disgrace to me and to the church. It is a disgrace to Jesus Christ. I don't understand why."

"Do you study your Bible every day?" the minister asked.

"No, but I do study it occasionally, whenever I have time."

The minister turned to a little baby lying in a carriage nearby, and said, "Suppose you fed that baby once in two hours today and once in six hours tomorrow, and then let him go without eating for three or four days because you were busy. Then you would go back and feed him every two hours the next day and just keep that up. Do you think the child would grow?"

"No," the woman said. "I think the child would die under that treatment."

"Yet that is just the way you are treating your soul," the minister replied.

Young people who are going to become doctors, lawyers, merchants, accountants or mechanics know that they have to study constantly to become proficient in their work. They read everything that they can get that will help them to understand their subject. They do more than read—they pore over the contents and master the pages.

A person who knows nothing about medicine would be an absolute failure as a doctor. A lawyer who did not know the law could never win a case. There is no short cut to learning the Bible—no easy way of discovering what it contains. There is only one way, and that is to accept the challenge to study the Bible.

As we approach God's Word, our prayer should be the words of Psalm 119:18: "Open my eyes, that I may see wondrous things from Your law." Remember, the reason for our study of the Bible is that we may become approved unto God (see 2 Tim. 2:15).

There is little use to read and study the Bible if we do not obey its teachings. Do you want to be "approved unto God"? If so, you must study His Word.

A Light in a Dark World

How much light we need in this age of spiritual darkness and confusion. It is often hard to know which way is right. You know how you feel when you go into a strange dark room. You haven't any idea what is there. You just grope around and are afraid that you might fall or knock something down. What a difference it would make if a light were turned on in that room! God's Word throws a light on all of our paths through life. God's Word, the blueprint for our lives, shows the pitfalls and ditches, the stones and rough places.

Daily Meditations

Sunday: Study to be approved unto God–2 Timothy 2:15; 3:15-17

Monday: Study to know God's will–Deuteronomy 6:6-9

Tuesday: Study to be fed–Deuteronomy 8:1-6; 1 Peter 2:1-7

Wednesday: Study to learn the way–Psalm 27:1-14

Thursday: Study to know how to live–John 6:48-58

Friday: Study for enlightenment–John 5:39-47

Saturday: Study under the Holy Spirit–John 16:7-16;
1 Corinthians 2:10-16

39

The Challenge: Follow God's Plan

If anyone serves Me, let him follow Me; and where I am, there My servant will be also. If anyone serves Me, him My Father will honor.
John 12:26

One of the real thrills for tourists in Rome is a visit to the catacombs. These are underground passages with recesses dug out for coffins and tombs. An almost endless series of tunnels connects the different rooms and sections. What a maze of turns and twists, ups and downs, backward and forward. Only an experienced guide could possibly find his way.

Visitors to the catacombs are conducted through the passageways in groups. Each one is given a long thin candle to light his or her way in the darkness. All are warned to stay close to the guide. Separation from the leader of the group or a wrong turn by an individual might end in a catastrophe.

Life is often such a journey. It can be very confusing at times and difficult to know just what to do. We hear people say, "I don't know which way to turn." Yet this feeling of confusion need not apply to Christians, for our God "will be our guide even to death" (Ps. 48:14). God's promise is that "your ears shall hear a word behind you, saying, 'This is the way, walk in it,' whenever you turn to the right hand or whenever you turn to the left" (Isa. 30:21).

When the Lord Jesus Christ called His disciples to follow Him, He promised to guide and direct them. "Then He said to them, 'Follow Me, and I mill make you fishers of men'" (Matt. 4:19). "Jesus said to him, 'I am the way, the truth, and the life. No one comes to the Father except through Me'" (John 14:6). Christ is willing to lead each of us all through life. It is up to us to follow Him. We simply need to stay close behind Him and keep watching Him.

When the Lord Jesus called His disciples to follow Him, they left their fishing nets and went right along after Him (see Matt. 4:18-20). Of course, we cannot follow Christ in the same way as the disciples did, for we do not see Him in person here on Earth. So what does it mean for us to follow Christ and His plan for our lives?

Follow the Leader

Actually, we follow Christ in a spiritual way by observing the same principles that apply to being a good follower of any leader. First, we stay behind Christ and allow Him to lead us. Sometimes, Christians do not wait for the Lord to show them what to do. They go ahead with their own plans and then expect the Lord to bless them. Are they following Christ? The Bible tells us that we must follow Christ if we would be His disciples (see Luke 14:27).

Christians are those who truly try to follow in Christ's way. They study the Word so that they might know God's will. They may not succeed as well as they would like, but they nonetheless press toward the mark for the prize of the high calling of God in Christ Jesus (see Phil. 3:14).

As a follower of Christ, you will often come short of what we aim to do or be. Do not be discouraged if you are not perfect. Christ knows your heart. He knows if you are trying faithfully to follow Him. Be careful not to compare yourselves to other people (see 2 Cor. 10:12). Do not follow a human pattern, but be "imitators of God as dear children" (Eph. 5:1).

One day, General Robert E. Lee stepped out the front door of his home. Snow had just left a fresh blanket over the earth. He took great strides, leaving an impression in the white snow with his huge military boots. A little voice behind him said, "Daddy, take shorter steps. I'm following you." Lee looked around to see his little four-year-old boy trying to stretch his short legs and make his feet fit into the very prints that the general had just made.

Even though you do not realize it, others may be following you closely and imitating all that you do. Surely this should be a challenge for you to follow Christ so closely that if others follow you, they will never be led astray.

Second, we keep our eyes focused on Christ. One characteristic of sheep is their tendency to follow the one just ahead. When sheep are being led along and the attention of one is diverted so that he strays off the path, all the sheep behind him will follow him instead of the leader.

People are often like sheep in this respect. Isaiah 53:6 says, "All we like sheep have gone astray; we have turned, every one, to his own way; and the LORD has laid on Him the iniquity of us all." Christians must keep looking unto Jesus and not be diverted by the actions of anyone else.

How can we keep our eyes on Christ? By studying God's Word and speaking to the Lord in prayer. It is important that we never lose sight of the One who is our leader. We cannot expect to keep our eyes on the Lord Jesus if we never follow His directions or take time to look unto Him.

Third, we stay close to Christ. A group of young people was visiting Mammoth Cave in Kentucky. As they started through the great cave, the guide mounted a rock called "The Pulpit" and said he would preach a sermon. This was it: "Keep close to your guide." It was a short sermon, but it was a practical one. The party soon found that, like the tourists in the Roman catacombs, if they did not keep close to the guide, he would certainly be lost in the midst of so many dark pits, precipices and tunnels.

There was an old captain who was called upon to pilot seagoing vessels safely into a very dangerous harbor. He never failed. He always missed the shoals and the rocks. He was asked one time how he knew just how to point the ship. He said, "Do you see that buoy ahead? Now look on and you will see a white post. Look still farther and there's the light from the lighthouse. I cannot go by any of them. No one is sufficient in itself, but when all three are in a straight line, it gives me my direction and I bring my boat safely into the harbor."

When the Word of God, the voice of the Holy Spirit whom Christ has given to be our guide, and the circumstances about us are all in accord, it is then safe for us to say that God is speaking, and we can follow in that path.

The Reward of Following God's Plan

The Bible is filled with true-life stories of men and women. In every case, those who obeyed God and followed His plan were blessed, while those who did not obey were punished. Unfortunately, the punishment for disobedience often affected others. Disobedience to God is sin.

Adam and Eve are known for their outright disobedience to God. What was the result of their sinfulness? "By one man's disobedience many were made sinners" (Rom. 5:19). "Through one man sin entered the world, and death through sin, and thus death spread to all men, because all sinned" (Rom. 5:12).

Children often fret around and whine when their father or mother tells them that they do not want them to do something. They often say that they don't see why they can't do it, but down in their heart, they really know that what their parents say is best. Sometimes, parents will let their children have their own way because they tease and urge, but we all know from experience that the best results usually come from obedience to our parents.

Occasionally parents may make a mistake, but most of the time they are right. God never makes a mistake in guiding us in His plan for our lives. We can always depend on Him, for His way is perfect (see Ps. 18:30). We may not understand why He guides us in certain ways, but He can be sure that He knows how everything will work out. We can trust our heavenly Father at all times.

God promises that those who obey Him shall have good success (see Josh. 1:8). Christ said, "Not everyone who says to Me, 'Lord, Lord,' shall enter the kingdom of heaven, but he who does the will of My Father in heaven" (Matt. 7:21). How important it is to obey God!

Abraham obeyed God even when he knew nothing about the land to which God sent him. When God told him to leave his home and his people, Abraham obeyed, not knowing whither he went (see Gen. 12:1-4; Heb. 11:8).

How could one man lead out hundreds of thousands of men, women and children from slavery under a great Pharaoh? Moses accomplished this tremendous task when he acted in obedience to God's plan (see Exod. 3:1–14:31). How could Joshua take the high walled city of Jericho with only seven trumpets made of rams' horns? When he obeyed God, the walls of Jericho fell flat (see Jos. 6:1-20). How could Gideon with his small band of 300 men, with torches and pitchers, rout such a great army? This seems impossible to us, but when Gideon obeyed God, the great host of Midianites fled in confusion (see Judg. 7:7-21).

Remember, God always keeps His promises. He will never fail to do His part. If we want to derive the benefit of God's promises, it is up to us to do our part. To know God's Word and obey it is the challenge that the Lord gives to His people, "For then you will make your way prosperous, and then you will have good success" (Josh. 1:8).

Obedience Is Hard

It is true that you cannot live a life of power and obedience at the same time. It is hard to give in and do what someone else wants you to do. From the time you were a baby, you have always wanted your own way. Everyone does. It takes time and discipline to teach obedience. How, then, can we accept God's challenge to learn to obey Him and follow His plan?

The answer comes from the fact that Christ does not expect us to do it alone. He has provided help. He has promised that He will live in us. Paul said, "It is no longer I who live, but Christ lives in me" (Gal. 2:20). Yet because Christ lived within him, Paul could add, "I can do all things through Him who strengthens me" (Phil. 4:13). Hand your life to Christ and let Him live in you. He will help you to follow Him. God has also provided the Holy Spirit to dwell within us. Christ said, "He abides with you and will be in you" (John 14:17).

You can learn God's will through study of the Bible and through prayer, and then through the empowering of Christ and the Holy Spirit, you can have the strength to do that which you know God wants you to do. Do not depend upon yourself; your own efforts will always fail. Rest in the Lord and know that He has said, "My grace is sufficient for you, for power is perfected in weakness" (2 Cor. 12:9).

THE RESULTS OF FOLLOWING GOD'S PLAN

A man was walking near a building one day and saw a stonecutter chiseling patiently upon a block of stone in front of him. "Are you still chiseling?" remarked the gentleman pleasantly as he went up to the stonecutter.

"Yes, still chiseling," replied the workman as he went on with his work.

"To what part of the building does this stone belong?" asked the gentleman.

"I don't know," replied the stonecutter. "My job is to cut the stones. The architect knows where each one will go." He then went on chiseling, chiseling, chiseling.

As Christians, that is what we should do. We may not see the plan of the Master Architect above, but each of us has our work to do and we should keep at it until it is done. We must follow the directions that the Lord has given us so that our work will fit into His perfect plan.

With Christ's challenge, "Follow Me," He promises that those who do will become "fishers of men" (Matt. 4:19). We follow Christ in order that others may be brought to Him. What a privilege this is! Proverbs 11:30 says, "The fruit of the righteous is a tree of life, and he who wins souls is wise."

Caleb, in the Old Testament, wholly followed the Lord, and as a reward he was given all the land his feet trod upon (see Josh. 14:9). Those of us who follow God's plan receive many rich and bountiful blessings. We experience joy, peace, confidence, success and, best of all, the commendation of our Lord.

Daily Meditations

Sunday: Follow Christ–John 1:35-51

Monday: Follow His voice–John 10:1-15

Tuesday: Follow to be fishermen–Matthew 4:18-25; Mark 1:16-20

Wednesday: Follow Christ fully–Luke 14:25-33

Thursday: Followers of God–Ephesians 5:1-17

Friday: Follow the light–John 1:1-13; 8:12

Saturday: Reward of following–Mark 10:23-31

Conclusion

What a wonderful view an airplane gives one of the great engineering achievement known as the Panama Canal. There the whole thing lies beneath you. One sees the two oceans and the steamers as they ply between the locks from one ocean to the other! What a different idea of the canal the flyer has by viewing it all at once from a height than that the passengers have in those great steamers as they move slowly along through this wonderful waterway.

This airplane view is the one we hope you have had of the Bible as you have read and studied *God's Plan: Finding Yourself in His Grand Design.* We have passed over rapidly from one cover of the Scriptures to the other and have seen God's great plan from one ocean of eternity to the other. All the mountain peaks of interest have loomed up before us. We have looked into the dateless past and forward into endless eternity and in it all have seen that *God has a purpose.*

The Bible is a wonderful volume composed of 66 books, written over a period of 1,500 years by 40 authors. Every subject in the world is discussed in its pages. We might expect to find it just a hodgepodge, but instead it is a book with one theme: "Jesus Christ." All the Scriptures speak of Him, and He is seen in every book. As soon as sin entered the world, a Savior was promised. The prophets told of His coming. The Gospels declare, "He is here."

All Roads Lead to Christ

There was once an ancient saying: "All roads lead to Rome." In a very real way, all the roads or events in the Old Testament lead to the death and resurrection of Christ. He was present at the time of creation. He had work to do in connection with the creation of the world. "All things were made through Him, and without Him nothing was made that was made" (John 1:3). As far back as in the Garden of Eden, God promised that a Redeemer would come who would destroy Satan (see Gen. 3:15).

During the Flood, we know that the ark that Noah made was a picture of Christ, who is the ark of safety for everyone who accepts Christ as his or her Savior. Judgment was brought about by the disobedience of the people when they built the Tower of Babel—a judgment in which Christ had a part (see Gen. 11:7 and note the plural pronoun in God's words concerning Himself).

When God called Abraham, the Israelite nation from which the Messiah was to come was founded. It was in Christ that all the nations of the earth were to be blessed. The apostle Paul tells us that the seed of Abraham was Christ (see Gal. 3:16). Later, God gave the Law to Moses. Christ came to fulfill that Law. He is the only One who could keep the Law of God completely.

Without a doubt, David was the greatest of all kings of Israel. Under his rule, the Israelites prospered against their enemies. And it was thorough his line that God promised that the Messiah would one day come: "When your days are fulfilled and you rest with your fathers, I will set up your seed after you, who will come from your body, and I will establish his kingdom. He shall build a house for My name, and I will establish the throne of his kingdom forever" (2 Sam. 7:12-13). As we continue to observe the Jewish nation in the Old Testament, we see that throughout all of its history, Christ is foretold.

God disciplines His children. For 1,500 years Israel was under the Law. God wanted to prove to people that they were sinners. He gave them every chance to obey, but they would not. Remember, the Law is like a mirror to show everyone that he or she is a sinner, and then as a "schoolmaster" to lead him or her to Christ (see Gal. 3:24). Christ is the only One who can forgive and cleanse us of our sin.

Jesus came to seek and to save that which is lost. He was the supreme sacrifice for us all. He was the Lamb slain once, and for all. In Genesis 3:21, the skins to cover Adam and Eve's nakedness meant that the blood of an animal had to be shed. We can follow this scarlet thread of sacrifice through the Bible until we come to the cross. Christ had to shed His blood to make a covering for our sin.

The Holy Spirit and the Work of the Church

When Christ ascended into heaven, He sent the Holy Spirit to the earth. The only responsibility God puts upon us today is that we believe on His Son. We do not have to *try* to be Christian, but just *trust* in Christ for our life and hope. Surely, people would be willing to accept eternal life as a free gift from God! But how have people behaved? Many have rejected this precious gift and rebelled against God. They have failed God. Here on the cross, where we see God's greatest manifestation of love, we see humankind's worst failure.

After Jesus departed this world, He left a group of people to continue His work. In the Old Testament, the Lord had worked through a nation and its leaders. Today, the Lord is working through a group of people who have been "called out" of the world as a separate people for His glory. The Lord Jesus Christ promised that there would be a Church. He told the disciples that upon the confession of His deity, the Church would be built. "And I also say to you that you are Peter, and on this rock I will build My church, and the gates of Hades shall not prevail against it" (Matt. 16:18).

The Church has always been a power for the Lord when it obeys Him in the task He gave to it—that of taking the whole gospel to the whole world. Someday, that Body of Christ will be complete. The Lord Jesus will come back and take all those with Him who believe in Him as the Savior.

God has judged humankind's failure each time before. He will judge them again for rejecting His Son and refusing the gift of salvation when He comes again. The result of this judgment is the casting of the wicked dead into the lake of fire. Then, after all the judgments are ended, those who have believed and followed Christ will dwell with Him through all eternity. "Then comes the end, when He delivers the kingdom of God the Father, when He puts an end to all rule and all authority and power" (1 Cor. 15:24-28).

THE GREAT COMMISSION

We will all spend eternity somewhere. The only question is *where.* That question, we know, is answered by whether we know the Lord Jesus Christ as our personal Savior. If we do, we shall spend eternity with Him. If we do not, we will have to spend eternity away from God.

For some of us, this question has been settled. We have accepted Jesus as our Lord and know where we shall be. But what of those around us? What of our families? What of those who live near us? What of our friends? What of them? Do they know the Lord Jesus? If we really realized that all who reject Christ will face God's judgment and be punished by everlasting death, we would be more anxious to introduce our family and friends to Christ. Instead, we are sometimes almost afraid to mention the Lord.

There is another way that we can have a part in making the Lord known and fulfilling His command in the great commission, and that is by supporting others who go as missionaries to the uttermost part of the world. We can support them by setting aside a portion of the Lord's money to send to them or to the mission board of our church. We can pray for the missionaries as well and get acquainted with some of them.

Why not commit to write them a letter and ask about their work, and then faithfully pray that the Lord will help them and keep their lives safe from dangers? And then, ask the Lord if He wants *you* to serve Him in some way here at home. Be sure that you ask the Lord what *He* wants you to do before you decide what *you* want to do.

All Things Are Possible in Christ

When you do make a decision, be sure to follow through. We often feel that we should make some sort of decision for the Lord, and so we say the first thing that comes to our minds. It is easy to promise something that we may never be called upon to do. But that is wrong. In fact, that is a sin in the sight of God. The people of Israel answered the Lord with the words that they thought were expected of them. But when the time came to perform the promise, they could not do it.

Don't make a decision just because you think it is the thing to do. Don't say things in a testimony meeting just because you think it will please someone to hear them. You are making promises to God. It is a sacred moment when you tell the Lord what you will do for Him. When you say the words, mean them and then look to the Lord Jesus Christ for the strength to do that which you have promised. If you depend upon your own ability to please the Lord and to perform what you have said, you will fail every time. But in Christ's power you can keep your word.

Remember the words of Paul: "I can do all things through Christ who strengthens me" (Phil. 4:13). These words are just as true for you as they were for Paul. You have the same promise that the Lord gave to Paul when He said, "My grace is sufficient for you, for My strength is made perfect in weakness" (2 Cor. 12:9). You can rest in this promise and say with Paul, "When I am weak, then am I strong" (2 Cor. 12:10).

Will You Take Up the Challenge?

Truly, God has a plan for this world and for your life. Will you embrace His calling and do the will of God? Will you follow the course that the Master Architect has laid out before you? Will you seek the guidance of the Holy Spirit, study the Word and look for His direction in the circumstances He brings into your life? It is not difficult to find God's plan for your life if you sincerely seek it. The real question is whether you are willing to *do* it. That question must be answered by each of us individually. How will you answer this challenge?

Bibliography

American Scientific Affiliation, The. *Modern Science and Christian Faith.* Chicago: Scripture Press, 1950.

Andrews, Samuel J. *The Life of Our Lord upon the Earth.* Grand Rapids, MI: Zondervan Publishing House, 1954.

Baldwin, Ethel May, and David Benson. *Henrietta Mears and How She Did It.* Ventura, CA: Regal, 1966.

Bouquet, A. C. *Everyday Life in New Testament Times.* New York: Charles Scribner's Sons, 1953.

Brotherton, Marcus. "*Teacher.*" Ventura, CA: Regal, 2006.

Burbank, Luther. "The Training of the Human Plant," *Century Magazine*, May 1907.

Cook, Robert A. *Now That I Believe.* Chicago: Moody Press, 1949.

Cruden, Alexander. *Cruden's Complete Correspondence.* Westwood, NJ: Fleming H. Revell Company, 1970.

Dugdale, Blanche E. C. *Arthur James Balfour.* New York: Putnam Sons, 1937.

Edersheim, Alfred. *Prophecy and History in Relation to the Messiah.* Grand Rapids, MI: Baker Book House, 1955.

Edersheim, Alfred. *The Life and Times of Jesus the Messiah,* 2 vols. Grand Rapids, MI: William B. Eerdmans Publishing Company, 1967.

English, Dr. E. Schuyler, ed. *The Pilgrim Edition of the Holy Bible.* Oxford, UK: Oxford University Press, Inc., 1948.

Hadley, Samuel H. *Down in Water Street: A Story of Sixteen Years Life and Work in Water Street Mission.* New York: Fleming H. Revell Company, 1902.

Havergal, Frances Ridley. *Kept for the Master's Use.* Chicago: Moody Press, 1964.

Huntington, Ellsworth. "The Valley of the Upper Euphrates River and Its People," *Bulletin of the American Geographical Society,* vol. 34, no. 5, 1902.

Lang, George H. *Histories and Prophecies of Daniel.* London: Paternoster Press, 1950.

——. *Israel's National Future.* London: Paternoster Press, 1952.

Mears, Henrietta C. *God's Plan of the Ages: Ninth Grade Student's and Teacher's Books.* S-91, S-92, S-93, S-94, T-91, T-92, T-93, T-94. Glendale, CA: Gospel Light Publications, 1958.

——. *God's Plan: Past, Present and Future.* Ventura, CA: G/L Regal Books, 1971.

Milman, Henry H. *The History of the Jews,* books XIV-XVII. New York: John Murray Publishers, 1883.

Morgan, G. Campbell. *The Parables and Metaphors of Our Lord.* Westwood, NJ: Fleming H. Revell Company, 1956.

Murray, Andrew. *Abide in Christ.* New York: Grosset & Dunlap, Inc., 1959.

Krey, August C. *The First Crusade: The Accounts of Eyewitnesses and Participants.* Princeton, NJ: Princeton University Press, 1921.

Paxon, Ruth. *Life on the Highest Plane.* Chicago: Moody Press, 1928.

——. *The Wealth, Walk and Warfare of the Christian.* Westwood, NJ: Fleming H. Revell Company, 1939.

Perrin, Bernadotte, trans. *Plutarch: Life of Alexander,* vol. VII. Cambridge, MA: Loeb Classical Library, 1919.

Phillips, J. B. *Letters to Young Churches.* New York: The Macmillan Company, 1947.

Power, John Carroll. *The Rise and Progress of Sunday Schools: A Biography of Robert Raikes and William Fox*. New York: Sheldon & Company, 1863.

Roe, Earl. *Dream Big: The Henrietta Mears Story*. Ventura, CA: Regal, 1990.

Ryrie, Charles C. *The Basis of the Premillennial Faith*. New York: Loizeaux Brothers, Inc., 1953.

Scroggie, W. Graham. *A Guide to the Gospels*. Westwood, NJ: Fleming H. Revell Company, 1948.

——. *Christ the Key to Scripture*. London: Pickering and Inglis, 1946.

Seiss, Joseph A. *The Apocalypse: Lectures on the Book of Revelation*. Grand Rapids, MI: Zondervan Publishing House, 1957.

Smith, George. *The Life of William Carey: Shoemaker and Missionary*. London: Murray, 1887.

Smith, Oswald J. *The Dawn Is Breaking*. Grand Rapids, MI: Zondervan Publishing House, 1920.

Smith, Wilbur M. *The Second Advent of Christ*. Boston, MA: W.A. Wilde Company, 1954.

Stalker, James. *The Life of Jesus Christ*. Westwood, NJ: Fleming H. Revell Company, 1949.

——. *The Life of St. Paul*. Westwood, NJ: Fleming H. Revell Company, 1950.

Stoner, Peter W. *Science Speaks*. Wheaton, IL: Van Kampen Press, 1952.

Tenny, Merrill C. *The Genius of the Gospels*. Grand Rapids, MI: William B. Eerdmans Publishing Company, 1951.

Torrey, R. A. *The New Topical Textbook*. Westwood, NJ: Fleming H. Revell Company, 1935.

Unger, Merill F. *Archeology and the Old Testament.* Grand Rapids, MI: Zondervan Publishing House, 1954.

———. *Great Neglected Bible Prophecies: Four Future Developments of Vital Importance.* Wheaton, IL: Scripture Press, 1955.

———. *Unger's Bible Dictionary.* Chicago: Moody Press, 1957.

United Nations, The. "Background Paper No. 27." Lake Success, NY: April 20, 1949.

Weizmann, Chaim. *Trial and Error: The Autobiography of Chaim Weizmann.* New York: Harper & Brothers Publishers, 1949.

Whiston, William. *The Works of Flavius Josephus.* New York: A.C. Armstrong & Son, 1899.

Explore Ancient Mysteries in a Fresh Way

How could Christ be fully man and fully God? If God is all-loving and all-powerful, why does He allow pain and suffering? Although we have all heard these questions before, and perhaps asked them ourselves, Jeff Kinley presents these age-old questions in a new light—one that speaks to today's generation and our perspective on the world. For this generation that is willing to linger in the unknown, Kinley does not really answer any of the questions he poses but simply comes to them with a fresh perspective, some hard facts and a captivating style that will inspire you to try to solve these mysteries for yourself.

Uncovering the Mysteries of God
Jeff Kinley
ISBN 978.08307.44251

Available at Bookstores Everywhere!

Visit **www.regalbooks.com** to join **Regal's FREE e-newsletter.** You'll get useful **excerpts from our newest releases** and **special access to online chats with your favorite authors.** Sign up today!

God's Word for Your World™
www.regalbooks.com